Language Unbound

Language Unbound

On Experimental Writing by Women

Nancy Gray

University of Illinois Press
Urbana and Chicago

© 1992 by the Board of Trustees of the University of Illinois
Manufactured in the United States of America
1 2 3 4 5 C P 5 4 3 2 1

This book is printed on acid-free paper.

Grateful acknowledgment is made to Yale University Press for permission to quote from Thornton Wilder's introduction to *Four in
America* by Gertrude Stein, © 1947 by Alice B. Toklas. The section of
the choreopoem is reprinted with the permission of Macmillan
Publishing Company from *for colored girls who have considered
suicide/when the rainbow is enuf* by Ntozake Shange. Copyright ©
1975, 1976, 1977 by Ntozake Shange. Grateful acknowledgment is
also made to St. Martin's Press, Inc., New York, New York, for permission to quote from *Sassafrass, Cypress & Indigo* by Ntozake
Shange, © 1982 by Ntozake Shange.

Library of Congress Cataloging-in-Publication Data

Gray, Nancy. 1947-
    Language unbound: on experimental writing by women / Nancy Gray.
    p.   cm.
    Includes bibliographical references and index.
    ISBN 0-252-01851-6. — ISBN 0-252-06211-3 (pbk.)
    1. American literature—Women authors—/History and criticism.
    2. Literature, Experimental—Women authors—History and criticism.
    3. American Literature—20th century—History and criticism.
    4. English fiction—Women authors—History and criticism.
    5. English fiction—20th century—History and criticism.
    6. Women and literature—History—20th century. I. Title.
    PS151.G78 1992
    810.9'9287—dc20   91-9876
                                                                  CIP

Contents

Introduction   1

1   Toward a Theory of Post-phantom Writing   9

2   The Language of Gertrude Stein   38

3   Looking-Glass Consciousness: Virginia Woolf and Dorothy Richardson   81

4   Interlude   122

5   Communities of Diversity: Ntozake Shange, E. M. Broner, Monique Wittig   133

Bibliography   175

Index   179

Introduction

Silence is golden, so the saying goes. If silence is golden, it costs too much. Women have been paying the price for a very long time. Breaking silence is seldom as simple and direct as it seems, for language and thought are not neutral givens arbitrarily accessible to anyone. They are cultural constructs, producing meaning according to social and historical configurations of value. In Western patriarchal culture, that production depends on Difference. Woman is Man's mark of difference. Woman is a means, an effect, a representation of the production of meaning that is language. She is a form of language—a carrier of meaning—for Man. When women take on language, it is She they meet. She steals their words. In Western patriarchal culture, good women are silent, bad women speak falsely, and no woman has a language of her own.

What is it, then, that is so powerful, so fearful and dangerous in a woman's words? The prohibitions against her have been strong. Among language users, it is women and slaves who have been outlawed. They have been kept from the writing and the reading of language, and when they have written anyway, their words have been trivialized or shunned. What happens when a woman not only uses words but does so on her own, as her own, as herself? What if she does not speak Woman in the doing? When a woman puts pen to paper as "herself," what is it there on the page? It slips, slides, changes shape, flies on the wind in the dead of night. It casts spells, speaks in riddles, is always elsewhere. "Herself" is intolerable to the culture that depends on feminized silence. Her words are read as chaos, non-sense produced out of lack or madness. They do not mean, but are hysterical gestures with sound effects. Don't listen. You will lose your mind.

What is remarkable about the women writers in the pages to follow is that they all, each and every one, have written exactly as if they could. What they have written does not follow the cultural script nor obey the codes of silence. It has been said that any woman who writes is a survivor. These women survive and more—they make words new by speaking as themselves. They break silence by what they say, by how they say it, by saying anything at all. They pay attention. Attention is the price they pay to put words on paper on their own terms. They look through and past Woman to language itself, to the specificities of their own experience, and by paying very close attention, enact what they know in voices so familiar they have never been heard before. Each has made sentences suited to her needs, using her own processes of knowing. Each is completely herself, and together they create interactive communities of words and experience so resistant to definitional categories of art or meaning that anything might be possible.

It is the business of feminist literary theory to break silence by breaking into and through the cultural codes that produce gender as access or obstacle to language. It recognizes the radical practicality of using everything, starting from where we are now, wherever, whenever, and whatever now may be. The need to understand how gender and its manifestations within concurrent structures of race, class, and sex are constituted by culture is a survival need. Those constructs produce very real oppressions of very real people, investing in distortion and denial to stop up their mouths. In the struggle away from oppressive paradigms of Truth and Meaning, everything counts. "Where we are now" is never the same twice, nor ever the same for any two writers. Learning to pay attention is a matter of learning to listen to all the voices—one at a time, interactively, all at once. If we do not, we can do little more than fine-tune the existing structures of hierarchic dominance that have produced a world bound to cultural ideals of power as conquest and possession, ideals that inform Western culture's very concepts of knowledge and meaning.

Experimental writing by women, then, is a term I use to work toward attentive disruptions of categories (of art, truth, meaning, identity, possibility). I use it to indicate writing that engages language not to (re)conquer or (re)possess The Word, but to enact radical interactions of subject and word. Because Western ideology depends on the silent presence of Woman, and because actual women are perceived as invisible without Her, then women writers who would write as themselves must find relationships to speaking that do not trap them in gendered accesses to language, art, or agency. As muse, primordial origin, eternal mystery, object of desire and loathing, Woman constitutes the enabling inspiration and the raw material of Art and Literature. Even as this constitution is given form in dominant-culture terms, removing potential speakers further from relationship to language when race, class, and sexuality are present as disabling features, Woman is still the figure standing ready to swallow up a woman's words or deny their very possibility. She is the phantom who keeps a civil tongue, ensuring that the relation between women and words is a familiar one, a relation to Man. It is she who conflates all the voices into one, the Eternal Feminine who functions as the silent underside of Civilization. As creators of literary art, women writers must confront and get beyond Woman not only as textual subject but as ideological nonsubject standing between them and their own uses of their own words.

Feminist theory demystifies Woman to demonstrate her existence as androcentric construct, to reveal the extent to which supposed universal categories of Art and Truth are functions of masculinized positions of agency and feminized positions of lack, to open our ears to the voices of actual women as artists and as subjects. When applied to Woman, subjectivity disappears. When applied to women, it collides with that most slippery of phenomena "female experience" to undo androcentric notions of thought, narrative, and action. Theorists such as Teresa de Lauretis, Catherine Belsey, and Alice Jardine, among others, have helped us to understand female subjectivity not as a corrective claim to Western humanism's (now devalued) "I," the site and center of knowledge and meaning, nor as postmodernism's alienated self, but as a process of experience in a material, historical context of shifting realities where female is in a specific relation to cultural constructs of sexuality. When subjectivity is continually constituted by contextual specificities of experience (always in motion, never fixed or definitive), Woman can no longer speak for/as women. Thus feminist theory gives us a way to read experimental writing by women with attention to the everydayness of experience, to a consciousness of actual female experiences in relation to iconic Woman, and to what de Lauretis sees as a shift from the notion of women as defined by sexual difference to female subject as a "site of differences." It is these attentions that inform my conceptualization of what I will call post-phantom

writing and my sense of the writers I deal with as vitally uncategorical.

Experimental writing, however, is a tricky term. It tends to imply a departure from a norm, and as such to cue a model of categorization the writings of Gertrude Stein, Virginia Woolf, Dorothy
Richardson, Ntozake Shange, E. M. Broner, and Monique Wittig
defy. It is also frequently recuperated as a means to invoke The
Feminine to retain the culture's investment in gendered constructs
of meaning. This is what happens when experimental writing is
defined as a preverbal, preconscious, nonrational instance of language use. It thus becomes an inscription of The Feminine and is
interpreted differentially as it is used by male or female writers.
That is, men's experimental writings are generally read as avant-
garde uses of The Feminine, wherein the writer has distance from
and control over the disruptive effects of his language. Women's
experimental writings, however, are more often read as instances
of The Feminine, wherein the writer is only expressing a female
essence of which she herself is a representative. Inevitably, then,
her writing is described as less skilled, less conscious, and altogether
less effective than his.

Because both Woman and language are figured in Western
culture as Man's access to Civilization, the conflation of women
into Woman removes conscious agency from women writers' uses
of language. Either they are read as imitators to varying degrees
of success or as innately suited conduits for the nonrational, non-
linear underside of the symbolic order. Occasionally women experimental writers are read as agents of a presymbolic language who
restore an ancient female (that is, nonpatriarchal) form to language.
However, this kind of reading is no less essentialist than those that
devalue women's writings as natural expressions of The Feminine;
it only valorizes what patriarchal culture has subordinated, thereby becoming an oppositional stance that confirms the very system
it is meant to refute. Furthermore, because such a reading looks
to a kind of prepatriarchal utopia for its effect, it does little to
help us realize in language the complexity of where we are now.
A "women's language" that is forced into existence by its very
suppression is a category of meaning already accounted for by the
system that silences women in the first place.

Insofar as the term *experimental writing* connotes that which
does without or makes untenable the assumptions of literary
realisms that naturalize cultural ideology to claim it as Reality, it
affords women writers an important means of leaving old gender

codes behind and breaking into language as experience, not as representation. The tension between the lived dailiness of experience and the ideological production of meaning opens up spaces for what Virginia Woolf referred to as the breaking of the sentence and of the expected sequence in writing. Because female experience is culturally shrouded in mystery or denied, its presence as itself, not as iconic category, in women's experimental writing uncodes the relationships among words, identity, culture, meaning, and subjects. This is what gets read as meaningless. However, uncoding does not engender chaos but frees language as a thing uncapturable into fixed classifications, in a state of continual movement, lively and alive. As such, it enacts presence from where we are now, historical baggage and all. Then what is unrecognizable from within the dominant cultural order takes shape for each writer, each in her way, as a presence of experience.

A language of one's own that is also language itself is not invented or so esoteric as to be inaccessible but a process of contextual experience, like subjectivity (in its least prescriptive incarnations). Language and experience become interactive, so that words are not merely symbolic but also experiential—experience itself. Each writer's language, then, is also (contextual) experience, is also language itself. It can tell stories that have been suppressed; it can enact "female subjectivity"; it can be just what it is as it is, using everything. The language of Gertrude Stein is so much just what it is that it can be any and all these things. Stein's remarkable freedom ungenders our accesses to language, uncodes our relationships with words, and teaches us to pay attention. It is for these reasons that I regard Stein's work as so relevant to any writer's attempt to write as a woman or about women without being trapped by The Feminine; it is for these reasons that I consider Stein's words so important to the conceptualization of any writing that would do without ideological limitations of form or language, thought or experience.

For Stein language is "a real thing." Her words continually break expected sequences, yet are always the most ordinary of everyday words. Her uses of them are both historically produced and free from antecedents, giving the reader the sense of encountering the utterly familiar in wholly original contexts. Stein's use of words is precise to the point of creating anew what we have always known but did not realize. Stein critics scurry to reformulate her words for easy handling into one version or another of communicable codes, but her work remains so much itself that it is not recuperable for meeting predetermined orders of meaning. Her use of language is so uncategorical that it frees us to read other women experimental writers not only as disrupters but as themselves.

Virginia Woolf's nonfiction provides me with the critical metaphors by which I read women's experimental writing. The Angel in the House, the phantom to be slain, her Society of Outsiders, and sentences proper to one's own use are all richly extensive images drawn from Woolf's critical re-visioning (to borrow Adrienne Rich's term) of women's work and writing. But it is her intentional crossing of the boundaries between fiction and nonfiction, her blurring of the distinctions between truth and fiction in the very structures of her writing, that helps me to think about female experience as also "a thing in itself," no matter how culturally inscribed. I have focused on her nonfiction (rather than her novels) because it is both and neither fiction and nonfiction—and because it is there that she sets out the confrontation between discourse and experience that allows her to speak "as a woman"; it is there that she interrogates the links between ideas and their formation, their relation to ideology, art, language, and life. Dorothy Richardson in a sense takes up Woolf's question, what is a woman, by producing narrative not only through but as "female consciousness." Her writing is so unfixed by place or expected sequence that she accomplishes a nearly atextual enactment of mind as process from within the specificities of a woman's experience. In her hands, writing becomes a politicized experience of consciousness that radically restructures gendered accesses to both meaning and female identity. Woolf and Richardson create narrative spaces for female subjectivity to come endlessly to life.

Ntozake Shange, E. M. Broner, and Monique Wittig make of that subjectivity "sites of differences"—or, rather, interactive sites of diversity. Shange refuses to choose among selves as definitions of her identity; race, sex, and class come together in her (writing), pull her apart, and finally are reclaimed on her own terms as contexts of experience rather than categories of being. She uses words culled from female traditions (spells, recipes, letters, stories) and recenters them in African-American heritages, mixing the languages of the page with the languages of movement and sound to make herself heard and to make herself whole. Broner breaks into patriarchal structures of ritual to find the many voices of women together. She searches through mother-daughter ties, Jewish history and myth, and the experiences of women under patriarchal rule to create what she calls "a house of women" in which language becomes a form of action as well as a symbolic system. Whether creating rituals of/for themselves, carrying out political demonstrations, or studying their own possibilities, Broner's women make a world in which they can live from the bits and pieces of the world into which they are born. Wittig breaks apart language and the categories of Man and Woman by making a kind of Amazonian war on the structures of form and meaning that produce patriarchal configurations of possibility. She uses the terms and functions of androcentric language systems to dismantle those systems. In so doing, she does not replace one system with another (the androcentric with the gynocentric, for instance) but creates in form and language the feasibility of an asystematic relation to language. Each of these three writers creates out of her own relation to diaspora, scattering and gathering what is known to her in the destabilized contexts of her experience.

For each and all these women, experimental writing is a choice for survival on her own terms. Individually and together, their writings resist not only the political and social structures of Western patriarchal tradition but also the very processes of thought by which those structures are put in place and maintained. They use form and language, experience, "post-phantom" possibility, sentences proper each to her own use, and everything that is not silence to utter themselves uncategorically. Stein's use of words as words remains for me an assurance that anything is possible. All these writers together enact possibilities gone begging in The Story of Man. Through them, boundaries are in such continual motion that they limit nothing. Through them, words take action and change what we know by involving us in the endless processes of knowing. Reading their words is a matter of paying attention, very close attention indeed. For these women's words will not meet our expectations. They are defiant and refuse to parrot or pander. In their presence we are not where we have been before, nor are we lost in alien territory. In the presence of these women's words we are, rather, always already elsewhere.

1

Toward a Theory of
Post-phantom Writing

In her 1931 essay "Professions for Women," Virginia Woolf lamented that when any woman sits down to write a book, she finds "a phantom to be slain, a rock to be dashed against" (*Women and Writing* 62). Woolf's phantom, of course, refers to her Angel in the House (so called after the title of Coventry Patmore's popular Victorian poem)—that pervasive and mythic figure of the eternal feminine that haunts any woman's ability to act or speak in the world. As Woolf so well understood, the phantom keeps a woman writer from "telling the truth about my own experiences as a body" (62). She is formulated by cultural ideology as an iconic image, imbued with the mysteries of life, death, beauty, and art. Civilization depends on her. But she is deadly to women. It is she who forces women to "tell lies if they are to succeed" in a world that depends on women's silence and invisibility as actual beings (60). With her in the way, Woolf saw that women cannot speak freely about "human relations, morality, sex" (59). Indeed, with her in the way, women cannot really speak at all.

Who is this phantom, then? Woolf described her as "intensely sympathetic . . . immensely charming . . . utterly unselfish. . . . She sacrificed herself daily . . . she never had a mind or a wish of her own . . . she was pure" (59). Should a woman not acquiesce to the phantom-Angel's demands, she is instantly catapulted outside woman's proper sphere. This has been the fate of all women who would speak truly as themselves, of all women culturally placed beyond the privileges of the ideal. In Western culture only white middle- and upper-class women can "become" the Angel, as it were, but all women are meant to aspire to her status, for she is the measure by which women are accepted or condemned. It is she who divides women from experience and from one another, she who confers language on Man and silence on all "others." Woolf felt she had no choice but to deal with her: "It was she who bothered me and wasted my time and so tormented me that at last I killed her" (58).

It was not an easy death, however: "She died hard. Her fictitious nature was of great assistance to her. It is far harder to kill a phantom than a reality" (60). Even after she has been dispatched, she has a tendency to "creep back," to stop women's words or to pronounce them falsely. For Woman is a fiction; she is not any actual person but Man's other side, an integral part of a system of oppositions by which patriarchal culture is structured. The Angel is her domesticated aspect. And since no thing is complete in this culture without its own opposite, she also comes in a Demonic version (known variously as witch, harlot, or shrew). Both Angel and Demon are necessary to the patriarchal order that produces and constantly re-produces them as the two faces of Woman, innately divided and divisive. Woman's evil side threatens chaos and disorder; she must be prevented from acting on her own and for herself—she exists to be conquered and controlled in the name of Civilization. Woman's good side is silent, chaste, and obedient; she is the emblem of Man's mastery over nature, his access to generative control and thus, again, to Civilization. The threat for women, we have been taught, is that to cross the line from good woman to bad will bring us a fate worse than death. It is the Angel, however, who defines both, constituting the bad woman who might say or do anything as the threat that keeps the good woman doing as she's told. Before she could use her mind freely to say what she knew, to be a writer, Woolf had to be rid of the phantom; as she said, "Killing the Angel in the House was part of the occupation of a woman writer" (60).

This is the business of experimental writing by women; being rid of the phantom is its most radical effect. It must be understood, however, that killing the Angel is not a matter of giving voice to the Demon, the spell-casting harlot with a sharp tongue. As Woolf knew, the Angel's opposite was not her only other choice. She understood, from the inside out as it were, that both sides and the opposition itself are part of the fiction, and all must go. But without the fiction, what is left? One might be tempted to say that the truth is left, but such a reply would only add to the original deception. As Woolf put it, "In other words, now that she had rid herself of falsehood, that young woman had only to be herself. Ah, but what is 'herself'? I mean, what is a woman?" (60). More than twenty years later, Simone de Beauvoir in *The Second Sex* would ask the same thing. With her investigation of this question, de Beauvoir revolutionized feminist thought—or at least made us hear what some women had already begun to say: Western patriarchal culture has for so long so thoroughly covered women in myth, has so efficiently used gender to conflate all women into Woman, the sexual category of Man, the Other, and the contrast by which a man may know himself as Self, that none of us can yet really know what a woman is. Woman blocks our view. And so long as this is the case, any woman's words will be compromised by their recuperation into already-gendered categories of meaning.

Even in the relatively open profession of a writer Woolf, for one, found the task of expressing "herself" far more difficult than it might at first seem. For Woman there is no herself that is not compromised by the split image (good/bad) that represents womankind. Any particular woman is neither Woman nor man, and only provisionally part of Man. Such is the power of fiction that Woman displaces the actuality of women's lives so pervasively, it is the actuality that comes to seem the fiction. Women together have often enough discovered this when their own perceptions of themselves have been comprehended only in the company of other women with related histories and experiences. Fictions, especially the mythic ones, are among the culture's most time-honored repositories for its valuables. Woman is crucial to Western myth as the fiction by which Man lives, indeed as the fiction by which he comes into being in the world. Woman is there for him, for Man, not for herself. As a writer Woolf (for one) knew that no so-called Realistic narrative could ever be sufficient to writing without the phantom stealing her words. Her only hope was to find new forms for telling what she knew. This she did. Still, she found the struggle, in a word, "severe." It meant confronting the problem of "telling the truth about my own experiences as a body," and that is the problem she believed she did not, perhaps could not, solve. But she, like so many other women of her time and since, did blur the boundaries between truth and fiction so successfully that the phantom, in either of her guises, no longer takes up all the space on the page.

Traditional narrative patterns can only repeat the fictions; they reproduce the cultural script. In form, that script relies on sequences of events moving forward in time in a logical progression, with characters divided into those who act and those who are acted upon. The whole of structural narrative theory (that which precedes post-structural deconstructions of the relation of form and meaning) is designed to discover and define the most basic components of narrative by which narrative itself can be identified. That is, Story is thought to exist only when it follows the delineated pattern, whatever its narrative medium. Claude Bremond (whose premises and conclusions are typical of structuralist narrative theories), in his 1973 work *Logique du récit*, examined narrative theory as it had progressed from the Russian formalism of Vladimir Propp to his own structuralist analysis, concluding that there is a "universal grammar of narrative" that can be applied to any narrative in any culture in the form of any genre (prose, poetry, drama, mime, dance, and so on). This grammar operates as does language, making Story possible only within a closed system of signs, or in Bremond's term, functions. What he seeks, and finds, is the something "real" in any story which is the autonomous structure that is the story itself. No matter in what form or version Story appears, it repeats this essential core of meaning through universal structure. Action is always the basic element of Story and must always occur in a logical, sequential pattern. Person or character is significant only in relation to action in its logical sequence. Bremond distills a system of "roles" from this relationship and posits it as universal because, he concludes, human experience can be narrated only through the relationship of person to action.

In patriarchal systems, of course, the relation of person to action is always gendered. That is, those who act do so out of a masculinized position of agency, while those who are acted upon fill the feminized space of recipient or enabling ground (as it were) on which action takes place. As Teresa de Lauretis (*Alice Doesn't*) has pointed out, this is a conceptualized division between man and non-man (human and non-human) by which the story of civilization and the conditions of human existence have been understood in patriarchal culture; because the historical and social practices of that culture have so pervasively associated man with the subject-position and woman with non-man, the very structure by which narrative seems to take on meaning is gendered. Structuralism's notion of narrative grammars is normed on a Saussurean model of language in which a sign (a symbolic device suggesting or standing for physical or conceptual phenomena, or indicating the relation-ship between phenomena and the symbolic forms by which they are expressed) can mean because of difference, its difference from other signs in the system. And since this system occurs only in a social relation, the concepts and events it communicates also take on meaning as relationships of Difference. Sexual difference, construed as the most basic naturally occurring difference (between man and non-man, ideologically formulated and not coincidentally defining the category Woman) becomes the model for all difference, dividing people into Self-or-Other/us-or-them, words into relational units of meaning, and narrative into sequential patterns of action performed or received by those who act or are acted upon, in language. Thus human identity, language, and narrative become complicit in a patriarchal system of meaning, producing gendered functions in logical patterns of linear progression that then are made to represent universal(ized) human experience.

This representation, however, is neither unproblematically human nor necessarily experiential. The works of countless writers who do not fit the Western cultural norm (white, male, heterosexual, Christian, and so on) bear witness to "human experience" as an ideological construct that is far from universal, but is historically and culturally produced out of a structure of dominance and concomitant submission. Moreover, a gendered hegemonic relation between categories of being or meaning produces all women and those men outside the dominant-culture norm as occupiers of a feminized (subordinate, less articulate) space. Even within that space, othered men may outrank (as it were) any woman, while those women most closely identified with the norm may outrank those most outside it. Difference, then, operates "differently" in relation to race, ethnicity, or sexual preference, yet preserves (universal) Woman as the measure against which (universal) Man is known. Insofar as experimental writing departs from the narrative patterns regarded as realistic in terms of their capacity to convey meaning within these representative parameters, it calls into question conventional categories of identity, language, and writing. Consequently, telling the truth of one's experience may not be deemed true or real if it disrupts or departs from traditional narrative patterns.

Because experience is culturally articulated before it is understood as communicable, we tend to translate experience into cultural terms. It is only when those terms seem not to exist "for us" that we find ourselves in the kind of severe struggle Woolf describes. Western culture harbors a deep suspicion of inarticulate experience; if it can't be or isn't reproduced as thought and (thus) language, we learn to know it as mystery, not as communication. We learn, in that case, not to know it all, but to feel it, by far a less "knowable" experience in that it takes uneasily to words. Mind and body, thought and emotion, are made separable; aligned with gendered positions of Difference, they function as representative divisions of agency and recipience. Mind belongs to (articulate) culure, body to (inarticulate) experience. (Man is then associated with the head, Woman with the body, and "female experience" becomes an unutterable enigma.) It is a lesson so relentlessly passed on as a kind of ordering mechanism for turning chaotic raw material into manageable data that we scarcely know how to experience without first translating experience into language or thought.

Realistic is a word we learn to use to describe the product of this process. When we say that a performance or expression of experience is realistic, we are saying that we believe it because we recognize it as something accessible to literal truth or accuracy. We accept it, in other words, as amenable to some universal law of nature, to some real something existent and functional in the world as the measure by which we know truth. We imply by our belief that universal principles are more real than immediate experience and that immediate experience has no real form or makes no real sense unless it can be fitted into the larger paradigm.

In the realm of literature, Realism is that tradition which assumes that literal truths and accurate realities not only constitute what we can know but also can be reproduced in representative forms of artistic expression that capture the essence of Reality. Language, written language in this case, functions as the shape—the representation—of that essence. Although we associate the term *Realism* with specific artistic histories, its influence as both a concept and a practice is far-ranging. Even from a Platonic perspective, the art of the poet or painter is an attempt to imitate the Real or True, however compromised by its dependence on image or appearance that in turn can operate only as conjecture and thus can never really be accurate. Whether in its metamorphoses as Aristotle's concern with how best to use the skills of artistic imitation for the moral good of the State, Wordsworthian pronouncements on the value of everyday real life and language in the hands of the poet of imagination, nineteenth-century naturalisms as antidotes to idealism, or contemporary trumpetings of "this is a true story" as a marketing tactic, the proper representation of reality—failed or successful, resisted or embraced—has been a persistent critical focus. And that focus has been based on belief in a something Real that is a part of Nature before and beyond historical-ideological reifications of it. The very discourse available to me for saying these things constantly turns back on itself for its own definitions and proofs: "real" means "true or actual"; "true" and "actual" mean "real or pertaining to reality." There is an assumed basis of common understanding that operates without denotative explanation and functions finally as that beyond which we believe we cannot go.

As Catherine Belsey points out in her 1980 work *Critical Practice*, however, realistic narrative or discourse is "intelligible as 'realistic' precisely because it reproduces what we already seem to know" (47). "Seem," of course, is the operative word, for despite Western culture's assumption that Truth must be ultimately universal in nature, our conceptualizations of it and the literary practices meant to embody it are social constructs produced in relation to time, place, and ideological motivation. Thus the cultural script that makes Woman seem a natural phenomenon already known to us even as it insists upon her nature as mystery incarnate, renders *a* woman, as herself (at once resistant to and in relation to her iconic signification), a being we do not know how to recognize. When we look for that woman, it is the distortion we see first, for any "she" who writes or is written drags the two-faced phantom with her. It cannot be otherwise in a system where women's problematic relations to the history of our production as image (as Woman) are covered over (by that very image) in the name of Truth.

For post-phantom women writers, then, realism will simply not do. Again in Belsey's words, "the experience of reading a realist text is ultimately reassuring, however harrowing the events of the story, because the world evoked in the fiction, its patterns of cause and effect, of social relationships and moral values, largely confirm the patterns of the world we seem to know" (51). To accomplish this, Belsey notes, "realism offers itself as transparent" (51). That is, realist fiction takes on the role of mediator between illusion and reality, offering itself as the illusion that reveals the reality, the fiction that tells us the truth—much like the role of the Angel-Demon in the production of female identity. For women truth has already been fictionalized to such an extent that women disappear from reality and are replaced by fiction-as-reality. It is only from within culturally inarticulate experience that women can see the fiction for what it is. This is an advantage insofar as the contradictions can become unavoidable with only a little concentrated attention to the gaps between truth and Truth. It is also, however, a very great obstacle in that it leaves the woman writer without a language "we already seem to know." The knowing this woman must find a way to articulate is outside the laws of conventional communication. She must use something other than convention to give it voice, for convention, especially the convention of realism, will only draw her back into the trap of silence where her fictional image "confirms the patterns" that silenced her in the first place. (It should be noted that placing gender or race at the center of even conventionally realistic narratives is also disruptive by its refocusing of what constitutes the real world. However, its conventional narrative pattern will at some level confirm Realistic expectations and thus will be recuperable into a special-case category of the Story of Man.)

Certainly women writers are not the only writers who have found realism insufficient for their work, though the effects of their departures from it have been received as especially problematic. The realities assumed by the conventions of realism have been found wanting, however, by both women and men. And despite the fact that, as Belsey notes (67), realistic fiction continues to be the dominant popular form of literature, the twentieth century has been particularly rich in writers who have rejected it or set it aside in favor of forms that actively resist formulation. Experimental writing has emerged both as a means to a more real reality and as a demonstration of the instability of the very concept of reality. And because avant-garde literary and artistic movements tend to disrupt convention and interrogate the terms of human action and identity in the world, such movements have offered women writers their best hope of breaking the strangleholds of gendered silence and conferred articulation.

The artistic and literary period occurring roughly between the turn of the century and World War II, known as Modernism, provided an especially active context for women writers seeking to break old bonds. Politically and socially, women were fighting for rights and pushing hard against old conceptualizations of "proper" womanhood. In the arts women were making themselves and their experiences of their world known as never before. Modernism is generally regarded as a time of global upheaval that altered perceptions of reality, fragmented any preconceptualized reliance on coherence or stability, and produced revolutions in artistic form and intellectual thought. Writers sought word-forms for human consciousness, dispensed with linearity of plot and time, and created voices and styles that interrogated the very foundations of what constitutes meaning, perception, self-in-the-world, and art. Such innovations are potentially well suited to dispensing with fictional Woman and investigating a/any woman as herself. But, as Woolf so astutely asked, what is "herself"? What is a woman? Because gender is culturally formulated to be so intimate to us all, to operate as the (seemingly) natural division of human beings wherein woman is the sexual subset of Man and the mark of difference on which he depends for his configuration of self, then women telling their own truths on their own terms has the power to be, at the very least, profoundly unsettling. Which, of course, is the point—and no doubt the reason why, despite the importance of their work, so few women innovators, to this day, appear in textbooks and anthologies of Great Writers.

Modernism continues to be preserved primarily as a masculinist phenomenon, regardless or perhaps because of the remarkable achievements of women who wrote against or without gendered expectations. The interrogations and innovations of this period are imaged again and again as effects of the cultural masculine, of the role of agency. Whole industries of literary study and criticism have sprung up around names such as Ezra Pound, T. S. Eliot, James Joyce: these men are read as shapers, innovators, bringers of the modern Word. D. H. Lawrence, Ernest Hemingway, F. Scott Fitzgerald: these men are perceived as warriors in the battle for a new age unfettered by the limiting conventions of the past. And therein lies the narrative pattern by which we learn to hear their words as important to The Culture.

War and combat (literally as well as figuratively), the wresting of self-possession out of the fragments of lost worlds, the claiming of new territory in the wake of the failures of conventional complacencies, one version or another of alienation and its redemptive relation to phoenix-like self-definition are the hallmarks of Western culture's "modern consciousness." They are also instances of acting-upon rather than being-acted-upon. They do not apply to all men simply because they are men; but because patriarchal constructions of identity and capability associate and even confuse masculine privilege with male beings, they do give men a kind of birthright access to the role of act-or. By the same token, they are decidedly not "womanly" activities. Even the independent modern woman who will not stay put behind gender lines is hard to hear, hard to see when transgression is assumed to be worthy only when heroic.

If a son wrests power from the father, he is deemed strong and able; indeed, such is the test of his right to manhood. But for a daughter, it's a different story. The father's power is not for her, and the power of the mother comes to her as a negative force to be controlled or overcome. Thus, when modern women such as

Virginia Woolf and Dorothy Richardson (to name only two) went beyond the exploration of modern consciousness into the dark and rock-strewn recesses of feminine or female consciousness (and even more problematically, female experience), their transgressions took on the taint of excess. And excess aligned with the enigma of the feminine is conveniently defused by interpreting it as anomaly or lack of control. Such labels prove useful to critics for speaking of women writers—if they are spoken of at all—in gendered terms. Thus we so often read of Woolf's lovely sen-tences or Richardson's frustrated polemics. Katherine Mansfield becomes a frail doer of small things, the power of which is owing to the influence of her reading Chekhov. Jean Rhys or Djuna Barnes are made nearly indistinguishable from speculations about their sexual lives, exploits, and preferences. Zora Neale Hurston or Nella Larsen, doubly othered by race as well as gender, are seldom even mentioned. And critics commonly scurry to proclaim Gertrude Stein a woman who wanted to be a man. Women writers who break new ground, who enact their own truths in their own words, are made safe through critical devaluation, denial, neglect, or reformulation according to gender codes. Their radical moves away from the language of Woman are seen as insupportable, dangerous, and downright unnatural.

Feminist critics, readers, and theorists have made crucial in-roads into the ideological assumptions of worthiness in literary development. They have been responsible for breaking old silences and bringing previously ignored women writers into critical view. In that regard, Shari Benstock's 1986 study *Women of the Left Bank: Paris, 1900-1940*, gives a useful overview of the women and men who shaped Modernist literature and of the largely inaccurate assumptions of male centrality by which that literature continues to be defined. *Writing for Their Lives: The Modernist Women 1910-1940*, by Gillian Hanscombe and Virginia L. Smyers (1987), adds to the picture by its examination of literary women in London and New York as well as Paris and by including excerpts from many previously unpublished letters that provide a sense of the network of support and influence these women created. Sandra M. Gilbert and Susan Gubar's *No Man's Land: the Place of the Woman Writer in the Twentieth Century* (Vol. I, *The War of the Words*) further extends our understanding of the gendering of Modernism by demonstrating male anxieties and subsequent attempts to regain control over the increasingly prominent position of women as shapers of social and literary contexts. Together these works not only demonstrate that Modernist women were far more instrumental in creating important new forms and concepts of literature than they are usually given credit for but also that the reasons for their neglect have little or nothing to do with the quality of their work and everything to do with gender as the structuring device by which to make meaning. For such women not only participated in disrupting old norms but often threatened to disrupt or dispense with the normative structures themselves. If these women were to be heard speaking "herself" into being, or making gendered accesses to meaning untenable, the whole Story of Man might collapse.

The Culture, however, has a remarkable capacity for co-opting or simply absorbing what threatens it from within. Certainly change does happen. We do read some women seriously now, when only a century or two earlier we could scarcely read any women at all. But the function of Woman as a fiction, as the language of fiction, has not really changed. The old codes still support masculinist rights of inheritance and accession to Self in Man's story. That is why merely learning to recognize women writers is not enough. We must pay very close attention not only to what women write but to the forms in which they write it and the spaces created in those forms for the writer to be, as Woolf envisioned her, only herself.

Of course we may say that some men too have questioned cultural gender and its effects, or that many women have not. We may say that the masculine and feminine positions constructed and narrativized by patriarchal culture need not adhere to men or women just because they are men or women. However, because these culturally gendered positions are inevitably associated with maleness and femaleness, the relation of men and women writers to them takes on differential possibilities. So long as Man is construed as the human while Woman is made a special case, then the cultural masculine position of agency aligns with subjectivity while the cultural feminine position is one of lack: lack of subjectivity, lack of consciousness, lack of agency. Whoever takes on the feminine enters a realm of silence. Thus, when women writers speak as if they always could, they seem to be taking up an impossible position, a position denied them by definition.

Women writers of the twentieth century have, nevertheless, been speaking just as if they could and creating a context of experience and literary innovation so mobile that definitional categories of language or form, as well as gendered accesses to either, become untenable. Gertrude Stein, for one, went so far in breaking cultural codes that her critics still don't know what to do with her. Her words are so often so completely not of "the system" that even the magic talismans female experience and feminine consciousness slide right off them. She has been simultaneously mythologized as an iconic character and popularized for her iconoclastic oddities. Her likeness has of late been showing up on Christmas cards and coffee mugs, and at least one bad-woman television character (on the old series "Dynasty") has been heard to invoke her name while imitating her verbal Steinese. Such phenomena are exemplary of the kind of mythic popularization that in effect silences a writer while keeping her name alive; they divert our attention from serious interaction with profoundly disruptive forces by redirecting it to safer outlets. We need never actually read Stein's words when a simple summoning of her name will do.

Yet somehow Stein's words remain resistant to co-optation. For this reason, her work is vital to any study of literary experimentation and any theory of gender uncoding. Lack simply is not relevant to Stein's writing. She radically interferes with cultural constructions of gender, language, narrative, and meaning. Her joyful ability to always be elsewhere when "what we already seem to know" is what's expected makes her work highly relevant to phantom-slaying, for she is unbound by the demands of representation and writes language as experience. Her words do not lend themselves to prescriptive conveniences but retain their capacity for being fresh and surprising no matter how often they are encountered.

Stein's contemporaries Virginia Woolf and Dorothy Richardson, among others, confronted representation and realism differently, by seeking to enter female experience onto the page where it might revolutionize social reality and artistic configuration alike. Women writers of the late twentieth century, in large part due to the work done earlier, have been further enabled to regard Realism as only one choice among many, and one not particularly well-suited to their own relationships with language. Writers such as Ntozake Shange, E. M. Broner, and Monique Wittig (among many) have added their experiences as postmodern outlaws of language use to the earlier uneasy alliances with Literature and have extended our notions of literary possibility and female subjectivity even further. All these voices, then and now, are not mere bids for equality in a co-optive system but genuine enactments of selves that do not comply with the expectations of Western cultural ideology. The work of these women writers, along with that of a great many feminist theorists, releases us from scripted categories of gender, race, class, or sex so that language and writing may be accessible to any of us, as we are.

To understand the relation of ideology and subjectivity to experimental writing by women, let's return briefly to Belsey's discussion of literary realism. For Belsey, realism "performs . . . the work of ideology, not only in its representation of a world of consistent subjects who are the origin of meaning, knowledge and action, but also in offering the reader . . . the position of subject as the origin both of understanding and of action in accordance with that understanding" (67). In other words, both realism and ideology produce (and re-produce) reality, but naturalize it as if it were simply the-way-things-are; as such it can then be inscribed unproblematically as human experience, monolithic and universal. Belsey derives her use of the term *ideology* from Louis Althusser so that it refers not to any particular doctrine of beliefs "deliberately adopted by self-conscious individuals" but to "the very condition of our experience of the world, *un*conscious precisely in that it is unquestioned, taken for granted" (Belsey 5). Ideology is inscribed in language or, more accurately, in discourse ("a domain of language-use") so as to produce "certain shared assumptions," not to signal the presence of any particular configuration of ideas, but rather to act as "a way of thinking, speaking, experiencing" (5). The work of ideology, then, is to conceal the *production* of what we understand as reality, positing it instead as already given. Since that reality serves the interests of the dominant forces of the culture in which it is inscribed, literary realism is, in Belsey's terms, complicit with a capitalist and liberal humanist world view that requires "subjects" who understand their place in the world as the consequence of individual freedom. These subjects are ideologically conditioned, as it were, to assume the world as a place of "non-contradictory (and therefore fundamentally unalterable) individuals whose unfettered consciousness is the origin of meaning, knowledge and action" (67). Realism's use of these assumptions then produces literary texts that rely on "the model of intersubjective communication" so as to act as "the guarantee not only of the truth of the text but of the reader's existence as an autonomous and knowing subject in a world of knowing subjects" (69).

We must pay special attention to the phrase "non-contradictory (and therefore fundamentally unalterable) individuals" in Belsey's description. Woman can never be non-contradictory because she represents the female classification of Man who is not-man; she is human, but not The Human. Women, then, (subsumed by Woman) can only be split, not-quite subjects, not real subjects. Ideology construes the subject position not only in terms exclusive of feminized access but also as "fundamentally unalterable." As the sexual component of Man, women can never be "autonomous and knowing subjects," can never engage in "intersubjective communication." As female persons in patriarchal contexts, however, women can speak from outside the construct or, more precisely, from its margins. Feminist critics and theorists have for some time been suggesting that this marginalized position can be enabling in that it affords a clearer experience of illusory realities *as* illusory. Nevertheless, as Woolf for one knew, the temptation to overlook the illusion and seek entrance into the reality it seems to offer is great. Furthermore, insofar as the margins are perceived as peripheral to (however disruptive of) the real center of meaning, then speaking from the margins may trap women in another kind of silence, that of the would-be usurper whose oppositional stance is already accounted for by ideological production. Reality will still seem to belong to someone else; her-self will still seem a contradiction in terms.

The problem of Western thought has always been how to know reality, the nature and purpose of being, the facts of existence. To that end, Western philosophical tradition has asked again and again, in one way or another according to the exigencies of historical development, how we know that we are and how we can prove that we know. This has inevitably led to an ideal of origins—a quest for knowing where we, existence, being began—and with it a logic of movement toward an end, preferably a transformative one capable of confirming the measure of material experience as representation of, obstacle to, or path toward Truth and Ultimate Meaning. Even current interrogations of the status and effect of the cultural production of this kind of truth frequently take shape in accordance with age-old quest patterns designed to reassure us that Truth is still there, albeit problematized by alienated anti-heroic movements toward and away from it in a world of lost innocence. That loss operates as the necessary access to the present while signaling a longing for a past that can never be recovered. Movement forward may entail movement backward, but ultimately must progress toward future resolution. (Impotence, even when valorized as the signifying mark of modern Man's existence, is the alternative. The androcentric sexual associations are not new.) The reward for the achievement of resolution, however theoretically suspect, is still release into some version of Knowledge, Truth, or Self—into that which has traditionally been Man's Destiny.

In his search for reality, the phenomenologist Edmund Husserl sought origin in "the transcendental Ego." This he conceived of as antecedent even to the physical world and capable of transporting the thinker into a "truer" realm than that possible in material reality—a kind of ultimate freedom to know. His disciple Jean-Paul Sartre would later reject this notion of transcendence and seek an interdependence between the ego and the world as a corrective of sorts for what he called the "escapist doctrine" of Ego as absolute consciousness. Sartre's quest for what makes experience or existence possible demanded a closer relation to "real problems" through a striving to determine the conditions that make the ego and the world essentially One—his "me" becomes an "existent," the origin and source of experience or lack of experience, of existence itself. (For useful opening discussions of these ideas see, for instance, Husserl's *Cartesian Meditations* and Sartre's *The Transcendence of the Ego.* It is not my purpose to trace the development of phenomenological and existential philosophy but only to indicate their place in the quest for an ideal of origins as a means to know reality.)

It took Simone de Beauvoir's understanding of the non-existence of Woman as a Self, of course, to call into question the whole assumption of Ego as source—source of meaning, knowledge, experience, even existence. For as Other to man's Self, de Beauvoir teaches us, woman is not allowed historical occurrence. Her only possibility is that of occupying the position of natural essence, the Eternal Feminine. Essences do not act in the world but are acted upon. As essence, Woman has no access to agency but is paradoxically divided from the human by providing the culture of Man with herself as human mater-ial. (*The Second Sex*, of course, offers a far more detailed analysis of the ramifications of this point.) It is de Beauvoir's ability to articulate the experience of Other that allows us to see Western Man's search for reality as an androcentrically ego-based construct.

Woman is a product of cultural gender. Gender splits human consciousness so that the act of knowing (and the condition of possessing Knowledge) comes about through the masculine position of agency in search of source, while the Other side is essentially unknown, unconscious, emblematic of the feminized space where source is sought. Psychoanalytic theory has taught us how to make these distinctions as if naturally. Jacques Lacan, building on Freud's theories of consciousness and sexual development, posits language in the place where the Freudian mother had been as the site of accession to Self in culture. This does not free Lacan from gender-complicit thinking, however; rather it merely reformulates an old structure and in the process confirms the patriarchal operation of

Woman as language. In his vision of human development, Lacan describes accession to culture as produced by a process of alienation from what he calls "m/other" through the articulation of "I" and its entrance into the symbolic order. This results in a loss of primordial and thus unknowable oneness, with the consequent acquisition of language as the cultural code mediating the relationship between the emergent Self or Subject and the (repressed) Other. (See *Écrits: A Selection* for a more complete Lacanian account of these processes.)

Significantly, Lacan locates the source of desire, the moving force of culture, in that Other, that lost lack of alienation that promises but cannot deliver wholeness. Instead the Phallus, Lacan's emblem of his "law of the Father," substitutes unity for wholeness, thereby resolving the crisis of loss and desire by repressing the source of desire and expressing it/Other as discourse under phallic control. Oneness becomes an a priori transcendent state forever sought and never achieved, simultaneously longed for and feared as the non-existence of the necessity of Self. This is how Woman, rendered inseparable from Other/not-Self, can be said not to speak, but to be spoken.

Both language and Woman, then, are spoken by man as representations of his desire for knowledge and creativity not predicated on a return to an origin where self-possession is irrelevant. Cultural ideology constructs Self as the agent of the human quest for knowledge, Woman as the Other (m/other) that forms the site of that quest, and the phantom-slaying woman writer as an impossible speaker of impossible experience. In her ground-breaking work *Alice Doesn't: Feminism, Semiotics, Cinema*, theorist Teresa de Lauretis unravels the central obstacle in the way of female subjectivity or agency interacting freely with language to enact unphantomlike experience. This obstacle is "the paradoxical status of women in Western discourse: while culture originates from woman and is founded on the dream of her captivity, women are all but absent from history and cultural process" (13).

The inscribing of Western cultural processes relies on the strategies of myth. As any dictionary can tell us, myth employs primordial types and recurring themes to appeal to consciousness through cultural ideals. Whether presented as history, philosophy, or literature, these ideals shape what can be told. In Western culture, any telling assumes an origin-telos pattern in which Truth is to be revealed by event, reason, or metaphor. As de Lauretis tells us, the cultural ideals Western Man creates constitute "a text which tells the story of male desire by performing the absence of woman and by producing woman as text, as pure representation" (13). That is, woman's presence functions as absence. She disappears as that part of the human which is herself (so difficult for man to imagine without jeopardizing his own unitary notion of self), and reappears *for* man as, in de Lauretis's words, "both object and support of a desire which, intimately bound up with power and creativity, is the moving force of culture and history" (13).

Desire and text, then, come together as the motivation for and shape of human beingness in the world, structured so as to be passed on as Culture. If Man is to be the creator and consequent heir of Culture, then the story of that being must be his. (How it got to be his and not hers, or even theirs, is another story.) When women, especially women of color or lesbians, place their own experiences at the center of the story, what can be seen is radically altered. That, of course, is the perceived threat of stories that do not repeat the reality created by white androcentric history and ideology. What must be obvious by now is that the Story of Man in Western culture is race and gender specific, though inscribed as universal paradigm.

Let us imagine man telling his tale. (As we do so, visualize the usual natural-history museum pictures of the evolution of Man: he is always light-skinned; the further away from his animal origins he gets, the more Caucasian is his appearance; he is never female, though he may occasionally be accompanied by a female.) In this tale, man begins by casting about for a beginning. (Every story has one.) He can't help but notice, perhaps, that his own life begins again and again in/on the body of woman. His own body does not produce as does hers. What's more, all of nature seems to produce and reproduce just as she does. Soon it's all he can see when he looks at her. It must be what she's there for. She and nature must be very alike. Her body, he perceives, marks her place in the world—indeed, marks her as place in the world, his place, the place where he begins, his first home. Now our storyteller is faced with a dilemma: how can he be he but still come from her? There must be another force at work. He will call it the mind of God, then eventually just Mind. If it is separate from body, her body, and has its own creative force, then body (her body) can become the field of creation, the ground acted upon while mind remains with he who acts. Of course without body (nature) there is no life. But mind has a life of its own and can act on nature to produce something more: it can create Culture. In the role of mind-creator, he can at last control the site of creativity she now represents for him. (He may even conceive of transplanting life from body to test tube, the ultimate victory of mind over body.) He can now begin to tell his stories, perhaps without mentioning her at all. He cannot completely deny, however, that he was once part of her. But by understanding her as a specialized being, he can take himself to be the inclusive One, the human, and make her his sexual (bodily) category. As such she is there for him as natural resource and bumper or protective device between him and nature itself. Thus she becomes both man and not-man, that most mysterious creature on whom he depends both as the place from which to start his journey into self and manhood and his prize at the end of that journey—or more precisely, his means to the prize through his re-possession of her body, of nature.

It is with just this sort of journey that de Lauretis begins her working out of the terms of man's story and the possibilities of female subjectivity in *Alice Doesn't*. Her chapter "Desire in Narrative" traces the development of mythic structure as it is manifested in both semiotics and psychoanalytic discourse. Her final chapter, "Semiotics and Experience," then takes up the question of what to do with the recognition that female experience is en-gendered by the historical and social dominance of one sex and concomitant oppression of an/the other. In her terms, the project of feminist theory is "how to theorize that experience, which is at once social and personal, and how to construct the female subject from that political and intellectual rage" (166). De Lauretis's work has been particularly important to my understanding of how or why postphantom women's writing can come into being. What follows, then, traces her influence on that understanding.

Man's story takes a mythic structure. It is a hero's quest given form and movement by his (the hero's, the storyteller's) desire to achieve successful passage from origin to end through an intermediary obstacle, a test of his mettle. What better obstacle than the mysterious creature marking the boundary between the hero's primordial past and his destiny? It can be a most complicated passage, but through the regulating strategies of myth it is brought under control, ordered so that no matter what its variants, it can still be identified as The Story of Man.

After examining the development of narrative typology in the structural analyses of Vladimir Propp and Jurij Lotman, de Lauretis is able to conclude that "mythical structuration" is responsible for a sciencelike classifications system based on sexual difference as the primary distinction on which all others depend. That is, myth's inscriptions of recurring types and themes divide human actions into the lawful and the anomalous by "reducing the diversity and variety of phenomena and occurrences to invariant images" (117). In Lotman, this arrangement (not unlike that of Bremond) produces a narrative model of myth/story in which characters are either mobile or immobile (can either move through narrative or are what de Lauretis calls "personified obstacles"), are reduced to two (the hero and the obstacle/antagonist), and exist in a two-function structure where the hero enters and emerges from a "closed space"—a space which, as de Lauretis quotes Lotman, can be characterized as a cave, grave, house, or woman, all with the corresponding features of "darkness, warmth, dampness" (118). Thus, immobile closed space provides the mobile hero with the obstacle he needs to accomplish passage from origin to end.

As she must, de Lauretis determines from this model that "the hero must be male, regardless of the gender of the text-image, because the obstacle, whatever its personification, is morphologically female and indeed, simply, the womb" (119). Consequently, as she goes on to explain, biological distinction in the form of sexual difference creates opposite pairs that derive from "the fundamental opposition between boundary and passage" wherein the female sex represents boundary and the male is transformed into "the active principle of culture" and "the creator of differences" (119). Thus, what she will later call the feminine position functions as plot-space, whereas the masculine position confers on the hero the movement of passage and transformation into Man. Narrative, that is, produces subjectivity as a hero's act of self-creation out of an idealized symbolic other. The morphological representation of this other in female-specific terms, moreover, conflates the (disorderly) diversity of women under the rubric Woman, that difference created by heroic man who then passes through her to become himself, subject and speaker of his own story.

Desire most obviously enters this process by way of psychoanalytic theory. As de Lauretis is at some pains to point out, it is no accident that Freud took his model of human development and identity from mythic narrative. The Oedipus tale provides an irresistible human drama based on the loss of an innocent past revealed only through the culmination of forward movement into the destiny of self-knowledge. As in so many creation myths, the cost of knowledge is high. The temptation to take it on must be powerful indeed. Enter Woman with her apple, her diabolic adaptability to another's desires, and her body as the very ground on which man will enact his loss.

(It should be noted that there have always been persistent rumors, and even material artifacts, that tell the story differently: woman as life force, personified as Goddess and acting on her own rather than through the agency of one more powerful, brings both knowledge and life to all human beings, not as a paradoxical punishment but as that which must be. Life and knowledge are interdependent and not susceptible to hierarchic power plays in her world. But of course the ideology of patriarchal culture recognizes this version of the story as wishful thinking—a kind of masculinity complex in which women recast the female as subject rather than object out of a misguided refusal to accept the-way-things-are.)

In man/Oedipus's story, once loss is realized, self-knowledge takes on the shape of Truth, transforming man/Oedipus into a superior being who has access to both nature and culture, both body and mind. And it is desire that first catapults him into this necessary loss. This desire may be thought of as the Freudian forbidden desire for mother as sexual being (which as a woman, of course, she must be by definition), as the Lacanian desire for the privileges of culture conferred by accession to language (the code mediating the relationship between subject and repressed "m/other"), or as the narrativized desire for meaning through resolution (created out of the construct of Difference that makes the hero's quest possible). Psychoanalytic theory takes Oedipal desire as the crisis wherein the boy encounters and overcomes obstacle to grow into man, while the girl encounters and *becomes* obstacle if she is to grow into woman. She must give up desire as not for her, but of her; she must learn to accept—or to be seduced into accepting, as de Lauretis tells us—the desire to be desired. Otherwise she is doomed to transgress on the boy/man's territory, which is herself, in the hopeless attempt to pass through herself as her own obstacle. As the object of man's desire, if she does not acquiesce to her function as territory, she must "act like a man"—a contradictory trap that can only turn her emulation of desire back on herself as its object.

Because woman is man's Other in this scheme, both man and not-man, her Freudian construct will make her vulnerable to continual alternations between the masculine and feminine positions of agency and recipience. She will never attain true subjectivity, but will always be, one way or another, man's quest(ion). Her semiotic reconstitution as a product of discourse leaves her no better off. It relegates her to the status of an internal essence that can be expressed only as the leftover excess of repression. That is, unable to speak as or for herself, the eternal feminine (repressed source of man's lost lack of alienation) can emerge only emblematically, as the ground or text of man's story, as what de Lauretis terms "pure representation."

But actual women are not Woman. Though indeed influenced, even captivated by Woman, actual female human beings are, after all, human beings. No amount of mythologizing can completely obliterate that fact. Myth has instead been put to use to take advantage of a woman's double/split life as human being and cultural icon. This double/split identity, with its potential for radically unordered multiplicity in its revelation of the contradiction between the two, is conveniently reorganized as a duality within a duality. That is, Woman is man's two-faced other. Not only is she his oppo-site, but she is always also her own opposite, either good woman or bad.

Even more problematically, if she is "not a woman" but a woman of color or a lesbian, she functions for Western culture always as the bad or not-quite woman who ensures the possibility and the desirability of iconic good-woman status by the threat of her seemingly oppositional position in relation to it. This is not a denial of "the other woman's" femininity so much as it is a divisive strategy to ensure the seductiveness of femininity in the service of Western Man. Furthermore, though the position of men of color and gay men is a feminized one that may produce important alliances between "othered" men and women, maleness, even culturally feminized maleness, is always accorded a birthright access to ascendancy based on its identification with the masculinized construct of agency. Thus, a man's feminization is considered deeply dishonoring, a serious emasculation by which to condemn him, yet which he may be encouraged to correct by acceptance of his birthright, even if in a devalued sphere. But a woman's feminization, in all its paradoxical dualities, is always understood as one version or another of her proper, her essential nature.

As women begin to articulate their experiences of these untenable positions, we find not only that the words for that experience are exceedingly difficult to come by but also that the very processes of reasoning by which masculinist culture allows transformation of experience into Knowledge tend to confine "women's experience" to the realm of instinct, and consequently to the realm of silence. But, however relentlessly the culture "hears" women as silent, they are not.

It is here, in the difficult relations between instinct and reason, experience and knowledge, that de Lauretis turns to Virginia Woolf's *A Room of One's Own* for enabling clues to female experience (and what to do with it) in the context of patriarchal culture. Woolf tells of an ambiguously fictional female "I" who, in the excitement of an onrush of ideas, forgets her place and trespasses onto a campus lawn where women are forbidden. The way in which the "I" discovers her error is the focus of de Lauretis's interest, for it is accomplished nonverbally but with perfect semiotic success. The "I" is confronted by a gesticulating Beadle whose outrage and indignation finally get through to the "I" as a signifying code translating her presence into female transgression. The sentence that de Lauretis finds most revealing is this: "Instinct rather than reason came to my help; he was a Beadle; I was a woman" (158, quoting *A Room* 6). The "I's" experience as a woman in a culture that understands her presence as (desired) absence is what allows her to make the connection between instinct and Woman.

De Lauretis calls our attention to the cultural prohibition against female access to reasoning. As Woolf's "I" dashes against the rock of the gesticulating Beadle (male enforcement of woman's place), she automatically interprets her understanding of the situation as "instinct rather than reason"—a far more womanly method of gaining information in the world. But de Lauretis notes that this instinct is actually inference, and that inference is the process of information-gathering on which reason is based. "And yet," she says, "to call it 'instinct' is not quite so inaccurate, for what is instinct but a kind of knowledge internalized from daily, secular repetition of actions, impressions, and meanings, whose cause-and-effect or otherwise binding relation has been accepted as certain and even necessary?" (158). Still, because "instinct" tends to connote "mindlessness," de Lauretis finds it necessary to designate the phenomenon in question by another term. The term she chooses is *experience*.

The choice is apt, for *experience* is a term both problematic and unavoidable if feminist theory is to ungender our access to language. For de Lauretis, experience does not mean merely what the dictionary might indicate (sensory data, the acquisition of skills, and the like), but "a *process* by which, for all social beings, subjectivity is constructed" (159). In an endnote she stipulates that others might call this process "ideology." Her reasons for using the term *experience* instead (while not directly explicated) have to do with the daily lived-through aspects of the process engaged in

by individuals in a social reality. It is through that process of engagement in a social context that one perceives as subjective "those
relations—material, economic, interpersonal—which are in fact social
and, in a larger perspective, historical" (159). Because the process is
contextual, it is "continuous . . . unending or daily renewed"; consequently, unlike the subjectivity of traditional Western humanism,
this subjectivity is "an ongoing construction, not a fixed point of
departure or arrival from which one then interacts with the world.
On the contrary, it is the effect of that interaction—which I call
experience" (159). In de Lauretis's terms, then, subjectivity is not a
production of ideology but of experience—of what she calls "engagement in the practices, dis-courses, and institutions that lend significance (value, meaning, and affect) to the events of the world" (159).

Now we can begin to see that the relation of person to action
(in societies as well as in narrative) might become open to women
not in their role as ground or recipient of action but as subjects
engaged in a continuous (unending, not predicated on beginning-
middle-end) and unfixed process of interaction. This interaction,
of which subjectivity is the effect, is based on the specificities of
women's experience in social-historical contexts. De Lauretis advises feminist theorists to keep in mind that this "female subject"
is neither the generic term ("the subject": "man") of patriarchal
discourse, nor the oppositional feminine subject ("defined by . . .
a natural sexuality, or a closeness to nature not compromised by
patriarchal culture") of those feminisms that seek to rescue Woman
from patriarchal experience. Rather, de Lauretis emphasizes, feminist
theory "must address women, not woman, and question precisely
that specific relation to sexuality which constitutes femaleness as the
experience of a female subject" (165).

By using Woolf's response to the gesticulating Beadle as a
starting point, de Lauretis helps us understand the subject and
social reality as semiotically constructed processes in a recipro-
cal relation to one another. Now she can finally re-envision the
project of feminist theory in such a way that the traps of essentialism are avoided and "the historical experience of women" (186) becomes the appropriate focus of feminist political and theoretical
practices:

> The question can now be rephrased in this way: is the female subject
> one constituted in a particular kind of relation to social reality? by a
> particular kind of experience, specifically a particular experience of
> sexuality? And if we answer that, yes, a certain experience of sexuality
> does effect a social being which we may call the female subject; if it is

> that experience, that complex of habits, dispositions, associations and perceptions, which en-genders one as female, then *that* is what remains to be analyzed, understood, articulated by feminist theory. (182)

What has happened is that de Lauretis has placed women, as social subjects who are also cultural (ideological) non-subjects, at the center of her inquiry. She has done so, moreover, with a feminist political and theoretical understanding that for women mind and body come together in spite of and because of the cultural ideology that separates them by denying women access to one while imprisoning them in the other. She has begun to look at women's experience (the process of subjectivity for a social being) itself. That experience, in both theory and practice, is undeniably constrained by an imposed world view that sees nothing—that is, only Woman—when it looks at women. And so it is appropriate that feminist theorists "deconstruct" or unravel the theoretical constructs that fictionalize women so thoroughly. However, if we are so seduced by the negative power of those constructs that we spend all our time focused on our rejection of or opposition to them, all we can really accomplish is a perpetuation of the very system we mean to change or dismantle. That is the function of opposition from within a hierarchy that recognizes meaning only in relation to oppositional pairs. It is necessary, then, to make the move de Lauretis makes: to ask our questions from within female experience, that most troublesome place of contradiction between Woman and women.

This shift from image to experience is what allows us to stop speaking Woman and speak as ourselves. It is precisely the shift that experimental women writers have been enacting. It must entail a connection between experience and language—for women, as social subjects. To theorize this connection, de Lauretis turns to current poststructuralist semiotic theory, that body of theory which moves our attention away from the classification of sign systems and toward an analysis of how signs and meanings are produced (167). She identifies two main emphases in semiotic theory, one a Lacanian focus on "the subjective aspects of signification" where the subject is an effect of language or the signifying process, the other semiotics of the social aspects of signification in which "culturally shared codes" produce meaning (167).

Because Lacanian theory relies on a feminized symbolic Other (or "m/other") as that which the subject speaks through the mediation of language, it cannot accomplish the shift we need; it re-produces

Woman in/as language. To see subjectivity as an effect of experience, in language, de Lauretis turns to Charles Sanders Peirce's theory of "semiosis," which she reads through Umberto Eco. Here she finds what she needs: an examination of the work performed by signifying processes through social practices. That is, rather than locating meaning in the subject, she is able to look at meaning as "semantic value" produced in the "practical, aesthetic, or ideological use" of signification in a social context (167). This is the shift that allows us to encounter transformation or trans-gression of cultural codes by individuals using those codes in social-historical contexts as social beings. De Lauretis is able to bridge the gap between discourse and experience by means of "dialectic interaction" between cultural codes and the processes of sign production. Thus she can project a theory of meaning susceptible to "ideological transformation" and "materially based in historical change" (172). This she must do if she is to elicit the interactive relationships among Woman and women, language, and experience.

Because, as de Lauretis has pointed out, women are "all but absent from history and cultural process" in Western patriarchal discourse, women writers who would speak freely must find a way to interact with the cultural codes "differently." The transgressions of experimental women writers, then, involve eluding Woman-as-language and enacting language through-and-as experience. This is what I have termed post-phantom writing. As Woolf noted, however, the phantom has a tendency to "creep back" even after she has been dispatched. De Lauretis's "ideological transformation materially based in historical change" is made difficult by a system of meaning in which ideology produces historical change as if it always originated inside the system itself. Since women disappear in that system, the social-historical process of female experience may be compromised by the very language available for its expression. It takes an "ungendered ear" to hear *through* the fiction that is Woman and begin to speak uncategorically. Though such speaking does not reproduce the cultural codes, neither does it happen apart from them, but with full awareness of them. This awareness is particularly volatile and empowering for women, standing as they do both within and without the culture's categories of experience.

Though gender would seem to be a category that applies to women and men equally but differently, it actually functions to cue the presence of the Feminine. It embodies women as Woman, gender personified. Based on a "natural" biological classification by sex, it performs the illusion of definitional description but is, of course, an ideological construction of characteristics designed to produce social patterns in line with patriarchal codes of meaning. Grammatically, "woman" is never a generic term for "human" but always indicates the sexual category of the human. "Man," which is the cultural inscription of the generic human, needs no gender marker. It is only when differentiating between the norm and the other that gender must be marked. Both "woman" and "sex" fulfill that function, reflecting the ideological alignment of femaleness and sexual status while maintaining the fiction that "woman" is a naturally occurring category of "human."

From inside the experience of being both female and human (complicated by race and sex as already-gendered positions in Western culture), women know the contradictions inherent in the construct. This is a kind of heretical knowledge. If acted upon, it could seriously undermine the larger construct Reality. Women will go about phantom-slaying, however, despite the risks of punishment and impropriety. It behooves the rightful heirs of the patriarchal order, therefore, to reformulate phantom-slaying as a bid for "equality"—an activity already accounted for in a hierarchic order that relies on progression by opposition. Thus, when questions of gender are brought forward for purposes of equality (women's rights, for example), they are often resisted with great energy, but are in the long run understood as meaningful insofar as they adhere to the terms of the existing system. Feminist political movements have historically been able to make some practical gains in this way—the vote, expanded civil rights, entrance into previously barred economic spheres—and the system remains intact. But when the very foundations of the system, its very production of meaning or identity, are made untenable, it is threatened with destruction—or, in ideological terms, with Chaos.

If, as Woolf imagined, a woman has "only to be herself" once rid of the phantom, that self will have no niche in the hierarchic order nor in the signifying system of Western patriarchy. That is why it is necessary to ask what "herself" might be. It is why "only herself" is so dangerous to dominant cultural and narrative order. Such a creature may come into the world uncoded. Neither good woman nor bad, not Woman at all, no longer special-case Man, not even a son in disguise making a bid for power, she must be Chaos. Dis-order must be her aim. But even those terms are safe categories of opposition in comparison with the radical dangers of "only herself." She would bring with her thousands of years of experience in the world; much of that experience would show itself as rage; all of it would be contextual, but not all of it would find a home in the signifying system that can recognize her only as one form or another of the Feminine. If she speaks neither against that system nor within its codes as is the case with Stein, she must be heard as madness; if she looks for her words in herself as do Woolf and Richardson, she will be accused of special pleading; if she brings outlawed traditions of othered peoples into the patterns of her very own words as do Shange, Broner, and Wittig, she will be accused of being a traitor or she will be said to be "speaking the unspeakable," and she will not be heard as saying anything real at all. This, then, is how cultural ideology works to stop up her mouth.

Cultural ideology makes itself invisible as what it is; it masquerades as explanation while it actually delimits and controls what can be conceptualized, how, and by whom. "Culture" and "ideology" come together not merely to indicate sets of beliefs bounded by national or ethnographic parameters, but to mark a paradigm of possibility, a "norm" assumed just to be there, like the air, everywhere. Western patriarchy produces a norm that is male-dominant and white-supremacist in its assumptions of Reality. It is based on a pyramidal structure of hierarchy in which a wide base supports a progressively more restrictive movement toward a very narrow pinnacle. That pinnacle's very possibility depends on values of conquest and possession. Movement upward is the only path to ultimate truth and is accomplished by joining, then displacing, whoever is above and moving a continually reconstituted supply of others to fill in below. While mobility may be understood as both heritable and deserved, it is birthright that guarantees a stable population of one (kind) at the top.

Race and sex are the most effective determinants of place since they are physically and genetically defined. However, even racial and sexual boundaries, it turns out, do not remain stable. There are far more variations among individuals than between categories, even categories ostensibly based on biological characteristics. Ambiguity and diversity, it seems, may be even more normal than the norm. To maintain rank, then, binary oppositions in hegemonic relations to one another serve to discourage disorderly tolerance for ambiguity. Civilization and nature, man and woman, mind and body, light and dark, become paired dualities of dominance and submission, with the first term in each pair as the one we learn to strive for against the other, which we must then control. Without something to oppose, we learn to believe, there is no going forward. The whole notion of civilization as an ever-increasingly beneficial control over nature depends on it.

This is Western culture's paradigm for knowledge and experience. It permeates the atmosphere. Woolf could not imagine "herself" without confronting it. None of us can. But we must remember that the paradigm is a construct, an effect of ideological production. Once discerned, the boundaries that shape it may be crossed, blurred, destabilized, or even done without. This is the work of the woman writer who would speak for and as herself. If the old codes of Difference are to be truly left behind, if women writers are to bring their minds and selves onto the page intact ("using everything" without having to choose among identities), then it must be possible to break into language through-and-as experience, not representation. Woman in Western cultural ideology is also representation and functions as language, as that through which meaning is conveyed. As such, a woman writing is like language trying to speak itself. If a woman, any woman, is to write in this context without being silenced, she will have to confront and evade Woman. Such a woman will have to find words that do not tie her tongue or speak in her place.

Breaking into language as experience may be the only way to enact words without having to slay and reslay the phantom. Once experience is understood as that process of subjectivity for a social being that de Lauretis envisions, this language-as-experience cannot be confined by categorical codes of predictability designed to further the quest for universal truth or self. We need neither deny nor depend on language's symbolic function and representational history; they are part of its contextual being. As a process of interaction with unfixed and continually shifting realities, however, it takes on a life of its own. It becomes a thing to which we can pay attention not to confirm "what we already seem to know," but to speak ourselves and our experiences into the open.

We may now see that when Virginia Woolf worried over telling the truth of her own experiences as a body, she was on exactly the right track. Twentieth-century experimental women writers have taken up the challenge of trusting the specificities of their own social-subjective processes in an ongoing and continually renewed effort to speak as themselves in a world accustomed to hearing women's voices as sirens' songs, shrews' complainings, mothers' lullabies, or not at all. Thus it is that we may find nonconventional possibilities in the words of nonconventional women writers. With the aid of feminist theory, we may read enactments of subjectivity where before there were only angels and demons. Each of these writers makes sentences proper to her own use; each writes language alive with her own experience. Stein opens our access to language by uncategorizing (and ungendering) her use of words. All these writers together stop the phantom in her tracks. No matter how often she creeps back, she will find that we have moved on and are elsewhere.

2

The Language of Gertrude Stein

Once when my sister and I were children we were presented with a small ball of mercury. The sight of it delighted us. We were told to pick it up, and so we tried. But of course it was not such a simple matter as that. Neither liquid nor solid, and both at once, it seemed to us a kind of thing that was not a thing. We each tried to take hold of it, but always at the moment of touch, at the moment of contact, it was elsewhere. I think now that's what I liked most about it.

When I sit down to write about Gertrude Stein, I think of that mercury, of that moment of touch. For of course in attempting to take hold of her words, to say what I know of them, in that moment they are always elsewhere. And yes, that's what I like most about them. Reading her words, simply reading them, is quite another thing. They are words and I read them. Nothing could be more obvious. It's writing about those words that is the problem—for they are never in the same place twice.

Now this business of taking hold of something, of fixing it in place and having it to carry around with one, can be a very attractive proposition. It seems to matter, to make sense of the world and one's place in it. But what have you got, after all, when you take hold of something, of an idea, a person, a thing? Do you have it then? Have you made it real by grasping it and finding its place in the scheme of things? Schemes of things are made things, systems by which we learn to perceive order and the meaning order is supposed to confer. The stability thus offered, the points of departure and return in your quest for place or identity, make sense only from within a closed system of meaning. What you've got and what you do with what you've got must operate within that system or it scatters rather than coalesces your sense of who you are in relation to the-way-things-are. What you've got, in other words, must translate into something known so that it gives you access to Knowledge, capital *K*, the kind that is there to lead you to Answer and Universal Truth.

The thing is, even that gesture of taking hold and every moment of contact it produces are mediated by matters impossible to fix in place. They are never the same twice; you are never the same twice. Nothing could be more obvious. But if in your struggle with knowledge you have learned to settle on a shape, to give it dimensions and a name, to test it against all other shapes and names to be sure of its points of difference from them, if you have, in short, made sure it will come when you call it and that you will recognize it when it does, then it will seem the same, and so will you. Then you can relax; the close attention first required of you may be relinquished. From now on you may see it without looking. Just as you know how to identify a friend in the distance without seeing her face, you may now come upon this bit of knowledge time and again according to your expectations, as if it were always there, there for you, there for you to know. But this is not an act of knowing; it is an act of possession.

This is important. For however tempting it may be to find a firm hold on Gertrude Stein's writings, I am persuaded that what she did with words was not an act of possession but a continuously attentive act of knowing—what Mary Daly in *Gyn/Ecology* calls "changing the nouns of knowledge into verbs of know-ing" (11). Stein paid attention. Her interaction with words made a process, an endless sensitivity to movement (experience rather than ideology). That is what paying attention is. And reading what Stein wrote is best done with that same kind of attention. Stopping to explain, to lay hold of or name, interrupts what is happening, as if it could become known by being made to hold still. But paying attention is movement, and without movement there is no life. At her most attentive, Stein made what she called her "lively words." They do not stand still nor do they lay claim to fixed states of being or of meaning. So naturally the moment one lays claim to Stein's words for her, they are already elsewhere.

Words are a kind of thing that is not a thing. There they are, sound and form. Written down they can be seen, even touched, though what one touches is hard to say. Yet words are also matter for conveyance, delegates sent to transmit, to stand for or tell about.

When Stein wrote, she ignored none of this and left nothing out. In this way, she wrote something that is not about something but is something. Or she came as close as anyone has dared. Writing about what Stein wrote, then, seems always somehow to do it a disservice. Using words with all their capacities intact and alive, as she did, is no mean feat. I admire Stein's daring, but am left with my own limitations. For as a critic reading Stein, what I am offering is a reading of Stein. And when we say "reading" in this way, we mean an interpretation, an appraisal or explanation of significance, an effort to represent the meaning of what we read. Even having adapted to the lessons of Roland Barthes's writerly texts and writerly ways, most of us continue to write-about as if words were objects to encounter only when they were written by someone else. We may say that now we know this writing-about is also writing-itself, but we do it as if the real thing itself were through and behind and beyond our words. We write-about as if it were a means to a thing without also being a thing, never the same twice and fixed in place only at the cost of stopping its movement.

So at best I try to keep my eye on the mercury at that profoundly ambiguous moment of contact. It is there and then that movement happens. It is the movement that keeps me looking. Perhaps it's only human to try to grab hold of what moves. My sister and I did finally get the mercury between our fingers, though it was hard to feel even then. We rubbed it on an old dime to make it shine more than any dime we had ever seen, and it stopped being mercury. Maybe one of us kept the dime to hold out and show to our friends. I don't remember. But I do remember the movement and the ambiguity of the mercury, the sense of touch that was both there and not. That has remained with me all this time. It is what I bring to my reading of Stein. As I write, as I write about what Stein wrote, I am aware of the difficulty of paying attention, of accepting movement without imposing stasis merely for convenient handling. Stein is the most uncategorical writer I have ever read. No name fixes her words in place. It's what I like most, and what is most troublesome, as I try to say what I know of her words without leaving out the know-ing.

Of course you might say why not invent new names, new languages but that cannot be done. It takes a tremendous amount of inner necessity to invent even one word, one can invent imitating movements and emotions in sounds, and in the poetical language of some languages you have that, the german language as a language suffers from this what the words mean sound too much like what they do, and children do these things by one sort or another of invention, but this has really nothing to do with language. Language as a real thing is not imitation either of sounds or colors or emotions it is an intellectual recreation and there is no possible doubt about it and it is going to go on being that as long as humanity is anything. So everyone must stay with the language, their language that has come to be spoken and written and which has in it all the history of its intellectual recreation. (*Lectures in America* 237-38)

Language has everything to do with Gertrude Stein. The English language, written down, by an American living her life in France, was Stein's intellectual recreation. Writing is what she did. But because her words seem to so many so unlike other words (though they are the words we use every day, simple and homey words, not at all difficult as words go), her critics tend to spend a great deal of energy calling them by other names. As a language user, Stein is frequently said to have gone to the limits and even beyond of possibility. Thus, there is and has been a persistent critical stance toward her work that seeks to make sense of it by super-imposing more familiar paradigms on it, then reading through the paradigms to discover the "real" Stein. In this way, her words are compared to cubist paintings or musical cadences, to childlike ut-terances at once innocent and knowing as only unintentional wis-dom can be. Or she is said to have found the key to language's primordial past, or to have invented her own language, or merely to have capitalized on an idiosyncratic lack of grammatical skill. Barring all that, she is proclaimed mad or disingenuous, writing nonsense and passing it off as profundity. It is hardly ever said that she simply used language—language with all its complexity intact.

As her words from *Lectures in America* indicate, Stein knew that mere invention or imitation would get her nowhere. She had her language and it was her task to know it well and use it attentively. Certainly movement and rhythm, shape and color were part of what she wrote. She would wonder if one could see sound. And the visual, the tactile, the auditory, *as well as* the abstract, were always there. Of course this can be said of language too, of language itself. It's all already there. As she tells us through Alice in *The Autobiography of Alice B. Toklas*, "the english language was her medium and with the english language the task was to be achieved, the problem solved. The use of fabricated words offended her, it was an escape into imitative emotionalism" (112).

Well aware that her readers liked to explain her work by claiming other media as her models (thus making her words safe by recasting them as imitation), Stein said that one has only one "métier"
no matter how avidly one enjoys other pursuits. Writing was her
métier, and "looking at pictures" was her pursuit. She did not consider herself an artist as a painter is an artist, saying (again through
Alice), "she cannot draw anything. She feels no relation between
the object and the piece of paper" (71). Of the theater (despite or
perhaps as a reason for her own plays) she wrote, "it goes too
fast, the mixture of eye and ear bothers her and her emotion never
keeps pace" (70). As for music, "she finds it difficult to listen to
it, it does not hold her attention" (70). She noted that her readers
frequently said that the appeal of her work was "to the ear and
to the subconscious," but she herself identified her eyes and her
mind as the "active and important" components of what she did
with words (70).

As for the subconscious, that demiworld so appealing to those
who prefer to explain her work as the product of trance-induced
techniques, she went so far as to claim, "Gertrude Stein never had
sub-conscious reactions, nor was she a successful subject for automatic writing" (74). This comment is aimed specifically at those
who would trace her method to her participation at Radcliffe in
psychological experiments in automatic writing proposed by her
teacher William James. (These experiments resulted in two articles
published in 1896 and 1898 by the Harvard *Psychological Review*.
The first, "Normal Motor Automatism," was written by her partner
Leon M. Solomons but listed her as co-author in recognition of
her participation. The second, "Cultivated Motor Automatism: A
Study of Character in Its Relation to Attention," was written by
her alone and stands as her first published writing.) Even at the
time, Stein did not believe "automatic writing" to be what the
experiments produced and remained far more interested in the
reactions of the subjects to the experiments than in the experiments themselves (Mellow 48-49; Wilder vii). More to the point,
however, because her part in these studies is frequently cited as
evidence for her writing as the result of "subconscious" or "automatic" states of mind, her comment in *The Autobiography* serves,
as does so much of that work, to give her equal time, as it were,
in the game of Explaining Gertrude Stein.

The fact is, Stein chose language as her medium. She did not
choose paint or music (though music was set to some of her words
by Virgil Thomson), but language. She could have chosen no medium

so vulnerable and so challenging, for we all, every one of us, lay claim to language. It is what we like to think of as that which, like opposing thumbs and upright posture, makes us uniquely human. We like to think that we have invested language—and that it invests us—with all of human thought, imagination, and identity. We have written it down as a record of "us" through time, complete with our universalized concepts of truth, fact, and who "us" includes. We distinguish human language from just any pragmatic set of signals exchanged between creatures and call it the only real language. It places us, we like to say, at the pinnacle of creation. With language we step away from the animals and into civilization. With language we make order out of chaos, meaning out of raw data, and identity out of our geographical and biological arrangements with one another. Mess with language and you mess with human beingness.

Gertrude Stein messed with language. Or, rather, she interfered with the culture's insistence on its orderly and representative functions. Near the end of her life she said in an interview for Robert Bartlett Haas, "I like a thing simple, but it must be simple through complication. Everything must come into your scheme; otherwise you cannot achieve real simplicity" (A Primer for the Gradual Understanding of Gertrude Stein 34). Stein used everything, rejecting nothing and basing what she did on an intensely close interaction with words rather than on linguistic conquest of uncharted territory. The ability to use everything may be precisely what confuses her would-be interpreters. As discussed in the previous chapter, we are heavily influenced by Western culture's preference for a system of meaning in which oppositional contrast in a hierarchic formulation leads to Truth and Answer. It is easy enough to see how Stein's readers, under such influence, would be seduced into selecting already-explicated paradigms (painting, music, etc.) as categories or keys to discovering hidden teleological meaning in her words. Such categories, however, can only reproduce what we have already been taught to know. The need to simplify by exclusion (making inclusion somehow suspect as less rigorous) creates tidy but artificial limitations for what we can encounter as real or possible. Stein knew this and used everything. It seemed only right. As she has Alice say of her, "she did not understand why since the writing was all so clear and natural they mocked at and were enraged by her work" (The Autobiography 32-33).

Yet Stein's reputation is that of an esoteric writer, difficult if not impossible to read, funny but altogether enigmatic. It is not uncommon for readers to refer to her words as fascinating but annoying. Her words are used both to mythologize and condemn her. And insofar as she is portrayed as not fully in control of what she wrote, her words cannot be read for their extraordinary "complex simplicity." Thus, while it is often enough acknowledged that what Stein did with words was remarkable, it is just as often concluded that she could not, after all, do what she did.

"Language as a real thing" is the problem here. We learn language as a vehicle for meanings or interactions between us. If it is also a thing in itself, available to anyone as raw material, then how can we be sure of its orderly use? That is, how then can we be sure we will know what it "means"? For Stein, language is what it is, nothing more and nothing less. And whatever one does with one's language, it is the language as one has it that one must work with. The writer does not create a new language, but writes in a language as it "has come to be spoken and written and which has in it all the history of its intellectual recreation." This language is *both* a real thing in itself and a means for conveying mind, identity, perception, and the many histories that produce our experiences of them at any given time. It is commonly said that Stein in her writing evaded time, dispensed with or secretly coded what we usually recognize as identity, attempted to make of words objects in themselves—in short, that she disrupted, mismanaged, or otherwise interfered with the prime objective of language: communication. This seems to be an unforgivable, or at least profoundly disturbing, transgression. Though much of her work is clear enough even to the most conventional of readers, and though even her most experimental writing uses the commonest of words, there is a persistent interest in preserving Stein's use of language as a puzzle to be solved, if not simply an anomalous outrage on the sensibilities of her fellow language users.

What then is language as a "real thing," an "intellectual recreation"? Language is a thing which is also not a thing. Written down it is there on the page and yet invisible; we learn to read through it to something else. As for reality, we have seen how slippery that is, how the intellectual traditions of Western culture have been aimed at naming it and fixing it in place for all time as a universal plumb line by which to know that we do exist and are not only named and defined but nameable and definable. We have seen how modern minds have called reality into question and revealed its relationship to language and narrative not as unproblematic representation but as a culturally motivated construct. Stein herself is often thought of as one who rejected the past to re-create the present. But it is more accurate to say that she neither rejected nor relied on the past, but stood firmly where and when she was, concentrating on all that she found there. As she said in "Composition as Explanation," "the only thing that is different from one time to another is what is seen and what is seen depends on how everybody is doing everything" (*What Are Masterpieces* 26). This is a way to talk about subjectivity (as does Teresa de Lauretis) as a process of interaction in a social-historical context. This is also a way to talk about time and reality as both constant and never the same twice; it is our interaction with them that constitutes what we know, or in Stein's words, that "makes a composition."

Stein's language is both full of history and free from antecedents. It is possible to read her words again and again as if for the first time. One is drawn into the ambiguity of her "intellectual recreation," finding the work of rethinking and the refreshment of mind-play (re-creation and recreation) equally and simultaneously likely. Her language is wholly of its own past and future by virtue of its complete presence or what, especially in reference to her early work, she called "the continuous present." And certainly there is a sense of playfulness in Stein; most any of her readers can hear the laugh in her work. What Stein called her "lively words" make a good example of all this. These are taken from the "Food" section of *Tender Buttons*:

> So then the sound is not obtrusive. Suppose it is obtrusive suppose it is. What is certainly the desertion is not a reduced description, a description is not a birthday.
>   Lovely snipe and tender turn, excellent vapor and slender butter, all the splinter and the trunk all the poisonous darkening drunk, all the joy in weak success, all the joyful tenderness, all the section and the tea, all the stouter symmetry.
>   Around the size that is small, inside the stern that is the middle, besides the remains that are praying, inside the between that is turning, all the region is measuring and melting is exaggerating. (479)

This is a passage to roll around on the tongue; or let the eyes take it in one word at a time. It first seems to talk to the reader in the way that writing does when it has a message to deliver. But it doesn't let you get too comfortable. Soon there's that flight into lyrical sound and an old "tyger" winks out at us. Then there's another shift in rhythm and one slows down to watch each word move on its own despite having come to expect a rhyme. Here the words become autonomous entities without giving up their involvements with one another. As for me, I get to "melting is exaggerating," and I laugh.

This language does not ask us to look through it for something else. This language is what it is and offers us contact as we are ready to accept it. Literary traditions and linguistic histories are not absent; neither are they paradigmatic cues to some right or real meaning. It is easy enough to imagine Stein's immediate experience of her surroundings as one reads, and just as easy to hear a purposeful and artful arrangement in her decisions on the page. What I notice most, however, is my own immediate experience of the words—they seem to ask for attention from all my senses at once. We seem to be in it together, these words and I. Stein has chosen and has placed her words so that they make movement, a live presence. They slide and stop, turn and talk, invite me in and let me choose my own part in the composition while they are what they are, always there but never quite the same twice. They neither depend on nor deny what comes before or after, but seem more like fully developed beings interacting as they must.

Stein often wrote of listening and looking until she could see the relationship in words and people. She claimed that she loved to diagram sentences and that it was the only way really to know them. She has Alice remark in *The Autobiography*, "I always say that you cannot tell what a picture really is or what an object really is until you dust it every day and you cannot tell what a book is until you type it or proof-read it" (106). Personal contact, one word at a time. I always think of Stein's process of writing as a kind of entering into language. She seems to look and listen, every day, until she finds the movement or being already inside the words, not the movement we are taught to expect, but that which makes the words real as words.

Stein's words are full of presence. It is difficult to take any of them for granted or to assume that one word will follow another in any way automatically. One is not asked to remember or anticipate in order to read (though of course there are also those narratives in which Stein uses a preposition or a conjunction almost as disinterestedly as the next person). Her words have in them all possibilities at each moment, not as fixed states but as a kind of animate energy always full of its moment so that locating it in a category to describe or explain it becomes merely convenient, and irrelevant. It is better to meet these words on their own terms,

like being part of a conversation in which you must pay attention
so that you respond to what you really hear rather than waiting
for the speaker to pause so you can say what you were already
thinking all along.

EYE GLASSES
A color in shaving, a saloon is well placed in the centre of an alley.
(*Tender Buttons* 470)

Selecting passages of Stein's writing to examine is always
somewhat misleading. Reading as many of her pages as one can,
continuously, is much more exciting. There is something in the accumulated effect that adds to their life. (The recurrent insistences
in the long passages of *The Making of Americans* and "Melanctha"
in *Three Lives*, for instance, become richly populated worlds of their
own the more one reads.) Writing about Stein's writing, then, can
feel uncomfortably close to critical appropriation of significance,
though her writing resists it more than most. Such appropriation is
undoubtedly a result of the act of writing-about; it is the move
made by an interpreter of writing. Yet Stein's words do not demand
such a move, and tend to confound it, though it is there to be
made if one chooses. But open response must not be tucked away
in the folds of critical tidiness. Certainly there are those who say
they are pushed away by Stein's words, and perhaps many of them
prefer a critical distance when they speak of her work. However,
it is just as easy and much more rewarding—though by far less
comfortable—to get one's nose, so to speak, as up close to Stein's
words as one can get it. This does require a willingness to keep
all one's faculties alert and open to surprise, as alert and open as
Stein must have been in writing the words down in the first place.
For as common as these words are, their effect is anything but
ordinary.

Writing presence with "lively words" is pretty radical stuff.
It has a certain resistance to any sort of containment. There is the
sense that it might do or be anything at any given moment. This
is no doubt what makes of Stein criticism always something that
somehow just misses the mark. It too often assumes there is a
mark to hit and that once hit, it will stay put. As we have seen,
language is not unmediated representation of reality, despite its
cultural and ideological investments in a window-on-the-world
function. Still, narrative theorists and literary scholars and most
anyone who likes a good old-fashioned yarn will find a sense of
security in the idea that words convey the realities we all have

access to because we all know what words already mean or can mean. That sense of security is not disturbed but only reinforced (or just enforced) by the volumes written to teach us how to read what we read.

Whole careers have been made demonstrating that all peoples use language, that all language users tell stories, and that all stories follow identifiable universal patterns by which we recognize meaning. These patterns are inscribed as narrative codes, then posited as essential to the existence not only of narrative (Story), but of communication itself. Without these codes (orderly sequences of time and event occurring in relational contexts of agency and receptivity), it is said that the transmission of meaning cannot take place. And without the transmission of meaning (i.e., communication), language becomes nonsensical or disappears. That, at least, is the structuralist's way of seeing it. It is a way of seeing that still holds popular sway despite poststructural interrogations of the very production of meaning. For we are doggedly loyal to the notion of language as first and foremost a tool for communication, as a transactive device effective only through the operations of linguistic law and order.

So it is that unfamiliar language, especially when it uses such familiar words as Stein's, is said to break laws and destroy order. In a culture obsessed by opposition as a means to unity, by the safety of universality as the assurance that even fragmentation adheres to prescribed patterns of meaning, a voice such as Stein's must be heard as profoundly dangerous. For rather than destroying to create anew, she merely enters the presence of language, coded baggage and all, as if she could express her experience of it just as she chooses to express and experience it. And into the bargain, her words are indeed most amazingly difficult to contain; no explanation for them quite does it. She seems to have found limitless possibility in language and for the most part to have been able to write it onto the page without interfering unduly with its unpredictable, lively movement.

We do love to read her words, those of us who do. Yet we often feel all too unsettled by what we read. Which of course is the point. Being unsettled thrives on movement and liveliness; it provides a perfect opportunity for paying attention. To be sure, many are discomfited by being unsettled and they seek to rectify the conditions that bring it about. Rectification abhors surprise; it takes on discovery (from the verb "to dis-cover," let us say) only as a precaution against surprise. Reading Stein involves an almost unconditional willingness to be surprised. She does not meet expectations, not even the expectation of meeting the unexpected. One doesn't if one really uses everything. And this requires a quite remarkably aware consciousness of what one is doing. Stein wrote simply by actively know-ing the complexities of language. She did exactly what she had to do: she wrote language as a real thing, an intellectual recreation. Reading what she wrote is best done with respect for her openness to possibility and play. Here are some of her words from late in her 1913 poem "Sacred Emily":

> Color mahogany.
> Color mahogany center.
> Rose is a rose is a rose is a rose.
> Loveliness extreme.
> Extra gaiters.
> Loveliness extreme.
> Sweetest ice-cream.
> Page ages page ages page ages.
> Wiped Wiped wire wire.
> Sweeter than peaches and pears and cream.
> Wiped wire wiped wire.
> Extra extreme.
> Put measure treasure.
> Measure treasure.
> Tables track.
> Nursed.
> Dough.
> That will do.
> (*Geography and Plays* 187)

On her 1934-35 tour of America, Stein noted, "and then everybody almost everybody likes a resemblance even when there is none" (*Lectures in America* 85). This statement occurs in her essay "Pictures" and refers in context to painters and painting. But of course what she has to say on the subject applies to her writing as well, including this piece of her poem. Stein is nearly always her own best critic. Here she is talking about representational art. She has just said that when people feel annoyed by a painting they think it is because of the way in which the painting represents what it is a painting of. She, however, believes the annoyance really comes from the fact that the painting exists in the first place by virtue of that which it represents—"and profoundly it should not do so" (84). The reason it should not do so is because, as she so simply puts it, "an oil painting is an oil painting." Nevertheless, a painting inevitably exists in some relation to the people, objects, and landscapes the painter paints. She speculates that most painters then spend their lives trying to escape this inevitability. It is this struggle, she says, to which everyone responds, liking or disliking what they see "depending upon whether they think the struggle is hopeless or whether it is not" (84-85). For those painters in whom she was most interested (such as Cézanne and Picasso), she doubtless found the struggle not to be hopeless. Nevertheless, the "naturally pleasant" human preference for resemblances makes everything "difficult very difficult."

A few years later Stein wrote in a similar way about writing in "What Are Master-Pieces and Why Are There So Few of Them" (published in 1940 in the volume titled *What Are Masterpieces*). She refers to the earlier essay's analysis of paintings as existing in and for themselves while the painter needs external things to bring paintings into existence. As she so often noted, this problem of the relation between the external and the internal occupied her all of her life. It is a problem of identity and of existence (perhaps even of origins, though not the dream of Origin as Answer), and it troubles the writer just as it troubles the painter.

In the later essay, Stein immerses us in the process of knowing what a masterpiece is by helping us to recognize what it is not. Recognition, in fact, alerts us to what it is not. Masterpieces are "things in themselves"; what they are not are remembered things. Recognition, as a product of memory, is what we learn to rely on as proof of identity and existence. But it is a misleading proof since it does not involve us in what is happening but only in what has happened or in a re-presentation of it. "These days," Stein says, people don't experience but only know what happens "by radios cinemas newspapers biographies autobiographies until what is happening does not really thrill any one" (*What Are Masterpieces* 87). We have learned, that is, to know our experiences and ourselves second-hand. (We have learned, one might say, to know without being there. This is how we can mistake cultural ideology for the truth of our experiences.)

Stein writes, "all this sounds awfully complicated but it is not complicated at all, it is just what happens" (89). Here she is asking us to pay attention. "Just what happens" is a presence. It cues a matter of fact while involving us in the moment, the moment that is never not now; it offers us a process of movement, an experience of attention. The thing in itself, experience itself, makes a masterpiece. If, however, you write by remembering, by trying "to remember what you are about to write," you are relying on used information (89). Remembering, constantly recognizing what you already know in order to know and say it, produces what Stein calls "secondary writing," writing that is dull, lifeless, and dependent on the external for its identity. And identity thus encountered traps both the writing and the writer in a kind of imitative code of representation: "and so they are not an entity but an identity" (90).

Identity (as this recognized and recognizable thing) becomes irrelevant in the act of doing or being. It has no beginning and no ending, and neither does what (at its best) is created without identity. The relation of production to product, however, of the internal to the external, remains problematic both for the writer and for what the writer writes. "I am I because my little dog knows me but, creatively speaking the little dog knowing that you are you and your recognizing that he knows, that is what destroys creation" (84). It is the work of law and order, the cultural codes of meaning and being, to produce experience as re-cognition. But it is being itself, doing itself, language itself as itself, that makes masterpieces. Like identity in relation to recognition, writing as an act of remembering is bound by artificial limitations. It is for the writer to understand those limitations from the inside out, as it were, so as not to become trapped by their seeming inevitability. The trouble is, even masterpieces, those things in themselves without beginning or end, "have to use beginning and ending to become existing" (89). The relation, however, that gives us access to art is not art. Consequently, Stein referred to the writers of her time as "desperately not having a beginning and an ending" (89). Like the painter who struggles to escape the inevitability of the relation of the painting to what is painted, the writer spends her life trying to escape the inevitability of the relation of the writing to what is written, of identity to recognition and language to identity. It is no doubt this struggle to which we respond.

If we look again at the lines from "Sacred Emily," we can see that Stein was well into her struggle. Here, as elsewhere, she presents us with the difficulty of liking a resemblance even when there is none, yet confounds rather than denies the associational preferences we bring to language. That is, she neither invents nor reproduces meaning, but enacts words as they are with everything intact. The composer Virgil Thomson, referring to setting Stein's poems to music, once commented that the meanings in her words were "already abstracted, or absent, or so multiplied that choice among them was impossible" (Mellow 369). This entering into language without limiting its possibilities is not arrived at haphazardly; it requires an exacting attention to what is, as it is. The words of "Sacred Emily," like most of Stein's words, may be read as written by one with what she called in *The Autobiography* "the intellectual passion for exactitude" (198). For Stein this meant that she could produce on the page "a simplification by this concentration, and as a result the destruction of associational emotion in poetry and prose" (198-99). It is in this concentrated exactitude that Stein struggled with "the thing in itself." (This concept, to which Stein refers often, is remarkably like what Virginia Woolf proposed in *A Room of One's Own* as "freedom to think of things in themselves" apart from the culture's assignments of identity. The striking similarity between the concepts as used by these two writers leaves one to wonder at their seemingly careful indifference to one another.)

In any case, things in themselves, complete with the irrelevance of beginnings and endings yet making use of "all the history of its intellectual recreation," can certainly be seen in "Sacred Emily." Concentration, simplification, and exactitude abound. There is precious little "associational emotion" except as one chooses to encounter it from inside one's own mind and experience. Stein's words do not refuse association, they merely do not depend upon it—and even go far toward becoming indifferent to it by the intensity of their own being and presence. These words are not remembered words, nor can they easily be reproduced by remembering them. There is that line of roses for which Stein is so especially remembered, but of course all that came later.

> Color mahogany.
> Color mahogany center.
> Rose is a rose is a rose is a rose.
> Loveliness extreme.
> Extra gaiters.
> Loveliness extreme.

The thing is, these lines use the most familiar of words, and even take advantage of familiar connections (roses, loveliness, color, for instance), yet meet no familiar expectations of meaning. This does not make them meaningless. They are what they are. They are words, words arranged on a page, and words are things in themselves as much as they are signs in a system constructed to make meaning. This might be a way to talk about nonrepresentational writing. Just as paintings exist as themselves though they come into being in relation to what is outside them, nonrepresentational writing can be said to use a linguistic sign system based on the function of relation though not relying on the codes of relation to exist as writing. In Stein's case, however, nonrepresentational writing may be more aptly termed "simply writing" in respect for its resistance to even merely descriptive nomenclatures.

Though categories such as nonrepresentational, abstract, or cubist have been widely applied to Stein's work, they are misleading as explanations of it. They are, by and large, attempts to translate Stein's words rather than to read them. Her friendships with Picasso, Gris, Picabia, her intense interest in modern painting, her written comments about what it is and what it does, all conspire to make comparisons between her writing and the painters' painting almost irresistible. She herself occasionally encouraged such comparisons. However, what is deceptively obvious is that Stein wrote words; she put words on paper, not paint on canvas. And words are so intimately allied for us with the human mind, with (as I have said) the concept of human beingness itself, that they are charged as no other medium can be with a kind of acculturated responsibility for representational accuracy. As writer Monique Wittig points out in her essay "The Trojan Horse," no one expects color, sound, clay, and paint to have meaning on their own. Literature, however, is an art of words; and words, even as raw material, are always already expected to mean.

Stein often referred to her word compositions in tactile or visual terms, such as buttons, portraits, or landscapes. This makes it all the more tempting to draw direct parallels between her writing and the modernist revolutions in the visual or plastic arts. The critic who takes on this task, however, invariably gets trapped into trying to force a separation of form and content in Stein's words to make them available as plastic substances like paint or clay. But as Wittig tells us, "in words form and content cannot be dissociated, because they partake of the same form, the form of a word, a material form" (49). While most critics who write about what is called nonrepresentational writing acknowledge this paradoxical excess, they also move to contain it rather than let it proliferate. Consequently, they must at some point conclude that it is impossible to use words as raw material for the artistic rearrangement of form to which conventional meaning does not adhere. This is a way to allow for the noncoincidence of convention and language while retaining convention in language as our only access to meaning. It is also a way to construct a project for Stein, then pronounce it a failure on the very grounds by which it was constructed in the first place.

Such machinations are indicative of the extent to which critics perceive Stein's words as mysteriously secret or coded, and thus in need of being "solved." Claiming them as experimental substances used to imitate cubist or abstract inventions seems at first blush just such a solution. To that end Wendy Steiner in *Exact Resemblance to Exact Resemblance,* for example, reads Stein's portraits as literary versions of portrait painting and compares Stein's use of words to a painter's use of geometric forms as "structural abstractions of real objects" (135). Once the abstractions, on canvas, become the objects themselves, the paintings become fully nonrepresentational. Steiner seems to want to apply this same principle to Stein's writing as a way to rescue Stein from meaninglessness. This operation is dependent upon reading Stein's words as meaningless in the first place, or what Steiner calls "a depiction of the author's thoughts in a manner not available to her audience" (130). She can then invest them with significance by restructuring them as literary cubism. But she is unable to allow words to slide between sign and object as she sees geometric forms doing. For Steiner, words are never not signs that must mean in relation to a referentiality outside themselves. And once she has constructed that referentiality for Stein as the painter's realm of nonrepresentational form, she must try to get Stein's words to act like paint. But they do not. So Steiner is ultimately compelled to declare Stein a failure on the basis of being unable to translate pictorial norms into literary ones. The translation, however, was always Steiner's, not Stein's.

Another aspect of this attempt to read Stein in terms of the plastic arts may be found in Michael J. Hoffman's *The Development of Abstractionism in the Writings of Gertrude Stein.* Hoffman first defines abstraction as a leaving out of elements of external detail to focus instead on "essences." He then finds in Stein's work a progressively more abstract reduction of lexical meaning in favor of something like "pure sound and syntax" (19). In works such as *Tender Buttons,* he sees Stein as "beginning to use words as plastic elements in creations that have no iconic relationship to anything conceptually recognizable in the external world" (153). This of course leads him to conclude that "abstract art, by the definition we have been using, is an impossibility, especially in writing" (176). The reasons for this lie in the relationship of external reality to words. Unlike Stein herself, who saw the struggle to escape the inevitability of the relation of the external to the internal as compelling and not hopeless, Hoffman is mired in the equation of language to external referentiality or association as its only access to meaning. For him language is communication and communication is referential. His definition of abstraction, applied to Stein, forces him to see her work as "an art that created its own reality" (178), then to find such a creation impossible precisely because words are "inherently associative." He cannot allow words to be both associative and things in themselves, especially not at the same time. His solution to the problem he has made of Stein collapses back on itself as he separates form and content to read her, then finds the separation untenable. He seems never to notice, however, that the separation is his and not hers.

Certainly the concerns of modern painting are not absent from the concerns of Stein's writing. One may talk of Cézanne decentering the canvas by making every part of it equal in value, of Picasso's vital reliance on the presence of his own vision, of art becoming an interrelationship of forms subject to the intellect and the laws of art itself rather than to the conventions of representation. One may even talk of a modernist dislocation of the complicity between memory and perception, and it would all be relevant to what Stein did with words. She herself wrote of her intense interest in what the artists were doing and of her participation in working out the theories behind such modernist discontinuities of convention. But attempts to discover equivalencies between her words and modern painting always get caught in a trap. That trap is a reliance on the convention of reading through language to something else. The literary-cubism school of criticism reads through Stein's words to the principles of the plastic arts and thereby intends to encounter her words as objects in themselves. But because they are words, that encounter entails a reformulation of them into impossibly empty signs to see them as objects at all. Thus, they are not read as or for themselves, but as occasions for extralinguistic imitation.

Stein is not an alchemist transforming words into things and things into words. Neither is she the inventor of a private language or a rebel against language altogether. She accepts language for what it is—a deceptively simple accomplishment on her part. When she uses words, she rejects nothing. Words are physical and auditory realities. Together they make communities, often as if of their own volition, complete with comings and goings, affinities, incompatibilities, moments of isolation and cooperation alike. Written, they have shapes, can be seen, and are tactile (as in ancient cuneiform, Braille, raised letterings, ideographs, even ink or type on a page, though less obviously so). But in addition, words conjure up sounds, images, and ideas inside our minds. We see, hear, feel, and touch words, just as we do events, things, and people in our lives. As the working parts of formal language systems, words also communicate according to the cultural codes constituted by their histories and their contextual uses. Words, that is, are both entities in and of themselves and symbols of cultural relationships and transactions. To write them, Stein did not choose one possibility over another, but chose them all, on her own terms. This makes her words both like and unlike any other words we know.

> A CARAFE, THAT IS A BLIND GLASS
> A kind in glass and a cousin, a spectacle and nothing strange a single hurt color and an arrangement in a system to pointing. All this and not ordinary, not unordered in not resembling. The difference is spreading. (*Tender Buttons* 461)

Thornton Wilder, writer and Stein's friend, makes it clear that she was well aware of the benefits and difficulties of attending to the lively interactions of all possibilities in words. In his introduction to her *Four in America*, he relates an incident at one of her University of Chicago lectures. A student asked her to explain her by-then most famous line of roses, first written in "Sacred Emily." Though somewhat lengthy, Wilder's transcription of her response is worth quoting in its entirety since it demonstrates Stein's playfully complex understanding of language and literature and her own relationship with words. As Wilder tells it, the student asked his question and Stein "leaned forward giving all of herself to the questioner" as she said:

> Now listen! Can't you see that when the language was new—as it was with Chaucer and Homer—the poet could use the name of a thing and the thing was really there? He could say "O moon," "O sea," "O love" and the moon and the sea and love were really there. And can't you see that after hundreds of years had gone by and thousands of poems had been written, he could call on those words and find that they were just wornout literary words? The excitingness of pure being had withdrawn from them; they were just rather stale literary words. Now the poet has to work in the excitingness of pure being; he has to get back that intensity into the language. We all know that it's hard to write poetry in a late age; and we know that you have to put some strangeness, something unexpected, into the structure of the sentence in order to bring back vitality to the noun. Now it's not enough to be bizarre; the strangeness in the sentence structure has to come from the poetic gift, too. That's why it's doubly hard to be a poet in a late

age. Now you all have seen hundreds of poems about roses and you
know in your bones that the rose is not there. All those songs that
sopranos sing as encores about "I have a garden; oh, what a garden!"
Now I don't want to put too much emphasis on that line, because it's
just one line in a longer poem. But I notice that you all know it; you
make fun of it, but you know it. Now listen! I'm no fool. I know that
in daily life we don't go around saying "is a . . . is a . . . is a . . . ."
Yes, I'm no fool; but I think that in that line the rose is red for the
first time in English poetry for a hundred years. (v-vi)

Yes, the line is just one line in a longer poem. And yes, it can
also be read as and for itself. If one is paying attention as one
reads, making contact one word at a time in the context of a great
many words together, then it is easy enough to see the redness in
the rose without having to rely on centuries of poetic traditions
of love, passion, and the prickly nature of beauty to do it. It's just
there, in the words, words repeated one after another in the way
Stein liked to repeat—for the insistence on intensity and indivi-
duality that is lost when words are isolated. "Everything must come
into your scheme." Even the nod to Shakespeare is there if one
wants it. This is not language devoid of history or tradition; they
help it "to become existing." But neither is it language that seeks to
extend, best, or overthrow what has been. It is language that exists
in the relations between socially produced meaning and materiality
of experience, in a continually shifting process resistant to univer-
sal(ized) identification or identity. As Stein wrote, "it is not extremely difficult not to have identity but it is extremely difficult
the knowing not having identity" (*What Are Masterpieces* 90).

When Stein says that when language was new a poet could
use the name of a thing and the thing was really there, she is
referring to that "vitality" in the noun that has come to be taken
over by naming as an act of definition and possession rather than of
evocation and attention. Part of our cultural mythology includes the
story that once upon a time a poet's utterance was magic. The poet,
having an especially intense relationship with words, could come to
know "the excitingness of pure being" in them and call out their
names as enactments of real things in themselves. For Stein the
magic is not just conjuring but an open (unpredetermined) concentration on life and movement. In "a late age," however, words
and names and sentences and nouns have become predictable; they
bring the baggage of their histories with them. And the writer
who only imitates history, one might say, mistakes the baggage
(the already-known) for the thing in itself. Consequently, we are

left with words that are only representations. They are stand-ins for lively beings; they have been rendered lawful and lifeless by their enforced dependence on memory.

Stein talks about this in her essay "Poetry and Grammar." There she says, "that is what poetry is it is a state of knowing and feeling a name" (*Lectures in America* 233). But the task of this knowing and feeling is made difficult by the fact that names of things become too familiar while the things remain what they are: "As I say a noun is a name of a thing, and therefore slowly if you feel what is inside that thing you do not call it by the name by which it is known" (210). To come to her "lively words" (the words of *Tender Buttons*, most of her poetry, portraits, and plays, as well as much of her most playful prose), and to keep her words lively, she wrote as if the language were both ancient and new, known and unknown at the same time. Language such as this could be forever coming into being. "Was there not a way of naming things that would not invent names, but mean names without naming them," she asked (236). Yes, there was. But it meant putting "some strangeness, something unexpected" into her writing. And this she did.

> Very fine is my valentine.
> Very fine and very mine.
> Very mine is my valentine very mine and
>   very fine.
> Very fine is my valentine and mine, very fine
>   very mine and mine is my valentine.
> ("A Valentine to Sherwood Anderson," as quoted in
>   "Poetry and Grammar" 239)

Indeed she was no fool. But for her trouble she has often been characterized as a kind of unthinking conduit by which her immediate experience of her immediate surroundings passed "automatically" through her eyes, brain, and ear onto the page. In this view, Stein is seen to concentrate on physical experience without conscious thought, then to record whatever words came to her during the process. Thus the Objects, Food, and Rooms of *Tender Buttons* become whatever she happened to see or hear as she wrote; poems like "Susie Asado" ("Sweet sweet sweet sweet sweet tea. / Susie Asado") become word-transcriptions of flamenco dancing, and so forth. Such readings unduly limit Stein's words; they suggest an unwillingness on the part of the reader-critic to stay attentive at every moment and a certain law-and-order bound need to contain Stein's freedom by capturing her words in convenient explications.

Thus she must point out to her Chicago audience that she is well aware of the difference between daily utterance and her rosy line of poetry. And she is well aware that no matter how deprecatingly the line is read, its readers nevertheless know it well and like to quote it. "They always say, she says, that my writing is appalling but they always quote it and what is more, they quote it correctly. . . . My sentences do get under their skin, only they do not know that they do, she has often said" (*The Autobiography* 66).

CHICKEN
Alas a dirty word, alas a dirty third alas a dirty third, alas a dirty bird. (*Tender Buttons* 492)

Yes, there is that about Stein's work which is somehow irresistible even to her detractors. It is often difficult to write about her without imitating her style—perhaps in part because her style is so free from imitation. Writers often lament the limitations of their languages and so are tempted to invent as if from scratch. There is much talk about this among those who would evade the limitations of patriarchal language by inventing a language free from the hegemonies of race, class, and sex. But as Stein knew, one cannot really invent new languages. What she did with words was something else. As she told her Chicago questioner, one must get "intensity" back into language by working in "the excitingness of pure being." Her ability to do just that makes her writing particularly relevant to the search for a way to give voice to experience unconstrained by ideological presuppositions.

You may take the words of your culture as you find them in your time and turn them against themselves, revealing their complicity in creating images designed to serve dominance and hierarchic privilege. You may use the words you have but apply them to hitherto denied or hidden realities, giving those realities public lives and thereby disrupting cultural complacency. These tactics very often work very well; other women writers have put them to good use. But these were not Stein's projects. She was after something even more radical, at the root of our access to language itself. She approached words on their own terms as well as hers, respecting their used and unused capacities alike. She looked inside them for their own being, without separating them from the sign system and its baggage, know-ing them without remembering them, listening hard for the vitality that keeps them from merely serving old masters in new ways. She gave each and any of us words of our own, by insisting on uncategorical uses of them. Here is Stein at work again:

> There is all there is when there has all there has where there is what there is. That is what is done when there is done what is done and the union is won and the division is the explicit visit. There is not all of any visit. ("Portrait of Mabel Dodge at the Villa Curonia," *Selected Writings* 530)

Because her words so often escape cultural codes of identity and meaning, they are unbound in ways that oppositional attacks on linguistic formulation cannot be. Because in her writing she never gives up anything nor takes anything by conquest, her words are only themselves in all their complicated simplicity. She left forced invention to the Logos-forgers, to those who would claim the territory of language and self for their own and offer it to others as re-mastered material dragged from the mire of conventional illusion. The modernist period, with its explosive social, political, and artistic upheavals, must have seemed an almost ideal context for reinventing meaning. And writers such as James Joyce and Ernest Hemingway took up the challenge in a longing for myth, which produced in their works an underlying determination to become culture's ultimate heirs by re-creating culture through their repossession of The Word as source of meaning and (new) order. Stein, however, is no one's heir, both by virtue of cultural gender and because of her words' insistence on being only what they are. She is as nearly free of myth in her writing as one can be. (That she herself has become such a mythic figure is doubtless a response to this as well as a familiar method of recapturing unruly female speakers into more proprietary iconic forms.)

For Joyce and Hemingway, however, each in his own way, freedom of expression is wrested from the laws and the fathers into whose world they are born(e). Their task is not only to take their rightful places as namers and definers of that world but also to demythologize their cultural forebears to remythologize themselves as new heroes in a new world. Joyce makes of his "Artist as a Young Man" a hero on a quest for mastery of language and the role of master that comes with it. His *Ulysses* (its reputation ever a thorn in Stein's side) produces narrative structure itself as an epic quest. And in *Finnegans Wake* he makes of the mother-tongue both source and prize for the writer/heir/hero who reclaims culture by reinventing its language. Hemingway, once Stein's friend and (she notes) pupil, relies on the adequacy of the written sign system to which he is heir, but uses it to recast himself as a tragic figure of modern loss who must reduce language to its bare bones to find a place for himself as its master. His writing is relentlessly marked by a sense of having to piece together from the broken parts of the larger-than-life hero a new man, a man who can look on the horrors of the world, sustain terrible wounds, and still rise with (as) the sun (son), complete with missing parts. It's as if he cannot forgive the modern world for killing off its heroes and must claim himself in heroic proportions in order to be at all.

For writers such as these, language is about possession and control. They are the ones looked to for definitions of modernist literature and the canons formed around those definitions. They fit nicely a tradition of hierarchized mastery that continues to be valorized in critical conferences of meaning such as Harold Bloom's "anxieties of influence" and Jacques Lacan's reculturalization of the human psyche in gender-complicit terms of speaking and silence. They are writers who are culturally reassuring, even as they disturb the complacencies of cultural conventions. They are not always good boys; but then, bad boys are a time-honored version of cultural hero.

Stein is frequently linked with both Joyce and Hemingway, the one as her imagined usurper of desired literary place and the other as her competitive friend whom she spurned when he became too famous or when Alice became too suspicious. Most any story about Stein's relationship to these writers contributes to the mythic impulses so handy for reconceptualizing her as a jealous woman; this is a move that discounts her uncapturable words by replacing them with a more recognizable image of cultural combat between Selves and Others. There is little doubt that she did indeed regard Joyce's work with animosity or that her break with Hemingway was charged with emotion on both sides. What she herself says about these writers, however, is instructive in terms of her own notion of enacting presence on the page. In *The Autobiography* she pairs Joyce with the painter Braque and quotes Picasso assaying of them both, "they are the incomprehensibles whom anybody can understand" (200). For Hemingway she reserved a degree of affection, but ultimately pronounced his work dishonest; she attributed his success to pretense, saying of him, "he looks like a modern and he smells of the museums" (204). Both remarks, even allowing for Stein's regret and anger toward their subjects, indicate her understanding of writing not as a territory to be repossessed from a lapsed past but as a lively presence to be experienced now. That is, invention or pretense cannot work. Being, really being where you are and paying attention can. The former may get you an audience but the latter gets you "the excitingness of pure being."

I am not saying that Stein had it all figured out. (I am not even saying that figuring it all out has anything to do with anything.) Nor am I saying that Stein was innocent of or beyond the oppressive assumptions of culture and its power plays. It is easy enough to hear the seduction of white male privilege in some of her words. She certainly was capable of summing up entire peoples and races in phrases all too accessible to Western patriarchal supremacist attitudes. She certainly seems at times to have rejected her own ethnicity and gendered experience, tossing off anti-Semitic and near-misogynist remarks all too unselfconsciously. On the other hand, her words are never without a keen, even intense interest in people for who they are. She never confuses "he" with "the human." Her personal affections and disaffections seem firmly based on the particular behaviors of particular persons and not on categories of identity, such as race, gender, ethnicity, or class. Even her faults and good points cannot be categorized or forced to conform to consistency. Though she certainly seems to have pursued the power conferred by titles such as "first" and "best," she also seems to have genuinely believed in her own remarkable abilities. I am not saying that her work is without its problems for those seeking the enjoyment of unfettered words. But I am saying that Stein's words keep us so richly off balance and make familiar assumptions so inconvenient that denying, ignoring, or reformulating them precludes the truly rare opportunity to see with new eyes and encounter the "intellectual recreation" of unconditional possibility.

> The sister was not a mister. Was this a surprise. It was. The conclusion came when there was no arrangement. All the time that there was a question there was a decision. Replacing a casual acquaintance with an ordinary daughter does not make a son. (*Tender Buttons* 499-500)

Cultural contexts do efficiently, perhaps because so pervasively, influence what we believe we can know or say. In Western patriarchal culture the word is made Logos (source of reason, order, intelligibility), woman is made icon (source for man's primordial origins), and subjectivity is conferred on he who can move from source to fulfillment. Even in the modern context of what Stein saw as a desperate attempt to escape beginnings and endings, women and words are taken as sources of meaning out of which subjectivity is forged. Both must be mastered so as to be controlled. As a part of Man but not-man, Woman threatens order with excess. As man's inscription of himself, language must reflect his containment of that excess. Woman as language user, then, must be denied access to subjectivity, making her in effect accessible to Man as language.

Feminist theory's analyses of such machinations are designed to reveal and resist them. That Stein's words offer such consistent resistance to the cultural codes of meaning makes her work especially relevant to a feminist theorization of an ungendered access to language. To understand the need for this access, we must turn to the difficult relationship between women and writing. Western cultural and linguistic conventions present language as a neutral sign system available equally to anyone. We are all, it is said, born into language. Our attainment of it marks our entry into the human community. But even in its spoken form, this attainment of language is valued hierarchically: men's speech is more important than women's; education produces better speakers than does the street or only life; white people speak the language while people of color speak in dialects. The human community, in other words, turns out as usual to be only a very selective segment—white, male, and economically mobile. This segment is universalized to function as representative of what is deemed comprehensively and really human. As is representational art, however, representational identity is oppressively exclusive. Both must be broken away from if the privileges of language are to be accessible to everyone. This is what experimental writing, at its most attentive, can do.

Language in its conventional written forms extends the exclusions even further. This may involve anything from distinguishing between literary high culture and just any writing to ensuring that access to writing itself is carefully circumscribed. Literacy is not only the emblem of civilization but also that which designates and empowers the transactors of civilization's business. Historically, women, like slaves, have been prohibited from transacting business or becoming literate. This prohibition has been based on female use-value as a means of transaction and women as prime commodities, though the culture has traditionally explained it as an inevitable side effect of woman's nature. This nature, of course, like the woman to whom it is assigned, is iconic, reinforcing its power as an ordering device. Thus, even after (many) women have become literate, women's transactions remain problematic. For if women can be transactors as well as the means of transaction, and that which is transacted, how can they ever "make sense"? The orderly conducting of a civilization requires the stability of reliable boundaries, both for containment and for the identification of transgression. (It is because no boundaries remain stable in Stein's writing that her work has such vitality as art and as a performance of free speaking.)

In a by now classic essay titled "Woman as Sign," Elizabeth Cowie demonstrates the cultural investment in woman as a form of language or transaction between men. Her reading of anthropologist Claude Lévi-Strauss's influential work on human kinship systems (*The Elementary Structures of Kinship*, 1969) reveals his category "woman" as a production of signification not biologically preexistent, as he assumes, but culturally motivated by patriarchal interests. Taking his cue from linguist-semiologist Ferdinand de Saussure, Lévi-Strauss understands "sign" as that (arbitrary) unit in a signifying system made up of "sound-image" (the signifier) and concept (the signified); it produces meaning by its relationship to—specifically its difference from—other signs in the system. As Cowie demonstrates, he then constructs a social human need to overcome oppositions between self and other, locating its resolution in the practice of exogamy, the exchange of women between men for the purpose of establishing relationship through difference. In the process, woman becomes sign. However, while actual women function as cultural signifiers, it is not the concept "woman" that is signified but the social contract between men that establishes both their relation to one another and the relation of meaning to the cultural construct of sexual difference. Thus, "woman" is that which is produced as the sign of meaningful social relation which is Difference. In effect, Nature cannot be transformed into Culture without the communication (exchange) of women. Cowie's project, then, is to make visible the *production* of woman as sign that Lévi-Strauss overlooks when he accepts woman as an already constituted category, which in turn assumes an already existent social structure (complete with sexual difference as that which makes social communication possible). Woman becomes sign, then, not due to any "natural gender position," as Cowie puts it, but because of her production and use in the cultural signifying system. (One might now see, as has Teresa de Lauretis, that Woman is not the object of representation, but representation itself.)

Gayle Rubin's essay "The Traffic in Women: Notes on the 'Political Economy' of Sex" takes Cowie's point further by focusing on the power garnered by men as the exchangers rather than the exchanged. Women, constituted as that which is exchanged and the very means making exchange possible, become in a sense the language that men speak. For Lévi-Strauss, in fact, women's function is so thoroughly that of sign that he must see them as misused if not communicated. But because a woman is also undeniably a human being, she is both speaker and spoken; this paradox then further produces her as man's mystery. Rubin goes on to note that by recasting woman as an already-occurring natural category for man's use and seeing exogamy as that which makes culture possible, Lévi-Strauss obscures the fact that the notion of "exclusive gender identity" is a product of the relationships that organize gender in the first place and not a natural difference. Consequently, shared human qualities between women and men are suppressed, effectively separating rather than joining the sexes in kinship and enforcing heterosexual relationships as the only lawful ones.

It is at this point that Luce Irigaray's reading of sexual relationship becomes useful. In her short piece translated both as "When the Goods Get Together" (in Marks and de Courtivron's *New French Feminisms*) and as "Commodities among Themselves" (in Catherine Porter's translation of *This Sex Which Is Not One*), she presents as the basis of Western economic systems an exchange exclusively among men of "women, signs, commodities, and currency" (*This Sex* 192). She then sees heterosexuality in effect as "nothing but the assignment of economic roles" in which men are the agents of exchange and women the goods exchanged (192). Sex or sexual difference exists only because it produces that exchange as the transaction of business between one man and another. The only relationship actually produced by the function of woman as sign, then, is a male homosocial one (or what Irigaray calls "masculine homosexuality"). In such a system, "woman exists only as an occasion for mediation, transaction, transition, transference, between man and his fellow man, indeed between man and himself" (193). The only way to account for the relationships among women in this system is to understand them as nonexistent except in male terms: "as soon as she speaks (expresses herself, to herself), a woman is a man" (194).

Irigaray's final question, then, is what if the goods (women) refused to go to market but instead established commerce (relationships) for and among themselves? Her implication is that the patriachal system forces women either to act (speak) like men (since women do not exist as themselves, ideologically speaking), or to get out of the system altogether (which the system cannot really allow if it is to stay in business). But there is another choice. In a lively and complex assertion of women as "multiple-centered" beings whose sexuality is diffuse and everywhere at once, Irigaray contrasts phallic reliance on concepts of unity, oneness, and sameness with an alternative female experience of "nearness" and diversity. This experience, however, cannot be enacted or spoken by the standards of the system that produces woman as commodity and language. As Irigaray draws connections between language and sexuality, she reveals patriarchal language as an enforcer of a discursive logic that values sameness or oneness in/as univocity. Female sexual difference is a construct which reinforces that univocity by serving as the means of establishing male-male relations. But if women "experience difference differently," "speaking (as) woman (*parler-femme*)," they may disrupt masculinized univocity in the expression of plurality and mutuality based on their own (actually) different experience of themselves (220).

Irigaray's project can be thought of as "gendering" access to language so completely that a kind of real difference is forced into the open. She envisions a displacement of patriarchal oppression through an excess of (female) plenitude. While her work is useful and invigorating, it is also sometimes trapped in notions of sexual essentialism (an overdetermination, one might say, of gender). She tends to conflate differences among women into female difference from men, a move that not only re-produces women in an ostensibly feminist version of Woman, but that can only repeat oppositional structures of change. I prefer to think of the possibilities of excess and plenitude in terms of ungendering our accesses to language—a "using everything" that makes getting a purchase on any stable category or formulation of meaning-through-Difference untenable. This seems our best hope of ensuring that any voice may be impervious to forced silence or valorized articulation. Irigaray's bringing together of woman, language, and socio-economic transaction, however, helps us to think about the relation of women to writing and of writing to the business of civilization.

Human history is said not to begin until the advent of writing; before that it is considered archeology or prehistory. However, the written records of civilization (the accounts, documents, chronicles, and "true stories") are prized not for their literary qualities so much as for their ability to transmit information. Insofar as it records and organizes the orderly conducting of societal affairs, writing assumes a privileged status in the history of civilization. Indeed, the need to transact business may be considered the origin of writing. A succinct summary of this view occurs in the British Library's 1984 exhibition notes on "The Story of Writing" (in use as a handout for the edification of visitors to London's British Museum). There we are told, "the purpose of writing is information storage. Each society stores the information essential to its economic and political continuation" (Gaur 1). Though human memory and oral tradition also preserve and pass on information, they are clearly less valued as reliable transactive devices than systematic written documentation:

> What type of information storage a society evolves or chooses depends largely on the type of society it is. Oral traditions have for long been adequate for the transmission of religious or secular literature. Hunters, food-gatherers (and a modern motorist) can manage perfectly well with simple picture signs. The need for a systematic form of writing is in many ways closely connected with the idea of property, its protection (state), exchange (trade) and administration (government). Trade and administration rather than religion and literature have been the foster-parents of literacy. (1)

Such statements are passed along as unproblematically factual information; they constitute Knowledge and are communicated as such. Here we learn that the real business of civilization is political and economic continuation, that the exchange and administration of property is the very reason human beings developed written language. The function of woman as sign, then, must contribute to trade, to the political and economic transactions that constitute society for Western culture. Given such a structure, it is little wonder that women are largely absent from recorded history; they may make that history possible but disappear from its inscription. Women do figure much more prominently in "religious and secular literature," though not often as its writers, literacy after all being a skill needed first and foremost by society's administrators. Women, in other words, are still part of the property.

Certainly literary language—poetry, narrative, story itself—has come to have a special status. No one is really expected to understand Literature without some specialized training. Poets in particular have been valorized as such specialized language users that their words are considered meaningful only to the most skilled among us. Even so, Literature too is subject to the transmission-of-information rule. The literatures we learn to preserve as our worthiest are those that, it turns out, transmit Western cultural values in stories as if representative of "the human condition." As we have seen, Woman is inspiration and material for such stories; but even as writers, women are too closely associated with her (as her) to be accorded the distance from and control over that material deemed necessary to be creditable transmitters.

Though the rules governing the acceptable production of literary form change over time, literary expression continues to be valued for its communication (transmission) of meaning. This is a way for it to take part in the civilized transactions of culture, to participate in the displacement of oral communication as the primary form of that transaction, even though it seems to have its roots in "religious or secular" expression rather than administrative exchange. Poststructural theories of language and narrative have sought to reveal these operations by looking at how meaning is made (rather than merely cataloguing its linguistic patterns). In so doing, the ideological investments in writing, language, and meaning have been brought under scrutiny, calling into account the pretenses to fact and neutrality covering the political and economic motivation for writing. One of the effects of such theories has been to re-locate meaning and its production in and as the text (writing) rather than in the transactive relation between language users. And one of the effects of this effect has been (at least seemingly) to embrace plenitude and excess as possibility rather than mere primordial chaos at the bottom of the hegemonic scale.

Jacques Derrida, for instance (in such works as *Of Grammatology* and *Writing and Difference*, both originally published in 1967), rereads the operations of language in culture to reveal writing as that form of language that escapes or exceeds predictable structures of communication. This is what Christopher Norris, in his theoretical overview titled simply *Deconstruction: Theory and Practice*, characterizes as the deconstructionist project of drawing out "the disruptive effects of language" to reveal Western culture's illusion of meaning as a product of pure reason located in Mind. It is Derridean deconstruction, in Norris's view, that breaks down or undoes the idea "that reason can somehow dispense with language and arrive at a pure, self-authenticating truth or method" (19). Behind this project, moreover, is what Norris refers to as the problem of achieving "a perfect, intuitive 'fit' between intention and utterance" (23). It is this problem that has structured linguistic and philosophical discourse, that has rendered literature as a particularly deceptive form of language (relying as it does on metaphor and "figurative devices" rather than reason itself), and that Derrida must confront by demonstrating that intention and utterance can never really coincide. In this way, Derrida can demonstrate the vulnerability of both spoken and written language to "misreadings," thereby releasing language into an endless "free play" of undecidability that makes order, opposition, and the distinctions they create untenable.

Like Derrida, Roland Barthes looks for linguistic plenitude in the written text, in writing itself. In his 1968 essay "The Death of the Author" in *Image, Music, Text*, Barthes displaces the term *literature* with *writing* as he posits the written text as "a multidimensional space" drawing its life from so many "centres of culture" that no limitations of form and intelligibility can be imposed on it without reverting to illusory humanist notions of self (the subject) as the source of meaning. Moving from structuralism to an atheoretical slipperiness, he celebrates writing as a self-conscious presence that never ceases to call its own origins into question. In a sense, Barthes continually re-writes himself by making of the written text its own occasion for being. In his terms, "language itself" takes the place of the person using it; that is, the "scriptor" exists only in that space which is the writing. For Barthes this authorial "death" allows a multiplicity of meanings to interact, not only making the reader at last truly possible but also "utterly transform[ing] the modern text" by bringing writer and text simultaneously into being: "there is no other time than that of the enunciation and every text is eternally written *here and now*" (145).

When Barthes declares writing an act of impersonality, he finds that it is language, not language user (author) which speaks. This would seem to bode well for a feminist disruption of Woman as language and help us to rethink women as speakers of language despite the pervasive power of the androcentric mythic and psychological constructs that keep women silent. However, this language that speaks is still conceived of as an effect of those very constructs, and is complicit with them. As Barthes turns to surrealism, for instance, to explain "the desacrilization of the image of the Author," he calls upon an endless "disappointment of expectation," multiply-written experience, and "the task of writing as quickly as possible what the head itself is unaware of (automatic writing)" to elicit the here and now of language speaking itself (144). This is a way of talking about liberating the unconscious to bring forth that which has been repressed by the structural codes of language. Woman, of course, has entered Western ideology as a kind of cultural unconscious, the image of primordial mystery and repressed human nature structurally coded to function as language. Insofar as Woman and writing are both understood as repressed by the cultural codes, liberating the unconscious onto the page merely releases Woman/the unconscious into/as writing. The noncoincidence of Woman and subjectivity is not displaced. Woman remains written/spoken/read text.

Barthes and Derrida have convincingly theorized the written text as the site of an endless, unfixed interaction of intention and meaning that (re)produces all the world as text(s) open to (re)reading. Their work does bring us closer to a realization of plenitude and excess as possibility. Nevertheless, textual space still functions as the instance of language and Woman still functions as a form of language. What happens when he who stands in the place of highest cultural privilege (as namer, definer, thinker) chooses to give up identity in favor of language, the very language that has made him visible as subject and conferred on him the right of agency in the first place? What happens when the language of Man is given free reign to speak in Man's place? How can the spoken among us tell when the change occurs? Have the speakers and the spoken now all taken up positions in/as the unconscious? If what has been repressed is now activated in/as text, does that mean that the Feminine is finally set free as the true plenitude of human identity, thought, and language? I do not see Derrida rushing to take up the feminine position; instead he shifts from castration to circumcision as the great wound signaling loss at the fringes of culture and producing language as the talismanic suture bringing the unconscious into conscious access. His is still a phallic world. The written word still clings to phallic privilege. And even as writer and writing conflate into a single instance, the feminized structure of plenitude and unconsciousness remains intact. A writer such as Gertrude Stein may "play" with language as freely as she likes—her text is still understood as *her* text rather than simply text; her "play" still meets the culture's ear as only a woman talking (Woman) to herself.

In an attempt to deal with this phenomenon, poststructural feminist theory has in recent years turned to texts such as Stein's, reading them through deconstructionist interests in the disruptive effects of language in hopes of rescuing the (a, any) woman writer from the silence of Woman. Marianne DeKoven's *A Different Language: Gertrude Stein's Experimental Writing* (1983), is a most industrious example of this attempt. Relying on Barthes and Derrida, as well as on a strong dose of Lacanian psychoanalytic theory, De-Koven discovers the secret to Stein's linguistic structure as a presymbolic, pluridimensional mode of signification that by its very nature is antipatriarchal. The reason it is antipatriarchal is that it is pre-Oedipal and therefore located in the "female" position as "the opposite of, the antidote to, patriarchal modes of signification" (xx). In DeKoven's work, "presymbolic" and "experimental" are made more or less equivalent terms, thus positioning all experimental writing, and certainly the modernist avant-garde, in whatshe refers to as "the location of women: patriarchy's repressed Other, and therefore its antidote" (150). For DeKoven, the very reason for experimental writing to come into being is that opposition to patriarchal modes of producing meaning.

Interestingly enough, DeKoven claims patriarchal modes of writing in the service of her own project of "mastering" (as she says) Stein's "alternative" language. She does so, she tells us, because these modes, unlike experimental writing, signal the "reason, order, determinacy, judgment, abstraction" appropriate to lucid explication (xvii). She goes on to assign the performance of Meaning to patriarchal signification by way of locating what she sees as female material and subversion in language at the lexical level of content rather than in linguistic structure. Consequently she is able to read Stein as a writer of female plenitude who performs Barthes's "jouissance de la texte" (a celebratory erotic liberation of the irreducible plurality of meaning) while bringing the repressed, presymbolic unity of Self and Other into the open.

DeKoven seems to want to heal a patriarchal wound of her own: to bring the ("female") unconscious and the ("male") conscious back together into wholeness. However, she relies completely on gendered categories and a patriarchal paradigm of opposition to do so. Consequently she can only locate both Stein and experimental writing in an antipatriarchal slot already constituted by the oppositional structure of patriarchy in the first place. In her reading of Stein, whatever is experimental is emblematic of the repressed, the unconscious, the lexical—all adhering to the female— while order, meaning, consciousness, and lucidity all adhere to the male. (The interchangeability of cultural gender with the terms *female* and *male* is not the least of the problems in such a reading.) In effect, she recaptures the plenitude she hopes to set free by making Stein's writing safe again as a presymbolic instance of patriarchy's repressed material: Woman.

Stein, however, preferred to speak of writing as very much of the conscious mind. She could be quite impatient with the notion of sub-, un-, or preconscious explanations of writing; she seems to have considered them merely obfuscating and far too dependent on enigmatic or hidden processes. "Just read the words on the paper," Thornton Wilder quotes her as saying. "Just read them. Be simple and you'll understand these things" (v). As for the term *experimental*, she disliked it as a description of her writing. In her words, "Artists do not experiment. Experiment is what scientists do; they initiate an operation of unknown factors in order to be instructed by its results. An artist puts down what he knows and at every moment it is what he knows at that moment. If he is trying things out to see how they go he is a bad artist" (Wilder vii). Her resistance to notions of experimental writing and the realm of the unconscious as its source seems primarily motivated by a strong sense of herself as a fully capable, conscious, intelligible language user. Reading her words as acts of imitation, automatism, oppositional rebellion, or presymbolic jouissance tends to ignore her own sense of presence and to contain her within practices that only affirm rather than disrupt culturally gendered accesses to language itself.

Stein makes it possible for anyone to realize a direct interaction with words and so with language. This is perhaps her most radical accomplishment. For however much language is imagined as universally available to all human beings, some language users are nevertheless imagined as unworthy or unlawful. In Western patriarchal culture, women generally, men and women of color, gay and lesbian writers are all aligned with unworthy unlawfulness. (Class, of course, cuts across all these categories, and each may shift its boundaries to include various others at any time; it should be understood that categorization pretends to be but never is a stable process of definition.) In Stein's writing, however, nothing is unlawful. Her perfectly common, everyday words, written with such uncommon integrity, interfere with the pretense that we all share language equally. Every critical cry of "she can't do that!" reveals the extent to which cultural inscription relies on ideological predetermination. It's as if Stein spoke the unspeakable— as if language were there to keep us safe from the unspeakable. But what is the boundary between the speakable and the unspeakable if not convention, a paradigmatic enforcement of cultural ideology? Stein's ability to "use everything" makes convention untenable. And once convention is made untenable, any speaking may be possible.

One might think that such an achievement would garner interest and praise from among those who profess an appreciation for dispensing with outworn pretenses. However, it is still not un-common for Stein as a writer to be denied language, even though her distinction is acknowledged in terms of her use of words. This method of silencing her goes something like this: Language is not really what Stein wrote, for her words do not make language but only refute it. This is because she does not use words to Com-municate. The only way to Make Sense of her, then, is to reread her writing as negation, a rejection of Meaning in favor of a perversely enigmatic privacy. She was so private, it is said, that only she could know what she was talking about. Or, as Clifton Fadiman put it in a particularly nasty review of her work in 1934, she "uses words in order to establish contact, as far as I can make out, with herself" (*New Yorker* 85). In 1975, the same sort of complaint was still being used, as when Walter Sorell (in his critical study *Three Women*) characterized Stein as a linguistic lawbreaker and, moreover, a rebel-lious daughter. According to Sorell, "grammar stands for law and order, for the acceptance of the past experiences of those who teach us this system of symbols" (106). Stein refuses this acceptance, he thinks, signaling her rejection not only of law and order but of patriarchal authority in general and paternal authority in particular.

This is one kind of story. It is not the only one, but it is an important one because it contributes so readily to the Stein-as-icon tradition aimed at keeping her writing contained within an already-known paradigm. Here she is assigned an image as a woman with only herself (and therefore nothing) as her writer's material, or she is merely made a naughty girl. And because she proclaimed herself a genius into the bargain, all the while chatting away with the most innovative artists of her day perched Buddha-fashion on a chair in her famous Paris apartment, her outlaw status is con-firmed. She is made to represent lack, lack of linguistic orderly conduct. She "carries" meaning, as an iconic figure of inspiration for other writers and artists, but not as a writer herself. The con-nection between Woman and writing that produces Woman as in-stance but not agent of language has everything to do with how Stein is read.

Stein was a woman. She was a woman and a writer, a woman writer who wrote not "like a woman" and not "like a man." This made her a most difficult woman and a most difficult writer. It has been very handy indeed for her critics and commentators to be able to speak of her in terms of internal processes, the un(pre/sub)con-scious, privacy and enigma, resentment at being denied cultural power, and as an ineffectual language user. These are ways to make her "mean" by reading her words as effects, one way and another, of the Feminine—as Woman on the page in an uncontrolled, raw form. It is a way to avoid reading her as herself, as she wrote, as a woman writing.

Now of course women do write and were writing long before Stein. And what women have written has not gone entirely without an audience. I need not reiterate here the extent to which, however, so much of women's writing has been relegated to the province of the immediately consumable, thereby precluding its standing the test of time (as the saying goes) to enter the ranks of Great Literature. Lest such claims sound somehow outmoded, we need only remind ourselves that women writers continue to be disproportionately absent from even updated anthologies of canonical literature, that women tend still to be regarded as more prominent in the "pulp" genres than in the "serious" categories of writing, and that when a woman writes she is likely to be given the label "subjective" as a pejorative rather than as a term indicating subjectivity. The operation of patriarchal privilege still translates women's abilities as forming a feminized base in nature from which masculinized intellect separates to confer meaning on the world.

Curiously enough, Stein has been both denied feminine status and captured within the cultural feminine position of lack. Her physical size, casual (one could say comfortable) style of dress, closely cropped hair, and frank enjoyment of her own abilities (otherwise known as her "monumental ego") have often enough been used as evidence that she was unattractive and unladylike. Add to these her relationship with Alice B. Toklas, frequently portrayed as oppressively controlling and husbandlike even when acknowledged as lovingly committed, and the picture that emerges is of a decidedly unwomanly woman. Such a woman, it is implied, must have been trying to be a man. This, of course, would make her unnatural, as unnatural as a woman being a great writer or language speaking itself. It should be no surprise, then, that with few exceptions her writings continue to be difficult to find, that she is known more for nonsensical or playful turns of phrase than for the importance of her work, and that her words are still explained away as uncontrolled internal meditations rather than read as well thought-out arrangements. As a woman writer she is made vulnerable to the category Woman. As a woman she is made the target of epithets designed to deprive her of womanhood.

As we know, Woman and actual women are not the same thing; nevertheless actual women cannot move about in the culture of this "late age" without being re-cognized/re-membered as Woman. This reproduces women's access to agency as a split or doubled condition of identity, neither one thing nor the other, yet both at once. Far from endowing women with mobility in the system, however, this condition of being everywhere and nowhere ensures women's transfiguration into enigma, the cultural riddle to be solved but never actually solved. Stein's writing is critically reformulated to function as enigma, a riddle in need of solution. Like Woman, it is named as that through which names pass but incapable itself of the function of naming.

"The name of a thing might be something in itself if it could come to be real enough but just as a name it was not enough something," wrote Stein (*Lectures in America* 242-43). In Woman, women disappear as "real enough" beings to appear as representative position markers of Difference. Without Woman, Man would collapse into men and women as if the two were fully interactive. Difference (sexual difference) prevents this collapse. It produces interaction between men as the business of civilization, relegates interaction between women to the realm of invisibility and silence, and constructs interaction between women and men as a demonstration of the normative dominance of Man. It is in relation to such a model that Stein's writing is read not as itself but as an impossible act of disruption.

Certainly Stein has been cast as male-identified, as one who rejected the (other than sexual) company of women as if she were (like) a man. Her literary ambitions and self-image have been interpreted as not just egotistical but inappropriate, out of bounds. Her conversations with the men, great and near-great, while Alice talked with "the wives" is a favored anecdote about her. Such characterizations serve to portray her as a woman wanting in on the real business of the world denied her as a female person, and to imply that she could not really compete but could only gain notoriety by association. As for her domestic life with Alice, it is either regarded as coded and purposely hidden, or it is discreetly overlooked (as if women together were not a real thing to see). Her many friendships with other women tend to be passed over as only indirectly of interest, implying that the men were much more important or that Stein didn't really like women or consider them her equals. Even her lesbianism is sometimes depicted as a kind of sexual inversion—after the fashion of psychological sex theories like those of Havelock Ellis, popular in the 1920s—in which she identifies inwardly with the male, inclining her to take the male role in life and relationships. And it has been said often enough that Stein was no feminist. Her own story (*The Autobiography* 78; Mellow 63) about purposely failing her final examinations in medical school because she was so bored, despite her friend Marion Walker's plea that she "remember the cause of women," is touted as proof that she cared nothing for feminist concerns.

It would be just as easy, however, to focus on the stories and anecdotes of Stein's regard for Mildred Aldrich, her friendship and fascination with Etta and Dr. Claribel Cone, her support and later rejection of Sylvia Beach, her long-standing and complex interest in Mabel Dodge Luhan, or any number of other women she knew and respected. It would be just as illuminating to speak of the very many female characters who populate her writings, characters such as Melanctha in *Three Lives*, Martha Hersland in *The Making of Americans*, Mabel Dodge in her portrait ". . . at the Villa Curonia," "Miss Furr and Miss Skeene" in *Geography and Plays,* Saint Theresa in *Four Saints in Three Acts* and everywhere, and of course herself and Alice in *The Autobiography of Alice B. Toklas.* These female characters are not incidental but central; nor are they there as retaliation against women's invisibility elsewhere but as complex, interesting, and lively beings in and of themselves.

The point is not whether Stein's gender loyalties redeem or condemn her but rather that gender is the public filter through which her work and life are passed to "solve" her, to get at her essence. For the essentiality of femaleness is ever a pressing concern in a culture ideologically bound by oppositional gender identity as the primary indicator of what is meaningful in human relationships and in human relationship to language. The separation of female lives from human lives forces an impossible choice between inseparable aspects of oneself, and reinforces the structure of patriarchal hierarchy that aligns the human with the male while devaluing the female. By linguistic as well as ideological association, female persons who appear in or use language are allied with the cultural feminine position of lack, particularly lack of agency. Stein is no exception. But her work belies convenient assumptions of gender limitations or boundaries. Indeed, it so thoroughly interferes with conventions of boundary-marking altogether that it seems unbound not only by gendered accesses to language, but by gender as a construct of meaning in language.

Just as Stein wrote words as "things in themselves," she was likewise engaged in knowing human beings as "ones" in themselves. This is what she called "learning being in women and in men." This phrase appears throughout her long work *The Making of Americans*, the work generally regarded as her attempt to scientifically classify all human beings in terms of what she called their "bottom natures." The book was published in both its full length of 925 pages and in an abbreviated version about half that long. It is far more instructive to read it as written, in its complete form. The accumulated effect of her pages of present-participial prose working through "bottom nature" in hundreds of nuances makes it clear that she did not perceive human identity as a product of cultural gender, nor that her theory of human "kinds" is amenable to a sense of human beingness as defined by fixed categories of possibility. She explores so many exceptions, combinations, qualifications, and environmental contingencies that it finally becomes apparent that her "dependent-independent" and "independent-dependent" kinds with "resisting" or "attacking" natures do not constitute a fixed categorization but a way of understanding human beingness as process. It is the complexity of interaction among people and among the aspects of one's own nature that holds her interest. In a similar way, her use of words, however much she diagrammed them, produces on the page a complexity of interaction that belies any convenient recourse to a determinate typology or code.

Reading this remarkable work in both massive and brief segments, allowing myself to come in contact with each word as it appears rather than in relation to my memory of what came before (a method of reading well suited to Stein's use of repetition/insistence and "the continuous present") has convinced me that the imposition of ordered schema in language or in human identity is not its point. "Bottom nature" emerges not as a determination of personality but as a resource for each individual's access to being who he or she really is. Each one may act according to internal proclivities (biological, environmental, both—Stein does not make us choose) and thereby learn to be a "completely whole one." However, having and recognizing one's proclivities does not mean having to act in accordance with them. Change and modification are ever-present, in relation to contact with others as well as in relation to circumstance or self-knowledge. Personality or "kind," that is, exists in an ever-shifting relation of experience to social-historical context, of interaction with others, time and place. Similarly, Stein's words constantly change and modify as they create shifting environments of contact with one another; they are in constant motion. Stein herself, as herself and author, interacts on the page with her characters, with the sentences she makes and the ideas she develops, with the reader. If there is a most relevant term for this work, it is not *typology* but *process*. At every moment Stein is actively engaged in "learning being":

> Always repeating is all of living, everything that is being is always repeating, more and more listening to repeating gives me completed understanding. Each one then slowly comes to be a whole one to me, each one slowly comes to be a whole one in me, slowly it sounds louder and louder and louder inside me through my ears and eyes and feelings and the talking there is always in me the repeating that is the whole of each one I come to know around, and each one of them then comes to be a whole one to me, comes to be a whole one in me. (*The Making of Americans* 300)

Whole and complete are not categories designating fixed or finished, but are continuously inclusive. This inclusiveness is in no way static; it takes everything into account and so is in a continual state of presence or liveliness. Stein's pronominal and participial sentence structures resist classification—of people, words, or meaning; they insist on a sense of movement in the arrangements of words as well as a constant close attention to "each one" in the midst of "every one" (each one, that is, in relation to every one). Stein never allows "kinds" to distract her from her interest in people and words in themselves. "Everybody is a real one to me, everybody is like someone else too to me. Resembling, in each one to other men, to other women, to other men and women, makes sometime a way of complete understanding of each one" (333). What she enacts is a contextual process that continuously constructs a whole in the interaction of its constantly shifting specificities. "This will be always then a longer and longer description always longer with my living and my knowing" (337). To know anyone well, as a complete being, she must understand all the ways of knowing and of being. Her use and arrangement of words on the page is part of the process.

> Now I am always hearing of ways some have of feeling living and they come crowding and I am resisting so that I can be slowly realising and always I am knowing I can never really be knowing all the ways there are of feeling living, all the ways there are of having living having meaning. I am knowing something of kinds of being in men and women, I could know sometime, if I could know completely all I could be knowing, all the kinds there are of men and women. I am comforting now my feeling by saying this thing in my complete feel-

ing again and again. I am beginning now a history of living, of feeling living, of living having meaning. (*The Making of Americans* 625)

Through active attention to process Stein insists on the lively interaction of all possibilities. She begins again and again, saying so as she does so. It is a way of continuing, not of stopping and starting. Even in this very early work (written more or less between 1906 and 1908 or 1911, but not published until 1925), Stein was dealing with what she later referred to in "What Are Master-Pieces" as "not having a beginning and an ending." *The Making of Americans* sets the stage: it defies categories even as it is immersed in them; it is a product consisting almost entirely of process, making producing integral to the writing; it is a history ("of a family's progress") that is independent of precedent. It was also a work exceedingly difficult to place with a publisher; and once published, it was ridiculed, puzzled over, praised, and used as evidence for Stein's literary inability even as it contributed to the growing reputation of this troublesome woman writer. Neither the work itself, its people, nor indeed Stein's use of language can be classified without distorting the complexities—the complex simplicity of using everything.

In the portraits, poems, plays, and "buttons" that followed, Stein retained her complexity as she subjected her words to the "concentrated exactitude" that came to occupy her so, creating intensely compact writings full of the presence, insistence, and avid interest in life-in-motion apparent in those early long, long sentences and paragraphs. As she left behind "associational emotion" to work in "the excitingness of pure being," she made it more and more possible for each one, every one, each one in the midst of every one, to realize a direct interaction with language. One may regender, may code and de-code her writing as much as one likes; one may strive to get her to conform to one version or another of Woman; but Stein will never make a comfortable fit with any prescribed category of being or of writing. Her words are too unpredictable for that.

When I read Stein's words there on the page, I enjoy myself. I have no doubt that Stein enjoyed herself as she wrote what she wrote. She was a woman who was a writer who wrote as if she could rely unreservedly on herself as one fully engaged in knowing life, language, and the life in language. She was herself. The fact that her work is so puzzling to so many is not the consequence of any intrinsic difficulty in it but of the ways in which we have learned to read through language and through Woman to the meanings made familiar by patriarchal values enshrined in hierarchic structures of truth and reality. Stein is of her culture and time, yet free of its mythologies. Her language is no more and no less than a thoroughly experienced "intellectual recreation." She simply paid attention.

> This one was always having something that was coming out of this one that was a solid thing, a charming thing, a lovely thing, a perplexing thing, a disconcerting thing, a simple thing, a clear thing, a complicated thing, an interesting thing, a disturbing thing, a repellant thing, a very pretty thing. . . . This one was one whom some were following. This one was one who was working. ("Picasso" in *Selected Writings* 334)

3

Looking-Glass Consciousness:
Virginia Woolf and
Dorothy Richardson

Everywhere in the valued, valorized words of the fathers is an immense need to force experience into fact, knowledge into objectivity, as if we all could, ideally, scientifically, recognize the world as the same thing, a repeatable phenomenon accessible to a common (that is, standardized) vocabulary of apprehension. There is a deep fear, a dread perhaps, of allowing experience a life of its own. It must be captured, tested, and put to the laboratory flame. It must be assigned proper names and battled over for rights of passage. It must become a tool, a device used to form and prepare, to construct the cultural edifices in which we are then to live. Otherwise, as itself, it is called chaos and used to frighten or condemn those who would meet it on its own terms.

Both Virginia Woolf and Dorothy Richardson, living among the fathers, sought to meet experience face to face, on its and on their terms. It was for them to pay very close attention to what they knew, in their bones and on their bodies, and to write it into words that would never acquiesce to mere fact yet would still ring true. To do this, they had to use everything, their minds, their senses, their very instincts—and to manage the information that thus came to them with a confidence denied them by societal right and custom.

We like to talk, indeed must talk of "female experience" when we talk of their works. But this is a disquieting term at best. And at best it evades any fix we attempt to get on it, resting annoyingly and tantalizingly as it does between the trap of self-serving propaganda and a misleading desire for revelation. One might all too easily understand such a term as a form of special pleading, or a kind of reconstruction of truth as it should have been. But it is much more than that. Female experience is, ideologically speaking, the presence always given shape as absence. Yet Woolf and Richardson, each in her way, took it on. It was what they had to do. After all, Freud had already set a relentless path toward his paralyzing question "What does a woman *want*?" It would be some time yet before Simone de Beauvoir would demonstrate so thoroughly that both the woman and the wanting are man-made images, forcing into the open the more relevant question, the question posed in the very structures of Woolf's and of Richardson's writing, "What *is* a woman?"

It was in the enactment of that second verb, "to be" (rather than "to want"), that Woolf and Richardson would confront the dangers inherent in both propaganda and revelation, to get beyond them and come to terms with the false claims to fact in either position. Only then could either writer clear the way for "herself." The old formulas available to them could only reiterate the myths, and the myths were increasingly stupefying for any woman alert to "my own experiences as a body" in a world that insisted on making of that body and the person it housed enigma incarnate. Female experience, in a social-historical context of relationship to culturally constructed realities, was precisely the problem. Each writer then, each in her way, looked to herself for what she knew, looked to herself despite the ideological improbability of "herself" as a real being, despite the essentialism of a scientific stranglehold on the nature of the female, and in the face of a profound patriarchal distrust of experience as anything more than unstable raw material suitable only for reshaping into those universalized antidotes to chaos, Fact and Reality.

Woolf, as we know, felt that even having killed off the Angel in the House, she was never able to tell the truth so long concealed under those ethereal skirts. Her writing surrounds experience, juxtaposing, contrasting, and ceaselessly connecting vast networks of human consciousness acting upon the world. The language she had first at hand came from a tradition designed to do without her. The forms in which that language had become known as literature admitted the truths of experience only in relation to the revelatory demands of event upon character. These were shapes one had long since learned to recognize. But Woolf, like so many "others," could not recognize herself or what she knew in them. So she headed straight for the undercurrents of language and form, intent upon her own right to what she understood as "the freedom to think of things in themselves." It was for her a demanding freedom. She often refers in her diaries to revising what she had written as a "sweating off" of unnecessary words. And there is a clear sense of her finished prose as honed to a fine point, stripped of everything but an exacting honesty, yet still rich, even luxurious, in its life on the page. She adapted language and form to her own confrontation with the phantom, creating textual space for experience to make possible a female subjectivity in the very interstices between sign and meaning. While her fiction enacts this possibility, her ambiguously nonfictional works *A Room of One's Own* and *Three Guineas* balance enactment and analysis to interrogate more directly the culture's production of woman as a specialized absence. Therein Woolf was able to activate both the connection and the contradiction between Woman and women. It is this activation that has the potential for pulling down the mythic edifices in which the patriarchal will to dominance would force us all to reside.

Dorothy Richardson took on her phantom in the creation of *Pilgrimage*, one of the earliest, longest, and most continuous attempts to speak "female consciousness" into being. Richardson, in the person of Miriam Henderson, never wavers in her conviction that this shadowy thing "herself" really exists or that women have always been true selves in their own right. But Miriam's material experience of herself as a female person in a male-defined world makes it clear that this self is barely, if at all, recognizable to the society in which she lives. She keeps herself real and present by fighting both the idealization of women and the scientific method used to give that idealization credibility. *Pilgrimage*, then, is a work of resistance. On every page Richardson/Miriam resists annihilation. At every moment she negotiates a cultural ideology that reads her, through gender, as a representation of the phantom in one guise or another. The work is written entirely from within Miriam's relentlessly alert and conscious awareness. Richardson allows no omniscient mediator in *Pilgrimage*, nor even in-character insight beyond Miriam's accumulated present moment. Consequently there is no recourse to external myth for meaning except as it creates slippages for Miriam between her sense of who she is and her culture's sense of her as a woman. We must rely only on Miriam's experience, from inside her ever-present realization of it. As this female consciousness interacts with the specificities and social realities of her world, it engages her, and us, in an endless process of subjectivity. The writing often seems almost atextual in its self-reflexivity, yet so particularized as to create a continuous sense of experiencing Miriam's subjectivity as if experiencing our own. By this method, Richardson radically interrogates gendered accesses to meaning, female identity, and the capacity of narrative itself to render female experience truthfully, or at all.

Woolf and Richardson, then, in taking on that need for "telling the truth about my own experiences as a body," were able to effect the shift from image to experience envisioned by de Lauretis, the shift that allows them to address women, not Woman, in a specific relation to sexuality (or sexual difference) as a cultural construct. The consciousness they put onto the page enacts a connection between experience and language wherein women are simultaneously social subjects and ideological nonsubjects. The tension and contradiction of this position produces an engagement between signification and social-historical context—between sign and experience—that makes possible a female subject unbound by conformity to generic subjectivity (Man) or the limitations of mere opposition to it. That is, Woolf and Richardson create subjectivity through female experience not as a feminine version of or counterpoint to the masculine but as a thing in itself, at once imbued with and apart from cultural significance as it has been historically understood. In so doing, they also put into play the adaptability and resistance of writing to gendered positions of meaning, thereby extending our ability to hear women's voices as interactive members of nondiscrete speaking communities.

Even so, Woolf still believed that telling the truth of what she knew as a woman eluded her. She located the problem in the cultural practices that closed so much of human experience to her on the basis of gender. A postmodern view of this problem might be that what was closed to Woolf were not only material-historical experiences but the experiencing of experience itself as itself. In other words, reality is an ideological construct, or at least our perceptions of it are so structured by ideology that our efforts to see it free and clear are always illusory. Nevertheless, most of the history of Western thought assumes reality to be there as a universal truth somehow amenable to scientific proof through a careful cataloguing of human experience reconstituted as knowledge. Therefore both Woolf and Richardson initially send their narrating consciousnesses in search of truth as knowledge, in the libraries, colleges, and newspapers of the culture. These searches, of course, yield a different kind of truth, namely that knowledge is what a culture chooses it to be and that it may have little or nothing to do with their material existence as female beings. Reality, in other words, is a constructed thing; it represents truth according to the motivations of the culture in which it occurs, not according to some universal repository of irreducible fact.

This, of course, is the power of Woolf's and of Richardson's concentration each on her own subjectivity as process in an ambiguous environment of shifting realities. Each blurs the boundaries, between reality and fiction, self and other, word and experience. If, as de Lauretis says, boundary is conventionally that opposition to passage which makes possible the transformation of the patriarchal subject into Self, and boundary is thus the place of the feminine, then it is only appropriate that Woolf and Richardson use their experience of boundary to evoke its fundamental unreliability as a parameter of truth for them.

In Western patriarchal thought, the truth of experience must be reordered as universal truth before contact with it can be risked. As the last step before transcendence into godhead (the realm of the Knower), universal truth acts as a panacea against a patriarchal dread of loss of control, feared as a fall into nothingness. Much current theory has taught us to interrogate universals and has given us ways to intervene in the social-ideological constructions that have made monolithic Truth so tantalizing. However, it has not gone far enough; whatever the interventions, they have tended to preserve control as masculinized right of passage, celebrating loss as the territory of alienation to be conquered by entering it, while protecting the articulating heirs of culture from its still-feminized silences. My own investments in postmodern feminism (or feminist poststructuralism, postdeconstructive semiotics, or maybe just feminist outposts) leads me to view control with a nervous uncertainty, sensing it as both a desirable resting place and an all-too-familiar trap. No matter how seductive, I know in my bones that control is not for me but about me. I cannot walk about, speak, or write as a female person in a patriarchal society without assignation to the cultural feminine position of chaos in need of control. So it is from my own experience of this nowhere/everywhere place that I speak as if knowingly about "female experience." Like Woolf and Richardson, we must look for a way to speak experience by speaking past the boundaries that produce Self out of a gendered female silence.

Certainly poststructuralist theories have helped us to see the illusions inherent in the old investments in Self protection; yet for the most part they have not really given up those investments.

The "in-vrai-semblable" (the implausibility of the truth of truth) current in French theory, for instance, is more a displacement of the usual search for identity and being than it is a genuine opening up of subjectivity. The quest has merely been moved to the unknowable and therefore seemingly more honest (i.e. "real") regions of the gaps or spaces between, behind, beneath, and inside experience. But this experience is still adapted to gendered structures of meaning, still resonates with the name of the Feminine, and thus still impedes our ability to read women or women's words as themselves. As feminist theorist Alice Jardine has noted in *Gynesis: Configurations of Woman and Modernity*, "there is, of course, the remote possibility that the non- or not-yet-subjects who are seen as closest to the presubjective maternal space (women, according to many analysts) will begin to speak—but then, Lacan might say, that is not language, but rather still only a symptom of language: *lalangue*" (107). Gender, that is, continues to determine not only the identity of writers/speakers themselves, but also the very construction of subjectivity in relation to signification, however modern in its alienated form. Consequently, the new alienation or "alterity" merely makes it possible to attack the Ego of old without endangering Man's position as self-creator.

Jardine's comment is highly relevant to a feminist post-modern reading of Woolf and Richardson, occurring as it does in the context of a discussion about "the speaking subject," that theoretical construct which locates, or concentrates, the subject in language. There has been a shift in the conceptualization of the subject from the Cartesian "cogito," or sense of identity as a stable, unified, noncontradictory site of meaning through cognition (a "master of its discourse, a Man" as Jardine says), to a function of language, or (in Lacanian terms) the symbolic. The old subject, Jardine reminds us, relied on the sign or language as a neutral and transparent "agent of representation" (45), providing a means for the subject to express or enact the meaning that accrues to "him." However, once the subject is understood as a function of language—that is, once language is understood as/through the symbolic order by which human beings become functioning cultural selves—then what is left out or suppressed by language becomes a pre- or nonverbal disruptive force, an unconscious acting as the absence by-and-against which consciousness takes recognizable shape (as self-recognition, we might say). This absence, by way of (psychoanalytic) theories of identity, is figured as the lost origin, the "(m)other" of Lacanian fame. It is the preverbal unity from which not only separation but the recognition of separation (the ability to distinguish ones—self and other), is necessary if one is to acquire language (culture) as a speaking subject. Thus it is that Lacan can refer to Woman as spoken but not speaking, still a symptom of language. Thus it is that Teresa de Lauretis must understand (cultural) Woman as representation, the presence of absence making subjectivity possible for Man. And thus it is that the term *female subjectivity* becomes a radicalized term.

French feminist theory (to call it by its American name) has helped us to understand that, again in Jardine's words, "the status of women is determined not only at social and political levels, but by the very logical processes through which meaning is produced" (44). Both Woolf and Richardson, writing so much of their work in a modernist atmosphere of destabilized notions of the ego or subject, also understood the determination of gender in this multileveled way. For them, claiming a process of subjectivity for and by women meant precisely an active resistance to androcentric logical processes, as well as to patriarchal social and political practices. Female subjectivity, then or now, is disruptive because it seems to put into play an impossible contradiction. For despite theoretical insistences that the "signing" of the unconscious or preverbal as Feminine is not sex-specific, still the function of sexual difference as the enabling factor in producing meaning makes alignments between sex and gender unavoidable. Or as Jardine puts it, "the investigation of how biological difference introduces the speaking subject into the play of language reveals sexuality as intrinsic to any theorization of any practice, especially literary practice" (45). Remember Lacan's *lalangue*, that symptomatic, presubjective alterity that escapes direct communication because it is rather the space for communication—the space in which literature (writing) and the Feminine are so intimately brought together. At its most privileged that space produces art on the page and reproduces the relation between Art and the Feminine as a function of sexual difference.

It is only by recognizing, Jardine believes, "the ways in which we surround ourselves with our fictions" that we can reconceptualize "the organization of sexual difference as grounded in cultural and political reality without positing that reality—man or woman, for example—as somehow preexisting our thought and fictions" (47). That is why merely revealing Woman in the master discourse or removing ourselves from the master discourse is not enough; such moves only reinforce that discourse. Or as Toril Moi envisions it in *Sexual/Textual Politics*, the positioning of women on the margins of patriarchal order reinforces the phallocentric view of women (conflated) as the representation of the "*limit* or border-line of that order." Woman then becomes "the necessary frontier between man and chaos"—and like any frontier, both-and-neither inside or outside. It is this split and doubled position, Moi believes, that allows "male culture" both to vilify women as embodiments of chaos and to elevate women as madonna-like protections against that chaos. "Needless to say," Moi reminds us, "neither position corresponds to any essential truth of woman" (167). Needless to say. But the phantom dies hard.

When the ego went transcendental and self-forgetfulness was the path to truth, the force of the phantom could still be felt. As the humanist Self (a.k.a. Man) has fallen into disfavor and been held responsible for the inhuman nature (as it were) of the modern world, still the phantom has remained. Under the tutelage of Lacanian theory, Otherness has simply been relocated as already present in the self. It can be detected as the enabler of the divided "I"—the age-old maternal touch (with its constant threat of blur-ring the distinction between the pleasures of nurturance and the pleasures of titillation) that separates the men from the boys. As modern Man has become increasingly engrossed in the wonders of self-alienation, "alterity" has come to seem a home away from home.

This development and its influence on a continuing patriar-chal belief in rational self-control brings us to what might after all be an expectable move: what Jardine calls the "intersubjective assumptions" of Self (or Same) and Other have become impure enough to be dispensed with just as it looked like such a thing as a viable female self might break into theory. Only One who has already adopted Self can throw it away because it is all used up. All to the good, we might say; at least gender may cease to be the weapon it has been. But as Jardine points out, "the space 'out-side of' the conscious subject has always connoted the feminine in the history of Western thought" (114). And it is this space to which the Ones turn. It would of course never do for the alienated self simply to return to the erstwhile primordial "(m)other." So as Man retreats, what Jardine calls a "neuter-in-language-without-sub-ject" steps forward, and the Feminine is once more signed Anonymous. We are assured that sexual constructs of identity are surpassed. Even a Lacanian Feminine should only remind us of something female. Nevertheless, this new "space of alterity," by virtue of its very access to signification, "always already must connote the female" (114). Yet remember, this female is collapsed in on it-self; there is no room for the chaotic specificities of contextual female experience, still so problematically real and accessible to so many Others.

In the wake of the breakdown of the phenomenological Self or Ego, we seem to be left with a posthumanist dive into the Feminine as the new frontier of knowledge and identity. This situation might at first seem to authorize writers such as Woolf and Richardson as forerunners of the post-Self self. However, we would do well to remember that this Feminine (at the) boundary of, beneath and behind the old order of Reason is paradoxically dissociated from both "female" and "experience." It is a manifestation of theory, and must be so if it is to function transformatively and not simply drop Man into the bottomless pit of enigma along with Woman. Theory rescues creativity from the whims of the Muse (always figured Feminine or Female) and delivers it into the hands of those who are able to interact (have fruitful intercourse) with the Muse from an oppositional or at least active alterative position as maker. In this way, the arts may safely be indulged in by men (as products of the cultural masculine)—even in posthumanist relation to the Feminine—without loss of Self-control and indeed with full retention of the privileges of generation and mastery.

The search for a safe self, a kind of universal-but-exclusive paradigm, it seems to me, is still going on. Only now we are to revel in its qualities of process, its altered path through "that which subverts it" such as Lacan's "Real" or Derrida's "écriture" (Jardine 149). The dream-of-mastery now being refused, the silence now being listened to is, once again, re-formed Man's version of the Feminine. And once again, just when it looked as though women's claims to experience might take hold and radically disrupt Reality, experience, reality, and truth have been discovered as illusions already disrupted by the un-mastered silence of the Feminine space. So once more it is the masters who choose to give up mastery for the freedom of this un-mastered space and who recapture the Feminine and its female associates for their own use in the doing.

What I have just said reflects but slides somewhat away from Jardine's notion of "gynesis" as a means to hear female speaking subjects. She uses that notion to unmask "Man's Truth" while at the same time undermining "the very conceptual systems that have posited it" (153). Along with theorist Julia Kristeva, Jardine understands Woman as "that element most *discursively present*" in the new theories (which concentrate the subject in language, thus making discourse the site of activity). Her overall project is to enter that space coded Feminine to accomplish "the transformation of woman and the feminine into verbs at the interior of those narratives that are today experiencing a crisis in legitimation" (25). That is, she wants to take advantage of a narrative loophole of sorts wherein gynesis becomes "the putting into discourse of 'woman' as that *process* diagnosed in France as intrinsic to the condition of modernity" (25). (Modernity here signals not just placement in time but also the complexities and conflicts of French and American postmodernisms.) By this method, she means to question the complicity between theory and feminism in "inscribing woman as the ultimate truth of and for modernity" (155), a complicity that keeps female subjectivity trapped in now-discursive essentialisms.

This is a questioning to which I lend my support. However, nomatter how necessary (and it is necessary) the recognition and revealing of Woman in the guise of a new discursive space masquerading as the demise of Man, it is nonetheless still a response (perhaps a reaction) to an androcentric model of meaning. It is still an exercise in phantom-slaying wherein the phantom constantly reappears and must be constantly reslain. I am not advocating a giving up of that move or a return to either "female" or "experience" as unproblematic realities existing side by side with cultural ideology. What I am suggesting is that "female experience" has never had a life of its own in patriarchal systems of thought—I do not mean a life apart from ideological constructs nor a life dependent on them, but a life both-and of itself and of its cultural contexts.

Female subjectivity and female experience have been understood in Western thought and its transformations only as a kind of feminist bid for equality or disruptive attention-getting that fills a ready-made slot of opposition. Now that they are surfacing in the very theories built on their suppression (as preverbal force or desire), they are recaptured by discourse, leaving femininity (feminine space) intact as enigma, but discovering it as source, if not enactment, of knowledge. Freud's "unconscious," Lacan's "Real," and Derrida's "écriture" all retain their association with/as the Feminine, becoming both the unrecuperable origin and the necessary object of Man's self-creation. The Feminine's seeming recuperation into discursive meaning through the offices of theoretical reinterpretation still leaves it imbued with the ineffable mystery of otherness. Like Art, it clings to instinct and experience only as raw materials out of which mastery and knowledge produce creativity. The very basis of the culture's intellectual valuation demands that art and the feminine, so intimately entwined, undergo transformation from experience into knowledge before they can be circulated as Meaningful. This is what theory purports to accomplish.

Woolf's *A Room of One's Own* and *Three Guineas*, and Richardson's *Pilgrimage*, function simultaneously as theory and practice, interfering with the hegemonic privilege of knowledge (what we already seem to know) as our access to experience. By seeking subjectivity in those experiences of the boundaries between truth and fiction—female experience as the culture has engendered, denied, and reincarnated it—and resisting the conflation of its specificities into the Feminine through the very strategies of articulating that experience, Woolf and Richardson use the instability of women's multiple accesses to both sides and boundary itself to make possible a relation between Woman and women that will not acquiesce to Man's Truth, not even alienated Man's altered Truth. They bring theory and practice together on the page, in other words, and so enact experience in writing. Their work does not re-produce female experience as a primary relation to Man but looks to the truths of experience for female persons in Man's world of Woman to find out what a woman is. Only in this way can female subjectivity engage interaction between sign and experience without reducing it to a unified vision of truth to be hegemonically wielded as Answer.

Woolf and Richardson, then, must use everything. Like Stein, they must pay attention to the speakable and unspeakable constructs of language alike; in the interaction between the two, "herself" may begin to become visible to each in her way. Woolf's trespass onto the grass at "Oxbridge" in *A Room of One's Own*, her "Society of Outsiders" in *Three Guineas*, Richardson's unclassified female consciousness throughout *Pilgrimage*, all take on Woman without reproducing her in language. This cannot be accomplished from within the stories of the patriarchy. Something "else" is needed. Although Woolf and Richardson accomplish similar effects in their works, the complexities of each make it necessary to approach those effects through each writer's work separately, calling attention as we go to particular points of contact. By this method, the relationship between diversity and similarity may begin to make possible a concept of female subjectivity that can be understood as what de Lauretis terms a "site of differences."

A Room of One's Own and *Three Guineas* may be read both as Woolf's critique of androcentrism and her vision of what female experience might yield were it given full textual (and social) space. That space is not something merely added to patriarchal structures but rather a new contextuality "proper for her own use." Woolf employs the very instability of women's multiple relationships to cultural identity to reveal how the culture produces difference as divisive rather than interactive. By de-constructing (as it were) this production, she is able to expose patriarchal hegemonies as motivated by a patriarchal desire for control and not, as cultural ideology purports, as natural categories of ability or limitation. She enters this ideology from her contradictory place as both a member of the culture it maintains and as an outsider. From that position she can use her experience of difference to establish connections, to "think back through our mothers" not only to claim a heritage of her own but also to imagine the possibility of speaking across differences. By the time she finishes *Three Guineas*, she has found her heritage of female experience, filled with lack as it is, to be so able in its access to the kind of knowledge the culture has devalued at its peril that her Society of Outsiders becomes her best hope for a kind of coalition politics of radical change. Hers is not merely a vision of equality but a rethinking of possibility in which systematic structures of inequality and opposition become undone at their roots.

Because her femaleness puts her authority as a speaker into question and allies her with the unreliability of Woman's words as far as the surrounding culture is concerned, she must not only strive to tell her own truths but must make the very structures of her texts part of her strategy to do so. So it is that what she calls "sentences proper to her own use" and "breaking the expected sequence" become as much a part of the truth of female experience on the page as what the words she chooses may signify. Each work purports to tell a story, but not a story with a beginning, middle, and end, nor even a story that reliably fits the categories of fiction or nonfiction. These stories do not follow linear paths, but pattern themselves according to the demands of their teller's engagement with process in the act of becoming—becoming experience, for example. These stories do not imitate the cultural formula of getting from a point of origin to a destination where Answer resides, but instead intertwine ideology and experience to, as Woolf says, "develop in your presence as fully and freely as I can the train of thought which led me to think this" (*A Room* 4).

In *A Room of One's Own*, published in 1929, Woolf invites us to share with her places and names she purposely sets at an unreliable boundary between fact and fiction. We wander with her through the campuses of Oxbridge and Fernham. We watch Shakespeare's sister hovering alive or dead at the crossroads of sixteenth-century London. We travel through the thought processes of the storyteller "I," an ambiguously real self who slips in and out between feminized absence and creative presence. "'I' is only a convenient term for somebody who has no real being," she tells us. "Lies will flow from my lips, but there may perhaps be some truth mixed up with them," she warns. "(Call me Mary Beton, Mary Seton, Mary Carmichael or by any name you please—it is not a matter of importance)," she advises between the lines (4-5).

From the start, *A Room* problematizes the cultural assumption of knowing the difference between reality and fiction, and thus of knowledge itself. Female experience belies the distinctions. Woolf's "I" will not and cannot use her words to hand over "a nugget of pure truth to wrap up between the pages of your notebooks and keep on the mantelpiece for ever" (3-4). Instead she can offer only her own experience of what she herself is in the process of knowing. By re-locating truth in experience, by depending on herself as a speaking subject who is also figured as a presubjective effect of ideology, she will leave unsolved "the great problem of the true nature of woman and the true nature of fiction" (4). That is, Woolf places truth, nature, and female being in a volatile and disjunctive relationship to one another that will not be stable enough to issue the usual prize of Answer as Knowledge. And that is the point.

It is in Woolf's use of contradictory engagements between woman as sexual icon and a female "I" with "no real being" whose presence is nevertheless powerfully iconoclastic that we can, as has Teresa de Lauretis, read Woolf's textual enactment of female subjectivity. When the transgressive "I" of *A Room of One's Own* walks on the grass at "Oxbridge" in a fever of excitement over an idea, Woolf has already begun to offer the effects of boundary-crossing as both textual and actual experience that can subvert centuries of feminized silence. At this early juncture the "I" is caught in the unladylike position of being not only intimate with Ideas, but of being stirred to action by them. The consequences are immediate and far-reaching:

> Instantly a man's figure rose to intercept me. Nor did I at first understand that the gesticulations of a curious-looking object, in a cut-away coat and evening shirt, were aimed at me. His face expressed horror and indignation. Instinct rather than reason came to my help; he was

a Beadle; I was a woman. This was the turf; there was the path. Only the Fellows and Scholars are allowed here; the gravel is the place for me. (6)

Instinct, like Woman, is the realm of nature and innate behavior. Reason is the foundation of civilization itself, setting Man apart from the animals and from his intermediary between them and him, Woman. Woolf's "I," having entered his territory both as a woman and a thinking human being, reasons through instinct to read the Beadle's behavior. The moment she realizes the horror on his face is aimed at her, she recognizes it for what it is. It is prohibition, and she runs up against it as if against a physical force. Immediately her mind translates the information her senses have gathered, providing her with the formulations the culture uses to erect and maintain its boundaries. She reaches the conclusion the Beadle is there to remind her of: "I was a woman." That is the category by which she is meant to know her place. But this "I," occupying as she does both the fiction and the reality of "woman's place," turns the category into a question.

If "woman" is both herself and the barrier that stops her in her tracks, its meaning must be more clearly understood. How else is she to go on? In the pages to come she sets herself the task of finding out as much as she can about this ambiguously real creature, woman. Her first stop is the Oxbridge library, where she is denied entrance altogether. She then gains the stacks of the British Museum, only to find that the heading "W" for "woman" is nothing more than a signifier for the anger and opinion of men "who have no apparent qualifications save that they are not women" (27). The repositories of the culture's knowledge having taught her only that men speak endlessly about women but say little that is useful or true, she finally turns to her own imaginative ability to trace a history of women that can put words in her mouth and ideas in her head without further interruptions from gesticulating Beadles.

"I" has at her disposal a wealth of what de Lauretis calls "daily, secular repetitions of actions, impressions, and meanings" (*Alice Doesn't* 158). This accumulation of experience encompasses social practices, ideological codes, and an endless variety of personal specificities. It is continuously constructed, however persistently the culture codifies it to fix it in place. The effects of an individual's interactions with it produce subjectivity. If that individual is a woman, her interactions will necessarily remind her daily, constantly, that sexual difference shapes her social realities. Hers is not a subjectivity mastered through the "cogito" or the heir's accession to language or even the alterity of self-alienation. It is a subjectivity of lived experience in a context that both produces and denies that experience. As soon as Woolf writes "I was a woman," she must ask "but what is a woman?" What she does with the sentences on her page reveals the answer to that question to be not a definitive "nugget of pure truth" but an endless process of engagement with actions, impressions, and meanings "caught and tangled in a woman's body" (50). That is, she seeks female subjectivity in the ideas and practices, both fictional and real, which are her legacy as a woman.

One of Woolf's first problems is to permeate the boundaries between fiction and reality. This she does both by turning to the fictions women have written for access to their realities and by telling us a story that is fiction and nonfiction at once in its narrative strategies, its images, its very shape and impact. As a woman writer, it is her business to break free of those structures so well suited to a phantom-intacta silence. We cannot fail to notice, then, that as we read about the development of women's writing that will produce the methods of Woolf's modern "Mary Carmichael," we are also reading an enacting of those methods by Woolf herself. When she brings us to Mary Carmichael "tampering with the expected sequence" so as to see something not seen before, we are aware that we have gotten there by means of a textual practice that also tampers with our expectations, thereby not only helping us to see what has been hidden but changing our angle of vision so that we may see it better.

When Woolf says of Mary Carmichael, "first she broke the sentence; now she has broken the sequence," she is calling forth a heritage or tradition passed from woman to woman, but unacknowledged (or un-known, as it were) by the culture at large (85). This tradition of breaking and tampering has been going on for some time. Little by little it has opened up important nooks and crannies through which we can catch ever more truthful glimpses of our own possibilities. And those possibilities are astonishing: "'Chloe liked Olivia,' I read. And then it struck me how immense a change was there. Chloe liked Olivia perhaps for the first time in literature. . . . All these relationships between women, I thought, rapidly recalling the splendid gallery of fictitious women, are too simple. So much has been left out, unattempted" (86). Mary Carmichael is turning away from the expected images to look with her own eyes at women alone and together. This act enables her "to catch those unrecorded gestures, those unsaid or half-said words" that release women from patriarchal poses (88). It is what allows us to begin to see women simply living and working—as themselves.

Like the relationships of literature's fictional women, the work of women who write literature has been distorted by neglect and misrepresentation. The new angle of vision Woolf brings to bear on that work reveals a history of female experience that signals the end of truth as a one-sided affair. Her tactic is a radically simple one; she merely puts women's words at the center of her story and looks closely at what they do. So long as she depended on the words of men stored in the libraries for her knowledge of women, she was trafficking in false images. What men have written about women, she tells us, is not really about women at all but about some danger to themselves. As theorist Mary Daly puts it, "for those who are . . . threatened, the presence of women to each other is experienced as an absence" (*Gyn/Ecology* xii). As Woolf puts it, "women have served all these centuries as looking-glasses possessing the magic and delicious power of reflecting the figure of man at twice its natural size. Without that power probably the earth would still be swamp and jungle" (*A Room* 35). It is this reflective function the words of men about women have so insistently attempted to contain and control. This they cannot do if the words of women begin to circulate freely:

> For if she begins to tell the truth, the figure in the looking-glass shrinks; his fitness for life is diminished. How is he to go on giving judgement, civilising natives, making laws, writing books, dressing up and speechifying at banquets, unless he can see himself at breakfast and at dinner at least twice the size he really is? (36)

Beadles, judges, soldiers—all the civilizers of Man's world—rely on Woman as a device. She is formed by them for them. In her eyes they mean to see only themselves. But there is another view possible. It is not a trick done with mirrors but an encounter among real beings. It forms a contextual history of shared possibilities by which Mary Carmichael or any woman writing can look to herself and her sisters for what she knows. After all, Woolf points out, "if you consider any great figure of the past, like Sappho, like the Lady Murasaki, like Emily Brontë, you will find that she is an inheritor as well as an originator" (113). What she inherits, however, is not that which accrues to the rightful heirs of the culture. It is rather an understanding of the necessity for paying the closest possible attention to "things in themselves" despite the impositions of the fictions of Woman in the story of Man. If "the average woman" is to develop "a prose style completely expressive of her mind," then what that woman is able to imagine must take its creative force from her own experience—not isolated or co-opted experience but experience in the context of related realities cumulative in the present moment (99).

Woolf's "I" credits Aphra Behn in the seventeenth century with making it imaginable for women to speak their minds. It was not until Aphra Behn earned money by her writing that women could change the conditions, material and ideological, by which they might speak outright, earning them the freedom to be rather more than less themselves. Before that, there are only traces of women's words left to us, in bits of writing here and there, in the signature of "Anon," and among the silenced. The great female Renaissance poet "Shakespeare's sister" must be imagined, given her absence from history. As for *her* sisters, they have all but disappeared, even from imagination. "When, however," Woolf speculates, "one reads of a witch being ducked, of a woman possessed by devils, of a wise woman selling herbs, or even of a very remarkable man who had a mother, then I think we are on the track of a lost novelist, a suppressed poet" (50-51).

Once conditions begin to change and (some) women get free enough to make their livings expressing themselves, the question of what form that expression will take inevitably surfaces. This is a question of the relationship of female experience to a female aesthetic, of what Woolf calls "the effect of sex" on both what and how a woman writes (74). Not only is it reasonable to suppose that her subject matter will be shaped by what she knows but her history of silence and captivity must also impinge on her use of language. Woolf looks to "the four greats," Jane Austen, George Eliot, Emily Brontë and Charlotte Brontë, to propose that a tradition of women writers exists in which "they wrote as women write, not as men write" (78). We may be unpracticed at seeing this tradition for what it is, since the culture has taught us to recognize value from an androcentric standpoint: "This is an important book, the critic assumes, because it deals with war. This is an insignificant book because it deals with the feelings of women in a drawing-room" (77). However, it is those very feelings, Woolf points out, the "training in the observation of character, in the analysis of emotion," that have produced the novel as a literary form and have made women such expert practitioners of it (70). Historically women's very survival has depended on such observation and analysis.

Still, Woolf says, the conditions of life in a patriarchal world have also made women into novelists who might have been poets or playwrights and have put bitterness into their words where only their art and truth might have been. Among Woolf's four, she regards only Jane Austen as having "consumed all impediments" so that she herself was inside every word she wrote, yet free of the hate, bitterness, fear, or protest that could twist those words into shapes not their own (71). Because, Woolf believes, Austen was able to write only and completely as herself, "the woman's sentence" could appear and take breath. In her common sitting room, seemingly against all odds, Austen "devised a perfectly natural, shapely sentence proper for her own use and never departed from it" (80). This intensely close match between (inner) experience and artful expression is not an imitation of someone else's experience—of experience closed to her—but is wholly her own. It is a crucial step. In the early twentieth century Dorothy Richardson would speak of this "integrity" through Miriam Henderson as "the realization of a bond, closer than any other, between myself and what I had written" (*Pilgrimage* 4:611). This bond, this relationship between female experience and the art of independent language, gives women access to "things in themselves" as never before.

As Woolf reminds us, however, so long as gendered limitations of subject or form are brought to bear on writers, there is no way to know what a woman's pen might produce. She has a history of novels behind her; but "who shall say that even this most pliable of all forms is rightly shaped for her use? No doubt we shall find her knocking that into shape for herself when she has the free use of her limbs; and providing some new vehicle, not necessarily in verse, for the poetry in her" (80). Woolf herself, of course, is just such a woman. We must remind ourselves that it was Woolf's struggle with the verb "to be" rather than "to want" that took her beyond the limitations of man-made gender. Like those whose example she had before her eyes, she adapted cultural realities to inner necessities (so like Stein's difficult relationship of the external to the internal) to "stretch" the sentence further than ever and create new literary spaces for female experience and subjectivity. As "Mary Carmichael" she uses the new flexibility of the sentence to invent shapes she herself can see, shapes proper for her own use.

We can hear Lily Briscoe, Mrs. Ramsay, and Clarissa Dalloway moving about just behind the scenes of *A Room*, reminding us of Woolf's other confrontations with the phantom Angel. Her written women know Woman well, but know themselves in relation to her even better. Woolf's own integrity, in her fiction and nonfiction alike, demanded of her a close attention to those unrecorded gestures gone begging under the name instinct and hidden from sight by narrative patterns designed for the story of man. She brings Woman and women together, clarifying the contradictions between them as well as the effects of one upon the other. The consciousness of a woman writing as herself with full awareness both of that self and of the culture's distortions of it creates a process of female subjectivity resistant to being swallowed up by the feminine or co-opted by the masculine.

We must keep in mind that the ideological constitution of Woman as Man's sexual category reduces female experience to illusion only from the phallocentric position of creator of the ideology. For women the action is multiplied rather than reduced. That is, as sexuality incarnate (ideologically speaking), women are both inside and outside the construct: as insiders, our dealings with sexuality are both complicit with and in conflict with ideological Reality; as outsiders, our knowledge of the lie comes from the inside of the conflict rather than from exemption as does men's. Add to this the myriad specificities of any particular woman's daily contact with cultural assumptions of her (as) sexual nature, and the reduction of her experience to illusion becomes a denial of her capacity to distinguish between the construct and herself. From a masculinized position of agency, this might be rethought as modern self-alienation. From the feminine position, however, it is only one more instance of "being disappeared" into the illusion. Woolf's stretched sentences, her transgressions of boundaries, and her continual blurring of the distinctions between reality and illusion, between experience and knowledge, between reason and instinct, constitute in her a refusal of silence and invisibility.

In the October 23, 1929, entry of Woolf's diary, she speaks of the publication of *A Room of One's Own*, predicting that "the press will be kind and talk of its charm and sprightliness; also I shall be attacked for a feminist and hinted at for a Sapphist; . . . I shall get a good many letters from young women. I am afraid it will not be taken seriously" (*A Writer's Diary* 145). Sex, politics, and the eternal feminine all come together in this remark, indicating Woolf's clear understanding that a common way to avoid taking a woman's writing seriously is to define it in relation to the mandates and prohibitions of gender, then condemn it on that same basis. Interestingly enough, she anticipates an eager audience among young women, perhaps the very women who might study Woolf's textual practices as she studied those of Jane Austen, to see what one might make of that question about being a woman in a world that defines "woman" by her limitations. What strategies might a woman employ to be herself, to speak as herself, even though so few have developed the eyes and ears to perceive "herself"? Who will speak with her? How will such a woman use the voice she has acquired, and to what purpose?

Woolf's voice, of course, brings art and politics together on the page, subverting the usual distinctions between them by slipping constantly between fact and fiction, multiplying and questioning the authority of the "I" so valued by Western humanism as a unified Self, and disrupting our conventions of expectation by involving us in a continually renewed process of thinking and knowing—all by means of the recording of those previously unrecorded gestures of women. Woolf is able to deepen and extend her critique of patriarchal sociopolitical systems by constituting the text itself as an active resistance to both the truths and the logical processes of those systems. The Beadles, judges, soldiers, even the brothers and friends who have so long relied on Woman as the reflection of their glory must wave their arms at phantoms; women have already begun to move off the path and move about elsewhere on their own.

The form and function of this elsewhere is precisely the problem Woolf goes on to address in *Three Guineas*, published in 1938. As World War II came closer and closer, Woolf applied her artful politics to the problem of how women might intervene in the dangerous situation brought about by what she called "aggressive masculinity." One of the text's central strategies is its demonstration of the effects of masculinity as a systematic will to dominance whose logical consequence is, at its extreme, war. The only hope for preventing this consequence is to remove the conditions that produce submission, thereby making dominance and the inequality on which it depends no longer effective tools for societal power and influence. This does not entail mere opposition, a move the existing structure is already designed to accommodate, but a radical restructuring of society in such a way that "independent opinion" may truly come into being. If such a development were to take place, dominance and submission would become relics of a former time; for independent opinion does not rest on the acquisition of external marks of status and power but on "freedom from unreal loyalties" (78). And who better to withstand the challenge of such a freedom than women, who have had so little experience of the privileges dominance seems to confer?

Woolf notes in a February 1932 diary entry that originally the motivation for *Three Guineas* came about through her reading of H. G. Wells's opinions on woman: "how she must be ancillary and decorative in the world of the future, because she has been tried, in 10 years, and has not proved anything" (*A Writer's Diary* 174). This attitude and its effects are also pointedly resisted by Dorothy Richardson; Wells (with whom Richardson had a liaison in her own life) is the Hypo Wilson character of *Pilgrimage*, Miriam's lover and friend who uses "scientific" views to silence Miriam's assertion of female autonomy. In *Dawn's Left Hand* Miriam has come to understand that for Hypo, "there was no place in his universe for women who did not either sincerely, blindly, follow, or play up and make him believe they were following. All the others were merely pleasant or unpleasant biological material." Women who opposed him he regarded as "misguided creatures who must not be allowed to obstruct" (4:223). Both Woolf and Richardson locate the impetus for this attitude in men's masculinity training—in the valorization of male dominance as a kind of birthright deemed natural and necessary to properly ordered, civilized society. This assumption of sovereignty over women as little more than decorative biological material that must be controlled so as not to obstruct is, for both Woolf and Richardson, at the root of "aggressive masculinity." For both, the task is to resist it through the development of personal, economic, and ideological independence, an independence that can ensure that "unreal loyalties" no longer rule human behavior.

In *Three Guineas*, then, Woolf proposes that women form a Society of Outsiders, structured otherwise than patriarchal society but working with men of good faith in the society at large to transform the divisive power of Difference (on which dominance and submission are based) into a coalition of interactive differences. In response to a man she imagines asking her, a woman, for help in preventing war (already an event "perhaps unique in the history of human correspondence" [3]) she offers that help, "not by repeating your words and following your methods but by finding new words and creating new methods" (143). Those new words and methods are enacted on every page of *Three Guineas*, giving form to what Adrienne Rich calls "re-vision"—the ability to enter an old story (as it were) from a new perspective. This, as Rich says, is an act of survival. It is a necessity for women, whose part in the old story has long been silent submission. Once women no longer take that part, the story itself must become new. That, for Woolf, is the re-vision that can mean survival for us all.

Because experience shapes and is shaped by ideological practices, it must be taken into account in any proposal for change. The outsider who is produced as such by a system structured on a hegemonic relation of insider to outsider is always trapped in a kind of complicity with that system; her difference of experience is always constructed as meaningful only in relation to the dominant values of the system itself. She must use that difference, then, to step away, to put into play the tension and contradiction of her dual/split role as both enabler and obstacle, source and prize in Man's quest for self and power. She must use her knowledge of both the inside and the outside to envision a structure whose boundaries are so permeable they invite freedom of movement and thought, not along formulated lines but for the sake of "experimental and adventurous" independence. Such independence does not fear loss and ridicule but encourages knowledge or work for the love of the thing itself. In this way oppression might be successfully resisted, for knowledge, work, and action would no longer make capital of privilege and disprivilege. Like the change that is immense once Chloe likes Olivia, this change also can "light a torch in that vast chamber where nobody has yet been" (*A Room* 88).

Woolf describes her Society of Outsiders as one "which must be anonymous and elastic before everything" (*Three Guineas* 106). Accordingly, it would exist "without office, meetings, leaders or any hierarchy, without so much as a form to be filled up, or a secretary to be paid" (115). Its "experiments"—for what else can we call the activities of such a society?—"will not be merely critical but creative" (113). It cannot be formed by those whose lives have been shaped by the privileges of patriarchal inheritance but must be free to achieve its ends "by the means that a different sex, a different tradition, a different education, and the different values which result from those differences have placed within our reach" (113).

This is not a marginal position but an enactment of autonomy informed by long and complex acquaintance with both periphery and center, achieved by a determined access to independent thought in relation to the very differences designed to prevent it. Speaking from the margins, however attractive such a move has sometimes seemed, is nevertheless a kind of confirmation of the boundaries of patriarchal order. It tends to secure that aspect of woman's place Toril Moi calls "the necessary frontier between man and chaos"—the borderland that is neither here nor there, occupied by beings that both embody chaos and act as buffers against it. This is the space Alice Jardine reminds us is conveniently figured as "outside of" the realm of the conscious subject that "has always connoted the feminine." This, of course, is the space to which the rightful heirs have always turned for sustenance; it is into this space Woolf's war correspondent has sent his request for help. But Woolf does not respond as expected. Her stand as an Outsider is a different matter. It is neither dividing line nor symptomatic of repressed material taking illusive shape. It is something else.

The nonstructure she envisions for her Society of Outsiders must surely seem nonsensical (chaotic) to one such as her correspondent; but as she tells him, there is already a model for such a Society in existence—a model that "far from sitting still to be painted, dodges and disappears," a model not provided for by the authoritative histories and biographies of the culture but only by "history and biography in the raw—by the newspapers that is—sometimes openly in the lines, sometimes covertly between them" (115). As proof of the viability of this model, she cites three incidents reported in the newspapers; she reads these incidents as experiments, for each involves women choosing not to participate in established practices of societal support and reward: a female mayor publicly refuses to aid the war effort; a woman member of the Board of Education rejects the awarding of trophies for winning teams in women's sporting events as unnecessary inducements since players continue to join the game "for the love of it"; and a new "paucity of young women" in church congregations is worried over as an indicator of "a remarkable change in [their] attitude" (116-17).

What Woolf is using as evidence for a Society of Outsiders are bits and scraps of female experience in a post-phantom era, an era in which women may encounter freedom not as license but as reliance on what they know for themselves. What they are after, she believes, is, "like Antigone, not to break the laws, but to find the law" (138). For as she once again reminds us, "when the lady was killed the woman still remained" (134). And it is the woman who must take on female experience, the very thing from which the Eternal Feminine is so thoroughly dissociated. The Feminine is not what Woolf, or Richardson either, brings onto the page but rather what both confront as they seek independent voices as female subjects who do not depend on altered preverbal spaces to hear themselves. It is not the merely "discursively present" Woman of the new theories of language subjectivity that they offer us but women who actively experiment and adventure in the land of discourse as they use words to "develop in your presence as fully and freely as I can" their own freedoms from unreal loyalties (*A Room* 4).

Woolf's Society of Outsiders, then, by virtue of its members' difference of sex, tradition, education, and values, achieves an "indifference" crucial to the nonsupport of war. Having discovered "herself" absent in the history of Western culture's libraries, campuses, politics, and professions, Woolf reclaims her deprivation as a radical freedom. In the mouth of her Outsider she puts these words: "as a woman, I have no country. As a woman I want no country. As a woman my country is the whole world" (109). For such an Outsider, there is little temptation to take part in "patriotic demonstrations . . . national self-praise . . . military displays, tournaments, tattoos, prize-givings and all such ceremonies as encourage the desire to impose 'our' civilization or 'our' dominion upon other people" (109). As she considers her options, it is to "this use of indifference" that Woolf ultimately gives her guineas, her support, and her energy. Otherwise, women will be merely joining men as purveyors of the ideas and practices that produced the problem in the first place. Her Society of Outsiders, then, is not a form of separatism but a use of that experience formed in the nooks and crannies of patriarchal constructs of possibility to envision a world where lack is not a weapon of dominance and where coalitions can be formed among people of independent ideas capable of creating a real alternative to annihilation.

We should keep in mind, of course, that the female experience on which Woolf relies is a kind of dominant female experience. That is, she is speaking as "the daughter of an educated man" to other daughters of educated men and to educated men themselves. Race and class for her are "normed." It is primarily through gender that she knows herself as an outsider. Woolf acknowledges this specificity of experience and presumes to speak only from within it. Her attention to her own particularity in relation to a nonunified, shared social construct is a realistically devised move, though one could wish that she had included in that particularity the deeper awareness, of which she was certainly capable, of race, ethnicity, and class as companion constructs to the otherness of sexual difference. While Richardson made a more pointed effort to do so in *Pilgrimage*, neither writer quite managed to overcome the terrible convenience of those privileges accorded to them by the class-structured, white-supremacist patriarchy in which they lived. Though Woolf briefly calls upon men to recognize the similarity in the fights against "the tyranny of the patriarchal state" and "the tyranny of the Fascist state" now that "you are being shut out, you are being shut up, because you are Jews, because you are democrats, because of race, because of religion" (102-3), she nevertheless speaks as if unaware that this new incorporation of certain men into some oppressions of otherness is not new at all. She has understood gender from the inside out, but has as if unwillingly collaborated with her own cultural chauvinism by leaving dangerous fictions about race and ethnicity virtually unquestioned.

Despite this limitation, however, Woolf's recognition of the closely allied interests of feminism and a peace movement committed to equality of rights for all human beings is an important step toward a viable coalition politics. The convergence of fascism and unchecked masculinism makes a coalition of resistance all the more necessary. And only from within female experience can she envision a workable coalition between women and men not blind to the value of that experience and its potential for realizing interactive differences. The Outsider's independence of opinion, honed by the daily practice of surviving the fictions, makes her a particularly able analyst of what passes for reality: "Inevitably we look upon society, so kind to you, so harsh to us, as an ill-fitting form that distorts the truth; deforms the mind; fetters the will. Inevitably we look upon societies as conspiracies that sink the private brother, whom many of us have reason to respect, and inflate in his stead a monstrous male, loud of voice, hard of fist, childishly intent upon scoring the floor of the earth with chalk marks" (105). This is not all that far removed from those analyses of race, class, and ethnicity in which sexual difference is understood as both a pervasive shaper of experience and a weapon used to further divide people whose survival has depended on a refusal to be divided. We must wait for the words of Shange, Broner, and Wittig, however, to see this sort of inside-out understanding put into textual practice.

Woolf's ability to see the ways in which patriarchal culture produces experience that can be read publicly only through ideological codes also allows her to posit private experience—the realm of the Outsider—as the tool by which to break those codes. "Though we look at the same things, we see them differently," she says to her male correspondent (5). She uses this double vision to present the public and the private in volatile relation to one another, yet without making one contingent upon the conquest of the other. To accomplish this not only in ideas and images but also in the textual strategies of the page, she continually invades her narrative with facts, information, and commentary taken from daily newspapers, biographies, histories, and the like in the form of endnotes comprising nearly a third of the book's length. In the original edition of *Three Guineas*, this tension between "the real world" and the writer's inner resources is further enhanced by a number of photographs depicting various scenes of pomp and ceremony by public officials of one sort and another. As one reads, eyes moving back and forth between notes, photographs, and text, the boundaries between the public and private worlds of fact and fiction become increasingly blurred. Soon they must all work together, creating a multivoiced text in which Woolf interacts with her own words, with actual and invented occurrences, with correspondents both actual and invented, and with her readers. Like the Society of Outsiders that functions both autonomously and in concert with others, this textual practice ensures an independence of opinion and freedom from unreal loyalties, uncommonly flexible in its ability to accommodate interactions among conventionally discrete signs and subjects.

For her trouble, Woolf was accused by friends and critics of the sin of forgetting her artist's place and transgressing into the territory of the overtly political. Despite the disturbances *Three Guineas* brought about, however, after its publication Woolf recorded in her diary a sense of release: "I need never recur or repeat," she wrote. "I am an outsider. I can take my way: experiment with my own imagination in my own way. The pack may howl, but it shall never catch me" (*A Writer's Diary* 282). This freedom to imagine as oneself comes about through Woolf's conscious and continually renewed understanding of what it is to be at once a cultural fiction and a material reality in a world bent on the reification of the fiction *as* the reality.

It is precisely this freedom that also occupies Dorothy Richardson throughout the more than two thousand pages of *Pilgrimage*. Like Woolf, she sought female subjectivity not as mere discursive presence (Man's not-man) but as attentive, contextual interaction between consciousness, cultural gender, and lived experience. Like Woolf, she enacted that subjectivity through a method or style that evades classification. And like Woolf, she resisted annihilation in the enactment. For Richardson, female consciousness on the page becomes an acategorical process in which language and subjectivity are simultaneously cultural constructs and things in themselves. Her work both adapts and disrupts narrative, recognizing it as an insufficient container for what she knew that nevertheless could be stretched and made flexible enough to record those previously unrecorded gestures of a woman who is always becoming "herself." In this work, Richardson devises a form that is more than a language of consciousness but rather an instance of language as consciousness, female consciousness, always in motion and never fixed in place.

Even the physical shape of this work evades conventional descriptive categories. *Pilgrimage* is the overall title by which the work is known, but also comprises thirteen subtitles Richardson called chapters but were published (and are still referred to) as separate books. The first eleven titles were printed between 1915 and 1935. In 1938 these were collected in a four-volume edition and the twelfth title added. And in 1967, ten years after Richardson's death, the thirteenth and final title was added to the fourth volume. *Pilgrimage* is now available in all four volumes, all thirteen titles, in a 1979 edition printed by Virago Press in London; but despite a complete 1976 edition published by Popular Library in New York, the work in its entirety continues to be difficult to come by in the United States. Richardson intended each book or chapter to be read as part of a larger whole, but not necessarily in linear or chronological fashion. She envisioned *Pilgrimage* as a kind of continuous process and readers free to begin anywhere and proceed at will; even the order of a book's pages was to her mind not fixed but variable. It seems only appropriate, then, that categorical nomenclature slips away when referring to this remarkable work. (My own page and volume references follow the Virago edition, consisting of volume 1: *Pointed Roofs, Backwater,* and *Honeycomb*; volume 2: *The Tunnel* and *Interim*; volume 3: *Deadlock, Revolving Lights*, and *The Trap*; volume 4: *Oberland, Dawn's Left Hand, Clear Horizon, Dimple Hill,* and *March Moonlight.*)

In her foreword to the 1938 edition, Richardson talked about the difficulty of finding an appropriate form for what she had to say. Any writer who means to render female experience or consciousness or subjectivity on the page, after all, has to contend with the pervasive figure of Woman, the very figure which so tormented Woolf that she concluded no woman could write without killing it. Richardson felt herself to be caught at a moment in history when her only literary models consisted of devalued "writers of romance" or men who wrote realist novels she characterized as "largely explicit satire and protest" aimed at "every form of conventionalized human association." She (characteristically speaking in the third person), "proposing at this moment to write a novel and looking round for a contemporary pattern, was faced with the choice between following one of her regiments and attempting to produce a feminine equivalent of the current masculine realism" (1:9). The latter choice seemed by far the better one; but as she wrote an odd thing happened. In place of what she called "the briskly moving script" of the first chapter (i.e. *Pointed Roofs*), there began to appear "a stranger in the form of contemplated reality having for the first time in her experience its own say" (1:10). As she gave this stranger voice, she became increasingly aware that it could not be contained by any of the "realist" fictions she had read, nor by autobiography, nor indeed by any form apparently at her disposal. It was, after all, a contemplated reality from inside female experience, a no-thing in the eyes of the surrounding culture.

What she then began to commit to the page seemed to her something that would never find a publisher but which gave her "a sense of being upon a fresh pathway, an adventure so searching and, sometimes, so joyous as to produce a longing for participation" (1:10). This writing took place between 1911 and 1913; by the time *Pointed Roofs* found a publisher in 1915, news had reached Richardson of Marcel Proust's "unprecedentedly profound and opulent reconstruction of experience focused from within the mind of a single individual" (1:10). Thus, she commented, France "appeared to have produced the earliest adventurer" and he, along with Henry James, was accorded "the role of pathfinder" (1:11). Richardson, however, continued to give her stranger her own voice, bringing out nearly a book a year at first; she also increasingly found herself accused "of feminism, of failure to perceive the value of the distinctively masculine intelligence, of pre-War sentimentality, of post-War Freudianity"—and, as if that were not enough, of work that is "unpunctuated and therefore unreadable" (1:12). While she supposed this last accusation to be somewhat justified, she at the same time proclaimed that "feminine prose . . . should properly be unpunctuated, moving from point to point without formal obstructions," and went so far as to cite Charles Dickens and James Joyce as likewise aware of this truth (1:12).

Clearly Richardson found it ironic, if not aggravating, that *her* feminine prose focusing on a mind from within should be found wanting while similar efforts by her male peers were hailed as important innovations. One cannot help but be aware, as the accusations Richardson cites demonstrate, that it was her focus not on a mind but on a female mind that got in the way of her critical reception. There she is, that female obstacle at the crossroads, still causing trouble; the more she works to remove obstructions for herself, the more she becomes an obstruction irresistible to androcentric cultural codes.

By calling her own written reality a stranger, she was in effect acknowledging that its like was not something even she knew how to recognize at first. But she did recognize its necessity. And though her work is frequently compared to "novels of consciousness" by modernist male writers, *Pilgrimage* cannot be read as that "feminine equivalent" Richardson herself abandoned when she saw what was actually issuing forth onto her page—the integrity Woolf so valued, the bond closer than any other between writer and writing claimed by Richardson through Miriam. In *Dawn's Left Hand*, Miriam finds her first real model of what such writing might be. She is reading a letter from Amabel, the woman whose life will seem so close as to be almost interchangeable with her own. In this letter, "no single word showed its meaning directly. . . . Yet each was expressive, before its meaning appeared. . . . When meanings were discovered, they sounded; as if spoken":

> It was this strange, direct, as if spoken communication, punctuated only by dashes sloped at various angles like the sharp, forcible uprights of the script, and seeming to be the pauses of a voice in speech, that was making the reading of this letter so new an experience. . . .
>
> Alive. These written words were alive in a way no others she had met had been alive. . . . Instead of bringing as did the majority of letters, especially those written by men, a picture of the writer seated and thoughtfully using a medium of communication, recognizing its limitations and remaining docile within them so that the letter itself seemed quite as much to express the impossibility as the possibility of exchange by means of the written word, it called her directly to the girl herself, making her, and not the letter, the medium of expression. Each word, each letter, was Amabel. (4:215)

There are no barriers between Amabel, Miriam, and the writing itself. Everything works together in a complex way that relies neither on expectation nor predetermination, but comes to her as a living being. This does not, of course, preclude its access to signification through the cultural codes; but neither does it take its ability to signify only from them. Rather, like Richardson's women living in patriarchal society, the writing is most alive in its dis-junctive relationships with the very codes of meaning by which it is to operate as communication. Because the writing does not direct Miriam's attention but demands it whole, she is able to respond one being to another. Form and content come together in a new way. The letter, like *Pilgrimage* itself, is no mere communication of some part of a life, but a written instance of that life:

> Real. Reality vibrating behind this effort to drive feeling through words. The girl's reality appealing to her own, seeing and feeling it ahead of her own seeings or feelings that yet responded, acknowledged as she emerged from her reading, in herself and the girl, with them when they were together, somehow between them in the mysterious inter-play of their two beings, the reality she had known for so long alone, brought out into life. (4:217)

This is the connection so close as to seem a "completeness of being," the same kind of connection Miriam feels between her-self and other women, only this time in writing. Richardson, as will Miriam, uses that writing to participate in a continuous, ac-tive process of female subjectivity. The words of *Pilgrimage* are "as if spoken" from inside Miriam's consciousness, in perpetual motion and never presented as the kind of knowledge that once formed will coalesce into a "thing" by which to set limits. Not only is there no omniscient arbiter of reality on Richardson's page, there are no passages that lapse into imagined or dreamed events; every-thing Miriam thinks can be counted on as her actual experience. The reader is given no special distance from Miriam by which to know truths hidden from her; we learn and grow as does she. So focused is the text on this process that it often does without cues to anchor it in externally recognizable scenes or events. We may be suddenly quite unsure of time or place, as in much of *Dawn's Left Hand*. This is particularly so during episodes of intense aware-ness on Miriam's part in which she pushes at the limits of what is known to further her access to her own know-ing. Such episodes catch us trying to expect what Richardson will not deliver: story, or even a woman's story. *Pilgrimage* does not reinscribe cultural truths or myths but enacts experience.

This is not the kind of writing Hypo Wilson (man of science, writer, thinker, husband of Miriam's old school friend and eventual-ly her own lover) advises Miriam to attempt. He tells her, "perhaps the novel's not your form. Women ought to be good novelists. But they write best about their own experiences. Love-affairs and so forth. They lack creative imagination." When Miriam responds by saying, "Ah, imagination. Lies," Hypo ignores her and goes on. "Try a novel of ideas," he says; "Philosophical. There's George Eliot." "Writes like a man," Miriam mocks. "Just so," says Hypo; "Lewes. Be a feminine George Eliot. Try your hand" (4:239-40). Not only does Hypo regard female experience as consisting only of "love-affairs and so forth," he sees it as without intellectual content—without consciousness— except as it can imitate what men do. He assumes that women are not and cannot be selves in their own right but must be guided by men, the creators who are free to take women as their creative inspiration. Miriam says of such men, "They seem incapable of unthinking the suggestions coming to them from centuries of mas- culine attempts to represent women only in relation to the world as known to men." Women, she says, "*can't* be represented by men. Because by every word they use men and women mean different things" (4:92-93). If men want civilization to work, "they must leave off imagining themselves a race of gods fighting against chaos, and thinking of women as part of the chaos they have to civilize. There isn't any 'chaos.' Never has been. It's the principal mas- culine illusion" (3:218-19).

Certainly *Pilgrimage* is not without descriptive detail and or- dered events, particularly in the early books or chapters. And we do follow Miriam Henderson through much of her life: we first encounter her as a very young woman leaving home to teach at a girls' school in Germany, go with her as she settles into a London office job that frees her mind for the hard work of living an inde- pendent (if impecunious) life, see her through a number of intense loves and friendships, search with her for that happiness which is a match between her sense of herself and the circumstances of her living, and leave her just as she is about to take up a full-time career as a writer. But this is not a representation of a life; it does not employ language, imagery, or events as focusing devices for revealing the shapes and truths of life we are already primed to recognize. Rather it is an immersion into consciousness; narrative becomes consciousness. Far from being a formless nothing, this is both a literary use of the sign system and an enactment of experi- ence, both a transactive device and a collapsing of the distinction between sender and receiver. Near the end of *Pilgrimage*, Miriam (Richardson) says,

> While I write, everything vanishes but what I contemplate. The whole of what is called "the past" is with me, seen anew, vividly. No, Schiller,

the past does not stand "being still." It moves, growing with one's growth. Contemplation is adventure into discovery; reality. What is called "creation" imaginative transformation, fantasy, invention, is only based upon reality. Poetic description a half-truth? Can anything produced by man be called "creation"? The incense-burners do not seem to know that in acclaiming what they call "a work of genius" they are recognizing what is potentially within themselves. If it were not, they would not recognize it. Fully to recognize, one must be alone. Away in the farthest reaches of one's being. As one can richly be, even with others, provided they have no claims. Provided one is neither guest nor host. With others on neutral territory, where one can forget one is there, and be everywhere. (4:657)

The completeness of contemplated reality; recognition of its ability to change and grow in the present even when it occurred in the past; the necessity of a solitude that is really an independence and that makes possible an equal interaction between beings where neither is guest nor host—all this produces an openness to the adventure of discovery, a forgetting of self-consciousness in favor of consciousness. We do not merely enter the world of the fictional character as in more conventional writing but share a process with her and with her author. She, her author, and the reader are almost interchangeable at times, in the sense of all participating moment by moment in the life on the page. Richardson's words invite us into a written presence so particular yet so connected that the "I/she" of the text seems almost to merge with the "you" it addresses. Even when characters return who haven't appeared for hundreds of pages, they are familiar; they seem to be part of our own pasts as well as Miriam's. At least that is how it seems to a female reader, to this female reader.

There are few enough instances in literature of the kind of recognition that has little to do with cultural scripts but everything to do with what is within ourselves, especially when that inner awareness is also cognizant of its tense relations to the culture's scripted expectations. Fewer still are those moments when a female reader does not have to compromise and negotiate her relationship with a text in a constant effort to overcome her implicit exclusions from it. Even when characters or writers are female, Woman threatens to take over. Culturally She is a vehicle for meaning and self; she is an essence whose essence is man's suppressed desire; her mind, her being, her name, her words are his; she is present only in relation to him. But Richardson's articulated consciousness is not a "feminine equivalent," nor a matter of reconquest of The Word designed to wrest meaning away from the forefathers in the service of one's own image. It is rather her enactment of writing the truth about her experiences as a body, a female body of thought and sensation in a world normed on the male. The consciousness Richardson writes confronts and strips away the workings of cultural productions of Man's meaning and self. It releases into the open an active engagement with those countless intellectual, physical, and emotional moments of a woman living in a patriarchal context, yet fully aware of herself as "herself"—independent yet deeply connected to others, able to discern the realities of women alone and together in those fissured spaces of the culture traditionally denied illumination.

For Richardson, as for her character Miriam Henderson, it is only through a full realization of the experienced self that she can begin to create art, not out of life, but that is life. Art and life come together in a conscious relationship so close that writing and experience are only falsified by categorizing them separately. This is the thesis of Gillian Hanscombe's 1982 study *The Art of Life: Dorothy Richardson and the Development of Feminist Consciousness.* Hanscombe reads *Pilgrimage* as experimental autobiography in which Richardson's realization of "the problem of being a woman" takes two parallel developments: "The first consists in how she lived her life, the second in how she wrote her fiction. Each may properly be called experimental" (25). That is, Richardson had to find a way to honor the intimate connection between art and experience even while recording it in a language generally hostile to it. Her "feminine prose," then, must break with expected sequences of time, event, and form. She avoids enclosure everywhere. The female consciousness she puts on the page is, in Hanscombe's words, "less committed than male consciousness to the demands of an external world which had been shaped by men" (28). Miriam is written in third person but moves to first person and back again without comment. Richardson freely employs repeated stops that appear on paper as a series of dots (looking very much like ellipses), which give her a more open access to thought processes as processes. As Hanscombe notes, there is a constant "expansion and dissolution" rather than a progressive development of character or story, though this nonconventional prose becomes increasingly adroit as Miriam's consciousness matures. The more descriptive, declarative sentences of *Pointed Roofs* become ever more flexible and concentrated in the middle books and beyond. Not only does this confirm Richardson's own sense of something new entering her writing by the end of the first book but it serves the purpose of, in Hanscombe's words, "accommodating Miriam's increasing complication of abstract thought and encompassing, too, subtler fusions between descriptions of the external world and inner reflections" (52).

The subjectivity Richardson brings to bear on her use of language is, of course, not merely personal but political. Miriam's solitude is not isolation, but a presence to herself and to other women. It politicizes experience and restructures gendered accesses to the meaning of experience. Miriam / Richardson never ceases to stand constantly in a new relation to the iconic fictions of the Feminine. In her dealings with the question of what a woman is, Miriam resists patriarchal epistemology. She rejects both men and women at first, yet thinks of herself as both male and female. In her world after all, if a woman insists on being fully human, she is said to be unwomanly; if she accepts femininity, she is denied full humanity. What she must finally come to terms with is a self that is both and neither male or female as the culture understands them, but that brings gender and self together in such a way that her female history does not disappear into imitation of the male nor into that separate sphere which is only another version of imitation. She says, "The deranging and dehumanizing of women by uncritical acceptance of masculine systems of thought, rather than being evidence against feminine capacity for thought, is a demand for feminine thinking" (4:378). What she must become, then, is only herself—a being without place or precedent in the myths and fictions of patriarchal thought.

Like Woolf's ambiguous "I" in *A Room of One's Own*, Miriam at first mistakes the culture's repositories of Knowledge for accesses to information that will apply to her own experience and help her to overcome the apparent disabilities of being female. She is aware that as a woman her form of knowledge is meant to be primarily instinctual and sensory. But she understands her intellect to be as demanding as her sensations and assumes that filling it with the "real" knowledge of the culture will put her in communication with others as an equal participant; one intellect would be much the same in kind as another, she thinks. She knows this is not what she as a woman is supposed to think. "I am something between a man and a woman; looking both ways," she says (2:187). Knowledge seems her surest way of understanding the duplicity of her condition.

Miriam seeks this informational knowledge first in the very place Woolf in *Three Guineas* found facts so revealing of the culture's fictions, in newspapers. Her father had never deemed newspapers fit reading for his daughters; but in *Backwater*, at one of her teaching posts, Miriam discovers them as a source of immediate information about the world. It comes as something of a revelation to her: "Of course; men seemed to know such a lot because they read the newspapers and talked about what was in them. But anybody could know as much as the men sitting in the arm-chairs if they chose" (1:243). She puts this idea to the test later, in *Honeycomb* where she has entered a private household as governess. Now an accomplished newspaper reader, she thinks this access to knowledge will allow her to communicate where other women only pose and pander. Secretly trying out one of the armchairs in the master's library, she imagines an encounter with him this way: "He would be sitting in the other arm-chair, and she would say, 'what do you think about everything?' Not so much to hear what he thought, but because some of his thoughts would be her thoughts. Thought was the same in everybody who thought at all" (1:367). But of course the exclusions of gender and class prove her wrong.

She will go on with her search in London's lecture halls, in intellectual discussions with Hypo, in tutorial sessions with the Russian intellectual Michael Shatov, who solicits her help in learning English and eventually becomes her suitor, and in Quaker meetings where silent contemplation seems to promise a purer or deeper knowledge than verbal performance has been able to deliver. But nowhere except in herself will she find what she wants because only her own lived experience can turn Knowledge into a process of know-ing. As she tells Michael Shatov, "facts are invented by people who start with their conclusions arranged beforehand" (3:214).

Nothing teaches her this lesson more clearly than the science so valued by Hypo Wilson. Science proclaims her, a woman, to be an "undeveloped man"—a "fact" she cannot accept, for it is quite simply unacceptable. "And the modern men were the worst . . . 'We can now, with all the facts in our hands, sit down and examine her at our leisure.' There was no getting away from the scientific facts . . . *inferior*; mentally, morally, intellectually, and physically . . . her development arrested in the interest of her special functions" (2:219-20, ellipses Richardson's). Miriam's response is initially an angry one that condemns men and rejects women who are complicit with them. "It will all go on as long as women are stupid enough to go on bringing men into the world," she says (2:220):

>   They invent a legend to put the blame for the existence of humanity
>   on woman and, if she wants to stop it, they talk about the wonders of
>   civilizations and the sacred responsibilities of motherhood. They can't
>   have it both ways. They also say women are not logical.

>   They despise women and they want to go on living—to reproduce—
>   themselves. None of their achievements, no "civilization," no art, no
>   science can redeem that. There is no pardon possible for man. The
>   only answer to them is suicide; all women ought to agree to commit
>   suicide. (2:221)

Patriarchal knowledge and its underpinnings are not only insufficient to Miriam's needs, they are designed to make her, as
she really is, invisible, nonexistent. They offer her a place only as
enigma, what Miriam calls "tricky femininity"—an illusion she
cannot live with, yet which trails after her cloyingly wherever she
goes. She is caught, as it were, between fact and reality. "Wit.
Woman's wit. Men at least bowed down to that; though they did
not know what it was. 'Wit' used to mean knowledge—'inwit,' con-
science. The knowledge of woman is larger, bigger, deeper, less
wordy and clever than that of men. Certainly. But why do not men
acknowledge this? They talk about mother-love and mother-wit
and instinct, as if they were mysterious tricks. They have no real
knowledge, but of things" (2:188).
    If she is to get beyond the myths masquerading as facts,
Miriam must go her own way. Otherwise she can be no more than
"the thing he thought he saw" (2:389). She thinks of women who
enter men's lives as "not themselves"—as, that is, Woman. "They
were in a noisy confusion, playing a part all the time," she says.
"The only real misery in being alone was the fear of being left out
of things. It was a wrong fear" (2:321). She embraces London as
the one companion that can ensure her independent solitude, char-
acterizing the city as "always receiving her back without words,
engulfing and leaving her untouched, liberated and expanding to
the whole range of her being" (3:272). In the city, she walks into
restaurants alone, takes up residence in one or another small room,
talks eagerly with friends, joins political societies, and earns a small
salary. She lives a freedom of her own making denied by the con-
fines of conventional womanhood. Still, Miriam longs for a nor-
malcy of connection, even as she is aware of its deceptions and
costs, and thinks to find it in the winter resort of Oberland, then
in the Quaker community of Dimple Hill. In both places she takes
a rest from the demands of her solitude, momentarily considering

marriage as a viable possibility. But the people of these worlds, she says to herself, "can be lived with only at the cost of pretending to think as they do. Not to think, but to live entirely in reference to tradition and code. Sooner or later, they discover that you belong mentally elsewhere as well as to them, and you become an object of suspicion" (4:252).

One of the most profoundly felt effects of tradition and code in the culture is gender difference. Miriam's awareness of her own difference is ever with her, though her attempts to see beyond her own cultural biases (while more deliberately present than Woolf's) are severely limited in their assumptions of white, middle-class norms. As regards gender, however, even in her intensest anger at men she is able to find moments of common humanity with them; but it is only with women she finds a connection so deep that she refers to it as a "completeness of being" and a "shared eternity" (3:545, 567). When her friend Amabel marries Michael, Miriam thinks of her as choosing to become "isolated, for life, with an alien consciousness" (3:545). Michael must experience the world as a man in a world defined by men. Even as a foreigner and a Jew in a nationally chauvinistic, anti-Semitic society, Michael is able to assume himself as heir to patriarchal assumptions of knowledge as Miriam can never do. Amabel, friends Jan and Mag, Eleanor Dear, the Quaker Rachel Mary Roscorla, and finally Jean, however, all know as Miriam knows, each in her way, always from a center of being that struggles daily with the fictions of living female in a patriarchal world. Miriam's connection to these women is, like her connection to the city, liberating and expanding. It is what confirms her sense of self, a self made possible by a solitude that in turn makes possible this connection that violates neither the self nor the solitude.

Because the female is always a suspect category for the culture, the living reality Richardson writes through the specificity of female experience is easily reformulated as feminist polemics or special pleading. But what Richardson accomplished goes far beyond a superficial reaction to the culture's systematic will to dominance by means of opposition. Miriam accepts as well as rejects both the masculine and the feminine as part of her. She uses this recognition to reorganize the structure of her relationship to gender so that it becomes not merely an androgynous vision but a new possibility for integrating rather than categorizing the demands of consciousness. In her 1975 study *Feminine Consciousness in the Modern British Novel*, Sydney Janet Kaplan locates this integration in

Miriam's access to competing gender roles. That is, women's ability to "absorb the diversity of experience in any given moment of time" is what distinguishes Richardson's conception of female consciousness (15). In Kaplan's view, Miriam understands that women, unlike men who organize experience in terms of power and control, are more likely to accept a nonhierarchic or "multi-leveled apperception of reality" which produces "a sense of life in motion" that is also a "condition of 'presentness'" (40, 41). It is this presentness that allows Richardson to see possibility anew from where she stands, using everything.

This is not a concept readily available from within gendered constructs of reality, as Richardson well knew. The culture all too conveniently provides ideological mechanisms for recapturing female uses of consciousness into old categories of The Feminine. A particularly revealing instance of this occurs in a 1960 study by Caesar R. Blake titled simply *Dorothy Richardson*. Blake evaluates Richardson in relation to James Joyce and finds her lacking. He regards both Joyce and Richardson as heirs to Henry James, but speaks of Joyce as having "seized" his method from James and "stripped it to its unconscious center," while Richardson "received" her method from the master and accommodated it to her needs by "gently prying it apart" (184). Richardson, Blake feels, is altogether too "self-contained" and "far less ambitious" than Joyce. "Unlike Joyce," he says, "who acknowledged the reality of the subjective and yet saw its further significance in the objective order of myth, Miss Richardson saw little order and hence little meaning beyond the individual's private . . . being" (190). Consequently, he concludes that Richardson "seems to speak for no major group" as does Joyce, and that despite *Pilgrimage's* historical interest, it is really no more than a "reflection of the general upheaval which brought forth the best of Eliot or Joyce or Lawrence, an upheaval mirrored by a perceptive woman" (190-91). Apparently women do not constitute a major group; they are too busy, it seems, still mirroring and reflecting the accomplishments of men.

Even in a supposed Feminine realm, this sort of construct must condemn women writers—by definition—to lack and failure. In his foreword to Blake's book, Leslie Fiedler (not unlike Stein critic Marianne DeKoven), defines experimental writing as Feminine, that which is man's but other-than-man by virtue of patriarchal order and reason. He sees experimental writing, then, as an expression of "the whole of man's undermind, the nonrational self" (xi). This is tricky territory for anyone; but whereas Joyce "has deliberately chosen to plunge into 'the abyss of the feminine sub-conscious'" and Faulkner "is driven" into "the minds of idiots" and "the hearts of women," Richardson, says Fiedler, "*lives* . . . in the 'abyss' to which Joyce or Faulkner only strategically resort" (x). In other words, Richardson cannot control this feminine material because she is feminine material. Though Fiedler agrees with Blake that Richardson's work is worth our attention, his praise is faint indeed; he refers to the finished product *Pilgrimage* as "not quite so monstrous as the pregnancy that produced it" (vii). Richardson's life as art, her enactment of "herself," is in Fiedler's view not only a "pale and dull" imitation of what Joyce or Faulkner do but it is a perversion of what women do into the bargain.

It is perhaps not surprising that two of the first critics to give Richardson her due on her own terms were also modernist women writers whose own work confronted the same phantom as did Richardson's. These critics were May Sinclair and Virginia Woolf. In an April 1918 review for *The Egoist*, Sinclair commented that "in identifying herself with this life, which is Miriam's stream of consciousness, Miss Richardson produces her effect of being the first, of getting closer to reality than any of our novelists who are trying so desperately to get close" ("The Novels of Dorothy Richardson" 58). Sinclair understood Richardson's method as one that allowed her to "seize reality alive," and with such intensity that she could blur the distinctions between the subjective and the objective in both fiction and reality (59). While this method was not entirely new, Sinclair noted, it seemed newer than what other writers were doing with it because of Richardson's ability to perfect a strict imposition of the conditions of life and thought, to avoid drama or narration in favor of letting the reality on the page develop as and for itself. This reality, she says, may be criticized as "formlessness," but is "just life"—life too intimate with actual experience to be carved up into convenient fictions. Instead Richardson takes on the whole and "plunges in . . . so neatly and quietly that even admirers of her performance might remain un-aware of what it is precisely that she has done. She has disappeared while they are still waiting for the splash" (57).

It is worth noting that Sinclair's application of the term *stream of consciousness* to Richardson's prose is the first such literary ap-plication we have. It is a term now, of course, more associated with the likes of Joyce and has become an accepted marker of the kind of modernist literature that seems to enter rather than censor or select its characters' thoughts and feelings. Thus it seems all the more remarkable that Richardson's name so seldom is brought forth in references or studies of such fiction. Richardson herself disliked the term, regarding it as only the leading phrase among many which made up what she called "formulae devised to meet the exigencies of literary criticism" (1:11). She found it, like other critical attempts to fix a writer's methods with names, insufficient as an expression or description of what was actually happening on her pages. Indeed, when reading *Pilgrimage* it seems clear that the best way to approach it is (like Stein's work) simply to pay attention; for it does both enact and demand the participation in which Richardson found herself immersed as she wrote. Author, reader, character, and the words themselves all interact in an ongoing process of consciousness that is also experience and that, like lived experience, is cumulative. Reading *Pilgrimage* is almost like living it.

Virginia Woolf was not as immediately enthusiastic about Richardson's work as was Sinclair, though in her first review in 1919 of *The Tunnel* she referred to Richardson as "one of the rare novelists who believe that the novel is so much alive that it actually grows," and said of her method that "it represents a genuine conviction of the discrepancy between what she has to say and the form provided by tradition for her to say it in" (*Women and Writing* 188). However, Woolf concluded that while Richardson had gone further than most in writing a living reality (what so-called realism fell so short of doing), nevertheless her use of words kept the reader "distressingly near the surface" and not enough "seated at the centre of another mind" (190). Early in 1920, Woolf still found Richardson too present in the text as an author, commenting in her diary that "the damned egotistical self . . . ruins Joyce and Richardson to my mind" (*A Writer's Diary* 22). But by 1923, in a review of *Revolving Lights*, Woolf was reading Richardson as one who "has invented, or, if she has not invented, developed and applied to her own uses, a sentence which we might call the psychological sentence of the feminine gender. It is of a more elastic fibre than the old, capable of stretching to the extreme, of suspending the frailest particles, of enveloping the vaguest shapes" (*Women and Writing* 191). She now distinguishes Richardson from other writers as one who "has fashioned her sentence consciously, in order that it may descend to the depths and investigate the crannies of Miriam Henderson's consciousness." This is a feat so innovative that it is "one for which we still seek a name" (191).

This sort of criticism must have been more welcome to Richardson, for it recognizes the implausibility of containing that searching, joyous, and participatory adventure she felt herself to have embarked on. Woolf, in fact, astutely acknowledged that when a writer refuses to present a human heart or mind as "a stationary body" to which we as readers have ready-made access, we tend to "retaliate" by claiming that nothing is important to the character, nothing is happening in the story. What we fail to see is what is actually there: "a body which moves perpetually, and is thus always standing in a new relation to the emotions which are the same" (*Women and Writing* 192). Such a reading is closely related to Teresa de Lauretis's analysis of subjectivity as a continual and contextual process of experience always complicated for women by the culture's constructs of sexuality. Richardson writes consciousness as her text, from within one female mind whose apprehension of culture through experience radically recenters identity.

The lives going on behind looking-glass fronts are seldom what they seem. Woolf, Richardson, and Stein, to name only three, have stepped away from the reflection and from the business of reflecting. The relation of the internal and the external, the blurred distinctions between the factual and fictional not only constitute a literary revolution but give voice to women writers as never before. If the specificity of female presence is to come forth not as the discursive presence of Woman but as itself, never the same twice, then the phantom must go. These writers seek their own realities in their most tenuous relationships to fiction. Only there can they rely on their own ongoing processes of know-ing. By recentering art and experience in the female, problematically feminized, they have begun to render boundaries permeable and interactive. They know how to know differently. This is important work. The words they speak, each in her way, help us to encounter differences as interactive; they help us to scatter differences into communities of diversity.

4

Interlude

What does it mean for each to speak, each in her way? When the language of patriarchal meaning is the language we are all said to be born into, the task is easily tainted with an unavoidable sense of complicity, complicity with that which would keep us silent. "We" and "us" become gestures fraught with as much threat as hope. Whose "we" is sufficient? How shall "we" take up the "dream of a common language" as Adrienne Rich suggested? She asked us to "re-vision" the past to find ourselves a present. We liked the sound of that, repeated it one to another, even learned to do it as well as to say it. "When we write for women," Rich said, "we imagine an audience which *wants* our words—which desires our courage, our anger, our verve, our active powers, instead of fearing and loathing them" (*On Lies, Secrets, and Silence* 108). Of course. How not? There is nothing so new in this. And yet everything.

It's an act of survival, women writing as themselves, for themselves and each other. We often say so. But this "common language"— I have to wonder what it would be. A language "we" can all know and understand. The phrase *what we have in common* is as often used to cover what we don't want to know about each other as it is an acknowledgement of our connections. Universals have always been designed to keep us quiet. How deep do the lessons go? Yes, we long to speak to one another; but whose language do we use? Or do we make a new language, with new words, a new grammar? I am skeptical. Very. Each her own language, I want to say. Language radical in its resistances to silence, radical in its "fit" to the needs of each woman who uses it. Language that has in it all its history, as Stein said of her language, yet does not yield that history without disrupting its claims to authority. Words forever in motion and sentences proper to her own use. A connection between writer and word so close that we cannot help but listen with all our senses at once—not for confirmation of what we know, not always with ready comprehension, but for everything that's there. Could it be as simple and as complicated as that?

Listen for a moment to Elizabeth Fox-Genovese. She is talking about the assumption of cultural privilege in authorship. "Feminist critics, like critics of Afro-American and third world literature, are beginning to refuse the implied blackmail of Western, white, male criticism" ("To Write My Self" 162). Blackmail? Interesting choice of words. I pay attention, eager for what will come next. "The death of the subject and of the author may accurately reflect the perceived crisis of western culture and the bottomless anxieties of its most privileged subjects—the white male authors who had presumed to define it." Indeed, I think, nodding at the page. "But it remains to be demonstrated that their deaths constitute the collective or generic death of the subject and the author." Yes, I say out loud, that's it. Still . . . couldn't this death signal new possibilities? Couldn't it mean breaking silence without having to imitate old masters? Fox-Genovese continues. "There remain plenty of subjects and authors who, never having had much opportunity to write in their own names or the names of their kind, much less in the name of the culture as a whole, are eager to seize the abandoned podium." Mm-hmm, I say under my breath. She's right, of course. But names again. And podium-seizing? Isn't that just playing into their hands? She goes on. "But the white male cultural elite has not, in fact, abandoned the podium. It has merely insisted that the podium cannot be claimed in the name of any particular personal experience" (163). Ah, there it is, that erasure in the name of the culture. She's unmasked it. It's the same old authorized subjects orchestrating their own rebirths, basking in their own alienation while pretending to speak for "all of us." Blackmail. If you don't buy into this "us" you will be voiceless, earless, eyeless. But of course that is what you are anyway, you whose claim to experience is "only personal."

The melting pot is and has always been a war machine. It pours down from fortified walls relentless streams of assimilation—assimilation to a white patriarchal norm, a norm with which white middle-class feminism has too often allied itself as if it were a cure for otherness. It is not. That norm functions to preserve otherness as the proof of its innate superiority. Assimilation operates to preserve boundaries between superior and inferior while seeming to transform them into something more. Whatever the norm cannot displace through assimilation, it destroys. It manufactures an endless supply of "them" to secure the position of "us." It has always done this. It cuts "them" down like trees to make way for Civilization in its own image. It builds towns over them, starves them, gasses them, buries them. It rapes them, takes them, and sells them off. It exercises power over them as the ultimate illusion of self-control. Remember. There is at least one them in every one of us. But the culture teaches us not to look, or if we must, to look away. It uses difference as opposition so as to keep all the "we's" isolated in their own acts of survival, each clamoring for equal rights of priority over all "others."

We cannot, after all, afford dreams of unification along patriarchal lines. This unification is silence in fancy dress. So the dilemma is as it has been, how to get our words into circulation without refusing someone else's, how to count on experience without using it to ignore all but the most familiar voices, how to use a word like *our* without any but the most disjunctive hints of possession. The history of female experience in (women's) writing has been short and explosive. When it is proffered as if it were a unified experience, a normed experience adhering to whiteness and middle-classness among women, its history is also distorted, insufficient, and destructive. That's why it's important to hear Teresa de Lauretis when she speaks of subjectivity as a process of experience in the unstable context of social realities. Race, class, and sex are simultaneously cultural constructs and specificities of experience. Individual consciousnesses also have collective histories. When both the individual and the community are retained, interaction is less likely to be divisive; it becomes less feasible to choose up sides without losing part of oneself. Gender has been an instrument of hegemonic control, conflating all women into Woman, then conferring the privileges of womanhood selectively by race, by class, by sexual preference. Identify yourself, we learn to say. I cannot speak with you unless I have a name by which to know you.

Both Elizabeth Fox-Genovese and Monique Wittig speak of sex and race as class. (Most of us are willing to see class as a social construct, and so can make the connection.) No matter how natural or given sex and race seem to be, they operate culturally as what Wittig calls "political and economic categories not eternal ones" ("One Is Not Born a Woman" 50). Because race and sex are physically apparent (usually) and genetically determined categories (more or less), they make effective representations of natural phenomena. As Fox-Genovese says, "sex and race more readily lend themselves to symbolization than does class"; they "more obviously define what we intuitively perceive ourselves to be: male or female, white or black" (162). But as Wittig says, "what we take for the cause or origin of oppression is in fact only the *mark* imposed by the oppressor" (48). Physical features are "marked by the social system" not as natural distinctions but as manipulations of such distinctions in the service of cultural ideals of power based on conquest and possession. Meaning is conferred on them through difference, culturally constructed and controlled. In Fox-Genovese's words, "even these basic self-perceptions are socially learned and result from acts of (re)cognition" (162). She and Wittig ask us to understand that a retreat into seemingly natural categories for a stable sense of identity is actually a form of self-erasure. Divide and conquer.

Wittig tells us this: "One feature of lesbian oppression consists precisely of making women out of reach for us, since women belong to men. Thus a lesbian *has* to be something else, a not-woman, a not-man, a product of society, not a product of nature, for there is no nature in society" (49). Fox-Genovese tells us this: "For white American women, the self comes wrapped in gender, or rather, gender constitutes the invisible, seamless wrapping of the self. Such is the point of gender in a stable society" (167-68). Then she goes on: "Slavery bequeathed to Afro-American women a double view of gender relations that fully exposed the artificial or problematic aspects of gender identification. . . . Black slave women had suffered the pain of childbirth and the sorrow of losing children and had labored like men. Were they, or were they not women?" (168-69). Used as what Barbara Christian calls "dumping grounds" for the sexual and labor functions from which "real" women must be protected, slave women stood at the intersection of race and sex where annihilation reigned. Denied sexual existence or voyeuristically consumed, lesbians have stood for neither man nor woman. The question, then, is still with us: What is a woman?

"'Woman' is not each one of us," says Wittig, "but the political and ideological formation which negates 'women' (the product of a relation of exploitation)" (51). Women, actual women of all experiences, must refuse not only the oppressions but also the seductions of the myth Woman. "Consciousness of oppression is not only a reaction to (fight against) oppression. It is also the whole conceptual reevaluation of the social world, its whole reorganizations with new concepts, from the point of view of oppression" (52). Fox-Genovese calls this the need to "bear witness to a collective experience" (166). Cultural ideology has taught women subjective necrophilia and pandering to the Feminine of Man's self-suppression. The languages in which we speak to one another, as ourselves and in full view of our histories, must not be used to reproduce the myth, but must use everything. This is how Teresa de Lauretis sees it:

> What is emerging in feminist writings is, instead, the concept of a multiple, shifting, and often self-contradictory identity, a subject that is not divided in, but rather at odds with, language: an identity made up of heterogeneous and heteronomous representations of gender, race, and class, and often indeed across languages and cultures; an identity that one decides to reclaim from a history of multiple assimilations, and that one insists on as a strategy. ("Feminist Studies/Critical Studies" 9)

Consciousness, then, emerges out of the particularities of collective contexts, "at the intersection of meaning and experience." It is responsive to the historical conditions and the specificities of presence that together produce it as a continuous process. "In this perspective," says de Lauretis, "the very notion of identity undergoes a shift: identity is not the goal but rather the point of departure of the process of self-consciousness" (8-9). Not only does this defy "an all-purpose feminist frame of reference" but the continued existence of feminism itself depends on the very differences its analyses of "women's heterogeneous subjectivity and multiple identity" can bring into interactive relation.

The shift de Lauretis sees is one we must, each in her way, understand from the inside out. It is, in her words, "a shift from the earlier view of woman defined purely by sexual difference (i.e., in relation to man) to the more difficult and complex notion that the female subject is a site of differences; differences that are not only sexual or only racial, economic, or (sub)cultural, but all of these together, and often enough at odds with one another" (14). If it is true, she says, that the female subject is "en-gendered across multiple representations of class, race, language, and social relations," then "the differences among women may be better understood as differences within women" (14).

Here is Audre Lorde talking about how this works: "I urge each one of us here to reach down into that deep place of knowledge inside herself and touch that terror and loathing of any difference that lives there. See whose face it wears" (*Sister Outsider* 113). She believes that it is not the differences that keep us apart but our failure to recognize the effects of our "misnaming" our differences. "For as long as any difference between us means one of us must be inferior, then the recognition of any difference must be fraught with guilt" (118). It is necessary to learn to resist the misnaming, to see more clearly to use differences interdependently without pretending it's really the same for all of us. This is what Lorde says: "Some problems we share as women, some we do not. You fear your children will grow up to join the patriarchy and testify against you, we fear our children will be dragged from a car and shot down in the street, and you will turn your backs upon the reasons they are dying" (119).

Gender is the construct that marks us all. All. We know where, and that, we are supposed to stand in relation to it. It is the model of difference as divisiveness. Instead of extending that model to the spaces between us, we can speak into those spaces, fill them up with ourselves, shout and laugh and rage and just sit and listen. Listen hard and pay attention. Very close attention indeed.

Louise Bernikow tells a story of lost friendship in the 1960s. It comes near the end of her chapter "The Light and the Dark: White Women Are Never Lonely, Black Women Always Smile" in *Among Women*. As a Jewish woman she knows first-hand the invisibility of being ambiguously both "light" and "dark." She has a friend named Barbara who is black. The revolution has begun and Barbara is dating a man who is a black revolutionary. They come for dinner to Bernikow's house where she lives with a man who is white. The two women have been friends long enough to be close friends. The two men talk. "They had between them a common ground called masculine culture," Bernikow says. "They could touch on this subject or that—sports, politics, the world— without establishing a personal connection. It was not required. They did not like each other, these men, . . . but still, they talked" (255). And what did the women, who did like each other, have in common? What was between them? They had personal connection and intimacy. It was not good enough. In the revolution they were expected to choose up sides, to separate definitively into light and dark, loyal each to her man, and speak to one another no more. The men were to be their relations. The women could have no culture between them. It is into *that* space, that space between women, we have begun and must continue to speak.

Make no mistake. Gender may be our common denominator as women but it does not make the stakes the same for all of us. Race and ethnicity produce alliances of survival between men and women in a racist culture that are different for Jewish women and women of color than for mainstream white women. Difference is multiplied yet again. And for lesbians, of all races or ethnicities or classes, sexual alliances are reduced to lack, a mark of difference so deep that when it is not denied it is imposed as a betrayal of nature and culture alike. "For women, the need and desire to nurture each other is not pathological but redemptive," Lorde tells us (111). Still we learn not to pass on to one another what we learn across our differences. Even within our differences, the otherness of women in relation to men is a deep division, a silence heavy with the violence "by which manliness can be measured." Those are Lorde's words again. "Womanhating [is] a recourse of the powerless," she reminds us (120). It apes the culture at large, coming at women from within their communities and from without. It offers power as a relation to sex and race. Hortense J. Spillers says that "sexuality as a term of power belongs to the empowered" ("Interstices: A Small Drama of Words" 78). Whoever would claim power must go through sexuality to get there. Any female body can be used as a conduit; race combines with sex to render the use of some female bodies, dark female bodies, as "the principal point of passage between the human and the non-human world" (76). Man at his most privileged.

Cherríe Moraga and Gloria Anzaldúa made a book of women's voices to take back the female body, all the female bodies. They made of *This Bridge Called My Back* safe passage for "radical women of color" who would, in Moraga's words, "this time—not use our bodies to be thrown over a river of tormented history to bridge the gap" (xv). As Audre Lorde, among many, has pointed out, just as women are expected to educate men about female experience, so are women of color expected to educate white women about the power of differences among women. So conveniently do race and gender partake of the same strategy of difference by opposition that "white women" and "women of color" are made to seem norm and Other, as if the differences were binary, as if they were only between us and not also within us. Moraga and Anzaldúa fill those spaces between women with, as Moraga in her preface puts it, "the pain and shock of difference, the joy of commonness, the exhilaration of meeting through incredible odds against it" (xiv). These are not the divisions already provided by passage through the dominant cultural order; they are not a matter of visiting alien territories to come away with information about others one may carry around as Self-protection. Rather, as Moraga says, "the passage is through, not over, not by, not around, but *through*" (xiv). The voices of the book become a celebration, painful, angry, difficult, and tendentious, but finally joyful and healing. Anzaldúa in her foreword calls out in two languages to those who would set forth: "Caminante, no hay puentes, se hace puentes al andar (*Voyager, there are no bridges, one builds them as one walks*)" (v). The building materials are words, each woman's words, proper to her own use, each in her way.

So I come back to the dream of a common language. What do I know of such a dream? I think of Judy Grahn who writes "from a House of Women Out Into the World" (*The Highest Apple* 58). She posits the artist's decision "to speak for women and to speak as a woman" as a most powerful decision, one that must include "*all* our selves" if it is to expand our processes of knowing in the world (58). She recenters the words of women marked Other even among Others, positioning them "in the ordinary and everyday" where they can interact openly rather than as categories of contrast. She says of Audre Lorde, "by standing in so many places, she is able to teach the philosophy of wholeness, of all our splintered selves that need to be brought together in love, in anger, in pain, in refusal to lie, in listening, in desire, in greatness of thought, in common understanding" (77).

I think of Mary Helen Washington who writes of tradition and the way it has been used to distort and reshape the literature of black writers in America according to the dominant model of androcentric white culture. She talks of Richard Wright and Ralph Ellison whose explosive powers were taken over by reviewers as contributions to "the universality of the invisible man's struggle," while the works of Nella Larsen, Zora Neale Hurston, and Gwendolyn Brooks were barely reviewed at all, often out of print, and condemned as too personal, anomalous, and incidental to be important to "the historical experiences of [their] people" (*Invented Lives* xvi). Never mind that black culture literally depended on the voices and actions of women for its survival, as Washington says; it is the men whose voices and actions count while the women are excluded, represented as misrepresentations. This is, she reminds us, "a model of literary paternity" (xviii). It takes its authority from the culture at large. Washington locates its logic of neglect for black women writers in a familiar place: as the heroines they write depend on the shared intimacies, support, and experiences of other women, female consciousness becomes the "center of the text," the empowerment of women through female relationships that are "an essential aspect of self-definition for women" (xxi). This, as usual, is read by patriarchal critics, black and white alike, as simply meaningless, without real content.

I think of Barbara Christian who points out that in her work *Black Feminist Criticism*, by institutional literary standards she is "studying a literature that is not a literature, written by women who could not be writing" (145). She studies anyway. Her ten-year-old daughter notices Paule Marshall's essay "Poets in the Kitchen" on Christian's desk and takes the opportunity to note that "whenever your friends come over, whether you're cooking or not, you all end up in the kitchen" (xii). "That's what Paule is talking about," Christian answers her; "she's telling us how she learned about language and storytelling from her mother and her mother's friends talking in the kitchen." "They're in the kitchen because they're used to it," the daughter replies. Indeed. It is among women that the words come into being, words they can use as their own, full of their histories of experience. Those histories are also laden with distorted imagery—the mammy, Sapphire, Aunt Jemima, whore, all counterbalanced by the queen, the Mother, "holders of the moral condition of blacks" (16). But in the kitchen, on the page, among women other stories circulate, women's own stories, in their own words.

I think again of Louise Bernikow moving attentively, painstakingly through the light and the dark. Dark Ladies and Fair Maidens—these are her signposts, the cultural constructs that must be resisted, especially in their internalized form. Otherwise they are there for use against herself and other women. She thinks about how the Jewish woman "represents double exile" (259); even at home, in a community of resistance to annihilation, she is "polluted, stained, menstrual" (257). She learns to hate herself and the Shiksa alike: "Folklore and film, high and low culture, Philip Roth and Woody Allen—all, in combination, are serpents on this subject and their hiss goes like this: not only is she good and you bad, but she is a different creature, nothing like you. She has power. You do not, cannot, will not" (256). "We have no plot," Bernikow says, "in which, as Jewish or Christian women, to set our experience of and feelings about one another" (260). So she is making space on the page, filling it with what she knows, with tensions and connections, between women and among women.

I think of Rosario Morales who says, "This society this incredible way of living divides us by class   by color   It says
we are individual and alone and don't you forget it   It says the
only way out of our doom   of our sex our class our race is some
individual gift and character and hard work and then all we get
all we ever get is to change class or color or sex   to rise   to
bleach   to   masculinize" ("We're All in the Same Boat" 91-92).
The only way to stop being Different, Other, is to lose yourself.
Your loss, the culture's gain. No amount of rising, bleaching, mas-
culinizing will erase difference; difference makes meaning. Not
only will you still mark white androcentric self-definition by your
assigned difference but difference will take up residence inside
you and demand that you choose among selves, none of them yours.
"I want to be whole," Morales writes. So she speaks what she knows
because, she says, "we know different things" (93). She is building
bridges as she goes, making passages through, not around or up
to or over the dividing lines, but through. She is refusing to be
silent or alone, and she is refusing to choose among selves.

The relation between language and Woman has been a crippling one. Woman does not speak, but is spoken, say the Law-
givers. If we speak at all, we must speak Woman. Father's Woman,
the eternal feminine who stands at the crossroads collecting fares
for passage to the other side of Other. Whose language is this?
The selves waiting to be claimed on the other side of difference
wear their alienation like badges of authority. This is the territory
women face. Enter it and disappear; refuse it and remain silent.
Difference conflates all women into Woman, but for women of color,
for lesbians, for all othered Others, Woman is an image doubly
distorted, doubly divisive.

As women writers work to bring shared communities into the
open, a radical recentering continually takes place. When the social
world of the text is not contained by Western patriarchal norms,
when a woman's consciousness is the world of the text, when
women together rewrite the text, it is not merely new realities that
come into language but a revaluation of language itself. Then who
speaks? Yes when women write for women we imagine an audience
that wants our words. Yes we want those words to be our own, for
us and each other. Dreaming of a common language may help us
to see into those places, unmarked and ill-lit, between us. It may
help to make bridges as we go. But the passage is still through,
not over. We are multicultural members of nondiscrete speaking
communities. There is no "we" that is all-inclusive, no "them" that

is not also "us." We each have our traditions, our encounters with phantoms, our struggles with silence and isolation. No one of us can do it alone, and no group of us can speak for or before us all.

I am as skeptical about a common language as I am about a new language. I listen instead for cacophony—for the sound of all our voices speaking at once, voices shifting, always in motion, now interacting, now pulling in on themselves to make room for their own powers. I imagine this cacophony as vibrant, one in which no assumption of knowledge is stable but depends on a continual process of experience, of language as experience, as action and enactment, using everything. To hear this language we must pay attention. We can't assume we already know what it means or even how it means; we can't stop listening while we prepare our own speeches. Women's "experimental writing" meets no prescribed code, but is in disjunctive relation to the culture's categories of reality and meaning. It makes possibility possible. It is a way of insisting on wholeness, not likeness. Its nonconventional cacophony seems our best hope of breaking silence by breaking into language itself, each as we are, each in her way.

5

Communities of Diversity: Ntozake Shange, E. M. Broner, Monique Wittig

Language is as complex and loaded as a spell. It carries intention and consequence, anticipated and not, yet is alive with its own energy. Like a spell, it takes shape both as itself and for a purpose; its being and its purpose are not separate and not one. Spells, like language, are always a bit tricky to handle; one can never be sure they will do one's bidding. Spells take action. Given form in language and by concentration of the will, they are of and interact with the experience of the speaker to become the experience of the listener. Once, it has been said, words cast as spells were considered a form of action in the world as real as any other. Now that action is regarded as superstition, a delusion borne of primitive ignorance and irrationality.

By tradition spells are the language of women—of witches and the "primitive" among us whose experience of the world is deemed mysterious, supernatural, as malevolent as it is prophetic, and outside the logic of Reason. Western ideology demands that such experience be contained as the mythic, dark, and other side of Reality. Speaking spells has been outlawed, punished, and kept under control as a sign of incapacity for Self possession. Only then can the effects be regarded as ineffectual. They are left to us as phantoms of uncivilized disorder, like the lost words that come to us only as images of "a witch being ducked . . . a woman possessed by devils . . . a wise woman selling herbs" (Woolf, *A Room* 50-51). Whoever speaks spells, woman or man, speaks from the feminized position of nonrationality. Their words can mean only from deep within and are therefore always potentially dangerous to order and reason. Wherever Western culture has encountered such language, it has burned it away, re-located it as the mark of savagery, reformulated it as a theological function of oppositional duality—if it is not the Word of God it is a Satanic seduction—or psychoanalyzed it as a hysterical gesture.

"When a woman thinks alone, she thinks evil," says *The Malleus Maleficarum* (43). It cannot be otherwise, for Woman is the body of Man and without him has no head of her own. Heinrich Kramer and James Sprenger, the Dominican Fathers of the Holy Roman Empire commissioned by Pope Innocent VIII to author *The Malleus* in the late fifteenth century, left us a deeply misogynistic record of a cultural ideology founded on the quest for perfection through purge and conquest. All evil, all obstacle, comes into the world through Woman. It is the body, not the head, that leads us away from Civilization. The metaphysics of reasoning behind *The Malleus* are fueled not only by insatiable religious fervor but also by the mandates of a cultural tradition that must create, name, and control mind and body (the rational and nonrational: man and woman, self and other) as effects of an oppositional relation in a hierarchy. That tradition has always required New Worlds in which to discover and possess, by extermination if not by "enlightenment," material Others as representations of the need to control by right of superiority and dominance. Western culture's inquisitions of purification have always sought to separate light peoples from dark, to rid Christendom (or the State) of its pagan/infidel roots, and to silence the ancient and feared female voice. In the recent modern world that voice is imagined as repressed, the mysterious and potentially dangerous content of the precivilized unconscious. It is not difficult to see how race, class, and sex have become markers for images of body without mind.

In the stories of Western culture, the pagan female dark side emerges as Chaos, the prerational origin of Man and civilization as desired as it is feared. It is the body unruled and unruly, desire itself. Reason orders chaos, and so is dependent upon it for its functioning. But the distinctions must be preserved; there must be safeguards against falling back into the primordial dream, that place where Knowledge has not yet divided man from woman and made him ruler of her (as) desire. The fall forward into civilization must not be negated by the fall backward. Boundaries, always in danger of being crossed and so also in need of being guarded, preserve and naturalize the distinctions that make difference, Man's mark of meaning, possible. Boundaries must not be permeable; the danger of not being able to tell the difference is too great. So the most honored stories tell tales of good and evil, sight and blindness, always activated at the moment of encountering the choice at the crossroads; the right answer is everything. That answer must confirm the cultural script; Knowledge and Reason must encounter and conquer Chaos. Death, desire, the unconscious, silence, madness stand just the other side of the checkpoints. A constant supply of occupants for the other side must be forever engendered if the proprietorship of Reason is to be maintained.

The Malleus warns, "They have slippery tongues, and are unable to conceal from their fellow-women those things which by evil arts they know" (44). A woman alone, women together, autonomous women, disobedient women, carnal women, "their" women, "our" women—all are subject to the taint, for no woman is ruled by reason who is not ruled by man. A woman's gesture, her look, an ungoverned word from her lips, even her very thoughts might cast spells. The power of the weaker sex, it seems, is of mythic proportions. It must be brought into submission, its words reduced to syllables of nonrational desire and its access to agency made a childlike gesture of imitation. Silence is a gendered tradition.

It is the business of writers Ntozake Shange, E. M. Broner, and Monique Wittig to break that silence, and to break it from within the multi-othered spaces of Western patriarchal culture that are so vulnerable to silence. To do this they call upon those forms of language most associated with the separated lives of women— spells, recipes, letters, the dance of the body, ritual without scripture, the mother's touch that wounds as well as heals, usurpation—not to reclaim them as "women's language" but to disperse the categories that enforce disabling distinctions. Like Woolf and Richardson they enact subjectivity as a process of female experience in language, but re-visioned so that they speak from a "site of differences" interactively multiple in its effects. Like Stein they use everything, but purposely imbue their words with stories of collective pasts suppressed by a culture of dominance normed on mainstream white, male, Christian, heterosexual models. They use culturally uncoded experience to reveal the oppressive operations of cultural codes. Each uses language as a form of action, each in her way mindful that the language she uses both excludes her and gives her voice at every moment of her utterance. These writers use words to permeate boundaries and make room for an unfinished, unfinishable wholeness of being. Each writes for survival by refusing to choose among selves.

Shange, Broner, and Wittig are especially concerned with both the splintering and the healing effects of language and tradition. For language, as the symbolic order of culture, divides us. It confers articulation on some and reduces others to mimes. Any woman who uses the language of the Fathers finds Woman there to speak in her place. Woman is an imitation of speech; she stands for meaning, miming the gestures the culture expects to see. But for Shange, Broner, and Wittig, even these gestures find scant purchase in the expectations of the culture. The black women of Shange's texts, Broner's mothers and daughters of Judaism, and the lesbian intervention of Wittig's warrior women confront language on multiple levels of exclusion. Telling their stories at all disrupts mainstream expectations; telling their stories as their own, on their own terms and in words of their own making, breaks the imitative code even further, giving voice not to mere alternative versions of Story but to what narrative hegemony has taught us not to hear at all. These voices would once have been among the first to be silenced at the stake; they have since been scattered into dusty, ill-lit corners of the dominant culture of Western patriarchy where they can be ignored both from within and from without. But Shange and Broner and Wittig each refuses exile, standing each on her shifting ground and using its motion to take action in words. The communities that shape their words are at once cohesive and dispersed. They write, one way and another, out of diaspora. Their words and the traditions they call upon, the very forms they put on the page, constitute continual movement among scatterings and gatherings. They write from where they are.

For none of these writers is equality an enabling position. It always reproduces access to the dominant structure that produced oppression in the first place. Neither is merely calling attention to the forced and enforced silences of othered peoples enough. The material, textual, emotional, and intellectual specificities of experience and possibility must be made active in and as language. This requires not merely revision or revolution but a bringing to life on its own terms what has only been imagined otherwise. Theorist María C. Lugones argues that adopting the terms of mastery—the words, images, and practices of dominance and dominant culture—means only "that we either use your language and distort our experience not just in the speaking about it, but in the living of it, or that we remain silent" ("Have We Got a Theory for You!" 575). She is talking about the relation of women of color to mainstream white feminism and by implication to dominant white patriarchy.

She sees change not as a matter of bringing all peoples into a universalizing language—an illusion of unity that in practice is only "your reduction of us to your selves"—but as a matter of insisting on one's own language(s) contextually (576). "Complaining about exclusion," she says, "is a way of remaining silent" (575). Speaking as oneself, using everything, is in effect far more radical than standing on one side or the other of equality in a system where equality is as often a term of nullification as realization. Cacophony is not chaos, nor is a common language a panacea. Each speaker activates her own words. Spells are never spoken the same twice.

In "foreward/ unrecovered losses/ black theater traditions" Ntozake Shange talks about using "everything we've got" to make her words alive to what she knows: "i cant count the number of times i have viscerally wanted to attack deform n maim the language that i was taught to hate myself in/ . . . yes/ being an afro-american writer is something to be self-conscious abt/ & yes/ in order to think n communicate the thoughts n feelings i want to think n communicate/ i haveta fix my tool to my needs/ i have to take it apart to the bone/ so that the malignancies/ fall away/ leaving us space to literally create our own image" (xii, virgules Shange's). Her language, then, is performance. She uses all her senses, not "just language," in her performances. She says she is able to do this because black culture is by tradition "an interdisciplinary culture" (x). Shange uses fragmented and broken threads of the past to understand the vitality of the connections that bring her people and her words, language and experience, together in the present, as presence enacted and performed.

Shange's texts are interdisciplinary too, intermingling words, song, dance, color and sound, oral histories, recipes, letters between women, joy and rage. In both *for colored girls who have considered suicide/when the rainbow is enuf* (1975) and *Sassafrass, Cypress & Indigo* (1982), Shange's rage is at the surrounding dominant culture, patriarchal and white, that tries to crush the many traditions of peoples of color who live in America as "subcultures." Her character Indigo refers to the African peoples who were taken from homelands and marketed as commodities in the "New World" as "the slaves who were ourselves." Shange's joy is for the perseverance of those traditions that survive against the odds, for their adaptability to the contingencies of lived experience, and for the passages they open through (not over or around) differences. It is women who bear the multiple marks of difference; and it is among women— sisters, friends, lovers, mothers, and daughters—that she locates the will for survival as a creative sustaining of life in the face of racial and sexual hatreds. Her women act together, not only to reclaim connections to ancient traditions but also to embody and occupy their own presence as completely as possible.

Like Shange, E. M. Broner brings women together from their places nowhere and everywhere to create new practices out of loss and erasure. She brings the world of the mother and the world of the daughter together on the page to open up fissures for a release into subjectivity that neither discards the past nor acquiesces to its restrictions. In *Her Mothers* (1975) and *A Weave of Women* (1978) she gathers the experiences of women on the page in songs, rituals, actions, and stories designed for a sharing of differences in the midst of a scattered and common heritage. In America and Israel, Broner's women test the lessons of Judaic culture. Exiles among exiles, they must mitigate the very heritage that has ensured their survival or disappear under its weight. They speak themselves into being in the ancient forms of questions and answers, songs and ceremonies, collective acts of renewal, revenge, and autonomy. They rework their words to fit their needs as disinherited legatees.

Broner's women are daughters of the Diaspora. For them the scattering of peoples that would force loss of tradition, knowledge, and strength brings them together to rebuild not what was, but what can be. The cultural and religious traditions of the Jews are strong threads, but threads that bind women to a gendered silence as well as to a community of continuity. From within that community, the women must break away to make gathering possible. As Broner says, they cannot simply return to the fold; for them, "there is no fold. They must enfold their own" (*A Weave of Women* 289). They know from experience that even boundaries within boundaries must be destabilized and made ineffectual if they, as women, are to speak and move about freely. Their words, Broner's words, cannot be confined by convention even as they partake of tradition.

Like Shange and like Broner, Monique Wittig brings women and women's words together as a gathering of new possibilities. Patriarchal culture everywhere has constructed Woman in and as language. Wittig, then, uses language to wage war. As language, Woman has no atextual place; as language users, women take up positions as warriors. In *Les Guérillères* (1969, English translation 1971) Wittig's women arm themselves with the terms of patriarchal language to wipe out what has been, to "start from zero" and begin again, with new texts that can be opened anywhere for new realities that can be anyone's. Wittig's words move free of the dis-courses they defy; they gather in a form that implies epic story but immerses the reader in dis-ordered descriptions and lists, diffused moments of thought or action without scene, plot, or character, without beginning, middle, or end. *Les Guérillères* is a textual effect; its words come off the page as palpable presences uncontained by the incidents in which they occur. Their violence is profoundly disturbing, like the violence of the system they set themselves against; yet they do not form a reversal of power but a radical scattering of power into unlimited possibility.

In her essay "The Trojan Horse" (1984) Wittig writes, "Any work with a new form operates as a war machine, because its design and its goal is to pulverize the old forms and formal conventions. It is always produced in hostile territory" (45). The symbolic structure of white male heterosexual culture produces the female body as coin, a communicable sign ensuring profitable relations among men. Even for those men culturally feminized by difference (men of color and homosexual men, for instance), the female body is still the icon guarding the boundary between manhood and complete loss of self. It is only women who have no self to lose in this system of meaning. So for Wittig it is women who must come together as a tribe, as warrior women who will take apart the construct. It is a painful process, demanding vast destruction as well as unlimited composition. But if language is to be open to any speaker, each in her way, the symbolic order must be broken and its material forms scattered into interactive diversity.

For all three writers the functions of dispersion and connection are interrelated. They structure interactions between form and content, sign and signification, capable of resisting hegemonic representation. Shange, Broner, and Wittig contextualize the tensions among differences that (again in de Lauretis's words) "are not only sexual or only racial, economic, or (sub)cultural, but all of these together, and often enough at odds with one another" ("Feminist Studies/Critical Studies" 14). Their works do not form a unifying voice but preserve the contradictions as part of the business of being others among others. Like Woolf they break the sequence; like Richardson they resist annihilation; like Stein they use everything they have; together they speak with slippery tongues, in many voices at once, refusing to conceal from their fellow-women those things which by lived experience they know.

Shange's writing is shaped by myth, tradition, and narrative, but is defined by none of them. Movement—language and experience in constant motion—is Shange's language: "i haveta fix my tool to my needs," as she says; "i have to take it apart to the bone/ so that the malignancies/ fall away." Shange must find a form of language in which she and her women characters can learn to be themselves rather than to hate themselves as she had learned to do in the languages of racism and sexism. The mother Hilda Effania in *Sassafrass, Cypress & Indigo* passes this advice on to her daughters: "Whatever ideas you have that're important to you, write down . . . but write them so your enemies can't understand them right off" (110, ellipsis Shange's). In both *Sassafrass* and *for colored girls*, Shange takes this advice. She cannot use language as if it were already understood; she refuses the separations that use of language forces on her and instead looks for connections with what is hers in the specificities of her experience. She uses her voice, her body, her mind, and words together, collectively, just as she uses the collective voices of women to perform her texts.

The movement that marks Shange's writing is a coalition of history, material experience, and linguistic signification. In tracing the development of black American women writers' uses of "African elements in relation to the concept of woman," critic Barbara Christian notes that "mobility of black women is a new quality in these books . . . for black women, in much of the previous literature, were restricted in space by their condition. This mobility is not cosmetic. It means that there is increased interaction between black women from the U.S., the Caribbean, and Africa, as well as other women of color" (*Black Feminist Criticism* 182). Christian argues (not unlike Woolf) that as this mobility expands experience it does not abstract or universalize texts in imitation of Western patriarchal forms; rather it incorporates multiplicity as a concreteness of specificity in experience that opens up connection and interaction among diverse communities of women. Shange's mobile and multiple words, genres, and characters stretch and break old restrictions of space as well as condition, using what she calls "alla my stuff" to "fix her tool" to her own needs.

In her introduction to *for colored girls who have considered suicide/when the rainbow is enuf*, Shange speaks of the need to reconnect what has been made separate. "The freedom to move in space," she says, "waz poem to me, my body & mind ellipsing, probably for the first time in my life" (xv). This freedom, furthermore, and the voice it makes possible for her, could not come about until she connected it "with the acceptance of the ethnicity of my thighs & backside" (xv). Rather than imitating existing forms, Shange resists

the constrictions of the language of the dominant culture in favor
of her own, shaped by her own history and experience. She calls
for colored girls a "choreopoem"; it is simultaneously stage performance and written text, dance and poetry, cultural history and fictional reality. She gathers everything together to enact experience
on the page and before the eye, both textually and dramatically.
She brings form and meaning, words and movement together in an
interaction that produces a wholeness resistant to iconic redistri-
bution or universalized imagery. In her words, "I moved what waz
my unconscious knowledge of being in a colored woman's body
to my known everydayness" (xvi).

Reading *for colored girls* does not disprivilege the lively action
of performance as does reading most other dramatic texts; while
it is not the same as seeing the choreopoem on stage, nevertheless
Shange's innovative use of language as a visual as well as auditory
and intellectual form retains its mobility so that the writing and
the reading alike seem to partake of all the senses at once. Shange
performs textual breaks with convention in her use of virgules,
ellipses, spelling, speech patterns, pace, and linguistically resonant
music. As in all her writing, in the mouths of all her characters,
Shange's language is not a closed sign system of meaning through
difference but an enactment of possibility through the tensions and
connections of multiplicity. It is a simultaneity of the concrete and
the abstract, of action and meaning.

But before movement can begin, silence must be broken. As
for colored girls opens, seven women dressed in seven colors stand
frozen in what Shange describes as "postures of distress." The "lady
in brown" confronts the other women with interrogations of their
silence and victimization. "Are we ghouls? / children of horror? /
the joke?" she asks (2, virgules mine). To animate them and hear
something besides the death screams racism and sexism have conferred on these women, the lady in brown calls out to them like this:

> somebody/anybody
> sing a black girl's song
> bring her out
> to know herself
> to know you
> but sing her rhythms
> carin/struggle/hard times
> sing her song of life
> she's been dead so long
> closed in silence so long

> she doesn't know the sound
> of her own voice
> her infinite beauty
> she's half-notes scattered
> without rhythm / no tune
> sing her sighs
> sing the song of her possibilities. (2-3)

Her call brings all the women to life. Throughout the choreo-poem they will scatter and gather, freeze in place and move about every inch of stage and text; they will speak in turn and together, sing as well as talk, dance as well as stand. Collectively they enact what Shange describes as "a young black girl's growing up, her triumphs & errors, our struggle to become all that is forbidden by our environment, all that is forfeited by our gender, all that we have forgotten" (xxi). There is no move toward a Western human-istic unified self but rather a simultaneous gathering and dispers-ing of many selves, many women, all as part of a whole that is never fixed in place as answer or solution but endlessly moves undeterred by discursive boundaries. This is what Teresa de Lauretis has referred to as "a multiple, shifting, and often self-contradictory identity, a subject that is not divided in, but rather at odds with language" ("Feminist Studies/Critical Studies" 9). This subject will give up no part of herself in the interest of someone else's need for her to be what is convenient. She insists on herself as a material reality in a culturally fictional context of representation. The lady in yellow puts it this way:

> my dance waz not enuf / & it waz
> all i had but bein alive & bein a woman & bein
> colored is a metaphysical dilemma / i havent conquered
> yet / do you see the point my spirit is too ancient to
> understand the separation of soul & gender. (48)

She (who is also they) keeps moving, pulling herself together from all parts of her possibilities. She knows disillusion and despair as well as she knows her own skin, but keeps moving. "I cdnt stand being sorry & colored at the same time / it's so redundant in the modern world," says the lady in orange (46, virgule mine). The culture around her gives her ample reason to feel sorry, but she must resist it or disappear. The names that pin her down are used as weapons of power, that power exemplified in the surround-ing culture as a means to maintain hierarchies of dominance and submission. They are names of oppression. Their use has harmed everyone and has distorted the possibilities of connection. They have left this woman, these women, with too many raw edges. "Ever since i realized there waz someone callt / a colored girl an evil woman a bitch or a nag," says the lady in orange, "i been tryin not to be that & leave bitterness / in somebody else's cup" (44, virgules mine).

One of the most reliable controls to prevent autonomy among Others is violence. One of the bitterest realities for Shange's women is that the violence turned on the black community by white society at large is in turn wielded against black women from within that community as well as from without. "Cuz it turns out the nature of rape has changed," says the lady in red; "we can now meet them in circles we frequent for / companionship," says the lady in blue. "We cd even have em over for dinner / & get raped in our own houses / by invitation," grieves the lady in red (20-21, virgules mine). Nor is love any guarantee against it. The lady in red, in a voice full of sorrow, tells the tale of beau willie brown who returned from Vietnam filled with rage to a street constricted by racism and poverty. His readiest outlet was the woman who loved him. He accused her of bearing children not his, beat her, and when "there waz no air" he "kicked the screen outta the window / & held the kids offa the sill"—then "dropped em" (63, virgule Shange's). Violence turned inward is a form of self-hatred; it makes survival all the more unlikely. The women of Shange's text can neither afford to give in to it nor to leave its effects unspoken.

Shange has been criticized for writing such scenes; she has been named a traitor to her people for speaking of the divisions within, for connecting the divisions within herself to those between men and women who have together been victims of oppression. This naming is also oppression. "A friend is hard to press charges against," says the lady in blue (17). But because the violence of sexism is any man's one sure access to some portion of dominance, Shange presses charges—the cost of silence is too great. This is the giving up that Shange's women and Shange's words must resist:

> we deal wit emotion too much
> so why dont we go on ahead & be white then/
> & make everythin dry & abstract wit no rhythm & no
> reelin for sheer sensual pleasure/yes let's go on & be
> white/we're right in the middle of it/no use holdin
> out/holdin onto ourselves. (47, virgules Shange's)

Resistance does not spring full blown from nothing, but takes shape from experience. When experience is hidden or denied, histories of resistance lose their power to inform our possibilities. Shange's words animate forbidden histories of all kinds as important forces to keep her women moving. As a child the lady in brown seeks resistance in the history of the Haitian TOUSSAINT L'OUVERTURE, "a blk man a negro like my mama / say / who refused to be a slave" (27, virgules mine). On her way to the freedom represented by TOUSSAINT L'OUVERTURE, she meets toussaint jones, a boy named for the history she has just discovered. Together they decide they can shape resistance from where they are: "no tellin what all spirits we cd move / down by the river / st. louis 1955" (32, virgules mine). The lady in green dances out another history as "sechita/egyptian/goddess of creativity/2nd millennium" (24, virgules Shange's). In a Natchez bar she is worn down, making do with oily crimson for her cheeks, waxed eyebrows, "sparsely sequined skirts," hard whiskey, and a broken mirror. But "sechita/had learned to make allowances for the distortions" (25, virgule Shange's); she dances in the dust and grime, ignoring the coins tossed at her by the men who watch, able instead to see herself "catchin stars tween her toes" (26). She is both distorted and made visible by her history. Remembering what has been forgotten gives her a dance of her own; but the only images left to her watchers are of Woman meant for them. To write her own history she dances in the spaces between image and reality, claiming both for herself, pain and joy alike intact.

The lady in red continues the legacy. Painted with butterflies and sequins, she "meandered down hoover street" as if unaware of herself but deliberately unforgettable: "& she wanted to be unforgettable / she wanted to be a memory / a wound   to every man / arragant [*sic*] enough to want her" (34, virgules mine). She acts out the fiction and the reality of herself as a woman, appearing in the heat of the day as seductress, rising at dawn to disentangle herself from the lover's "arms & legs that trapped her" and make a bath "of dark musk oil egyptian crystals / & florida water to remove his smell / to wash away the glitter," finally emerging as "herself / ordinary / brown braided woman" (35, virgules mine). Now unrecognizable to the man who followed her home, she writes "the account of her exploit in a diary" and cries herself to sleep (37). She is everywhere and nowhere in history, in the stories of a culture, in her own stories. Her walk through the world that history and those stories have produced is at once illusory and real, a recognition of being all these women and none. It means negotiating dangerous territory. But to rite, to be "herself / ordinary / brown braided woman," she must use everything.

This is no easy task. The words, the images, the very connections she reaches for are of her but not for her. To make it otherwise she must pay attention. "Somebody almost walked off wid alla my stuff," says the lady in green. She is surprised by how quickly she gave it up and by the fact that the thief doesn't even know what he's got; when he looks at her, he sees only what is his. But the lady in green knows: "my stuff is the anonymous ripped off / treasure of the year," she says (54, virgule mine). She takes it back, puts her own name to it—"ntozake 'her own things'" (53)—and steps forward into her own words. "If ya really want it/i'm the only one/can handle it," she says (54, virgules Shange's). It is herself after all, all of her selves together, who make her survival possible.

These selves come forward on the page in a dance of interaction that accumulates and intermingles individual experience in relation to collective histories. No one voice is enough, and the voices together do not overshadow the individual speaker. Everything is necessary to each and to the whole. At the end of *for colored girls* Shange forms a circle of women who speak all at once in all the voices available to them; together they affirm themselves as they dedicate the work to "colored girls who have considered suicide/but are movin to the ends of their own rainbows" (67, virgule Shange's). The conditions of their lives have not made survival easy; speaking those conditions is a matter of ensuring survival. The very shape and movement of Shange's words make use of those conditions. In her own words, in her own way, she enacts her sense of herself as a woman whose names are many and can't be contained.

Shange's resistance to silence disrupts normative language and story alike. As a language user, she interrupts flow and expectation by listening carefully for those sounds she knows as her own. As a storyteller she relies on events usually absent from conventional narratives of Western culture; by centering Story in the lives and traditions of black women, she performs the act of re-visioning much as Adrienne Rich has described it—she looks back to see with fresh eyes and enters the text from a new angle. As a performative writer she patterns her work on the collective interactions of many genres together, giving voice to women whose differences and connections take action not only in writing but in the spaces between text and experience.

For women that space has been so long neglected that it has come to seem a place of profound mystery. As women illuminate its nooks and crannies, as Woolf pointed out, we see what is there but as if it were entirely new; and so it is, dislodging as it does old assumptions about what can be seen. In *Sassafrass, Cypress & Indigo,* Shange begins with the mystery, but as if it had always been just another language to use. "Where there is a woman there is magic," she writes. "If there is a moon falling from her mouth, she is a woman who knows her magic, who can share or not share her powers" (3). Indigo, the youngest of three sisters and forever older than her years, is such a woman. She, like Shange, is rewriting the language that would cripple her; she is using magic to make a passage through what is seen to what can be seen. She only looks mad from the outside; from the inside she is making a language she can use. "Indigo seldom spoke. There was a moon in her mouth. Having a moon in her mouth kept her laughing" (3).

Cypress, the middle sister, is a dancer. For her the language of the body is the language she must use to know herself as she is. She is an explorer in motion, refusing the limitations she has been taught are hers. "At the barre she smiled at all those pelvic muscles, hearing her mama whispering that she had better work hard, because the white folks didn't want to see a colored woman fly of her own powers" (161). Cypress does not stay at home but moves home from place to place as she dances with the Kushites Returned in San Francisco or with Azure Bosom in New York City. She is learning the magic of "articulating what women had never acknowledged: our bodies are not our destiny, but all freeing-energy" (141). She uses this energy to keep herself and the histories of her people alive.

The eldest sister, Sassafrass, is a poet and a weaver like her mother. "When women make cloth, they have time to think," she says, "and Theban women stopped thinking, and the town fell" (92). Sassafrass is a rescue-worker. She covers her walls and clothes herself with stories of African-America woven by her own hand. She makes tangible the fruits of her mind, "certain of the necessity of her skill for the well-being of women everywhere, as well as for her own" (92). For her this is a language of interconnectedness, an act of will by which to overcome the separations visited on women and people of color by the legacy of slavery and the barrenness of white patriarchal rule. The motion of the shuttle through the threads on her loom "conjure[s] images of women weaving from all time and all places" (92); it brings together lost histories and new stories so that nothing may be forgotten.

Mother to these sisters, Hilda Effania passes on the lessons she has learned. She teaches her daughters how to cook, how to weave, and how to believe in their own talents. She is a preserver. Her recipes and letters intersperse the text, seasoning it with words of wisdom that are marvels of connections missed and made. She reminds them to believe in "the progress of the race" and admonishes them to maintain "good Negro Christian" behavior as a way to advance; she sends her support of their choices, reminds them to act like ladies, find good husbands, and "keep your distance from women with so little to do they stay around each other all the time" (154). Of course it is precisely among the connections between women that Sassafrass, Cypress, and Indigo learn what they need to know. But it is Hilda Effania's preservation of a safe home to which her daughters can always return that allows them to risk the choices they make. "You come back to Charleston and find the rest of yourself. (smile) / Love, Mama" (220, virgule mine). Hers is the language of memory, one generation to another. It is in constant danger of being lost and must continually be adapted to ever-changing realities; but without it this family of women would scatter and disappear.

The traditional skills of women shape Shange's text. They are skills passed on from mother to daughter, from Africa to America, and are shared or not according to how well each woman knows her powers. Shange says simply of Indigo, "She made herself, her world, from all that she came from" (4). Each of these women does so. Since "all that she came from," however, is so often devalued and unspoken by the mythic logic of the surrounding culture of dominance, the makings and sharings of these women constitute a radical construction of know-ing that breaks the conventions of what is known. Indigo is aware of the need for this from the beginning: "There wasn't enough for Indigo in the world she'd been born to, so she made up what she needed. What she thought the black people needed" (4). What is needed in Indigo's world is "Access to the moon. / The power to heal. / Daily visits with the spirits" (5, virgules mine). To that end she writes incantations, casts spells, makes and talks to dolls, apprentices herself to the wise old men and women of her community, brings forth sounds on her violin that change people's lives, and finally brings forth babies as a practicing midwife.

Indigo is the one in her family who most directly uses the languages of the sorceress to make a world that will not demand her demise. Shange says of her, "She was particularly herself. She changed the nature of things. She colored & made richer what was blank & plain" (40). She is the healer who can laugh even better than she can speak, who can see most clearly by moonlight, and who can make her will felt as if it were a deed or tangible presence. These powers are crucial to her survival in a world that relies on her captivity. Her feelings take action. Her actions take names, like headings in a book of recipes or spells: "Moon Journeys, cartography by Indigo" (5). Each time Indigo learns more of the world, new spells appear on the page. They mark her safe passage through that world.

"Marvellous Menstruating Moments (As Told by Indigo to Her Dolls as She Made Each and Every One of Them a Personal Menstruation Pad of Velvet)" (19). On the appearance of her first menstrual blood, Indigo tells her mother that stars are falling from between her legs. "This is Charleston, South Carolina," Hilda Effania tells her; "Stars don't fall from little colored girls' legs. Little boys don't come chasing after you for nothing good. White men roam these parts with evil in their blood, and every single thought they have about a colored woman is dangerous" (22). "To Rid Oneself of the Scent of Evil" (30). When she buys her first Kotex at Mr. Lucas's store, she is nearly raped by him. She has been in his store hundreds of times, but this time is different. This time her presence causes trouble; it is a female trouble. "Mr. Lucas took a step toward Indigo, like he was looking for the woman in her" (29). Indigo runs and Mr. Lucas remembers that even if she talks no one will believe her, witch-child that she is. "Emergency Care of Open Wounds/ When It Hurts"; "Emergency Care of Wounds That Cannot Be Seen" (50). Her insistence on her own way of seeing is translated as a form of madness; yet everyone who comes in contact with Indigo feels her power. She is the gatherer-thread, the link between worlds, collecting bits and pieces as she goes, shaping and continually modifying them into whole fabric. "Hilda Effania knew Indigo had an interest in folklore. Hilda Effania had no idea that Indigo was the folks" (224).

It is of course this same "folks" whose heritage Sassafrass weaves into cloth and Cypress dances into motion. But for them it is the revolutionary sixties, black power, flower power, and "experimental living" that offer opportunities to find and set their own parameters. Sassafrass is comforted by the words of dead women blues singers as she waits for Mitch—jazz musician, lover, and addict—to find his way out of hurt and destruction. She takes him with her to the New World Found Collective to live among priests and priestesses of ancient African traditions. But Mitch's wounds are too deep, and finally she must leave him to give birth to their child at home with Mama and Indigo. Cypress samples love the way a cook samples ingredients, looking for just the right combination. With the dancer Idrina she finds a letting go, woman to woman, which breaks her heart; but she learns to honor her "third-world" body in dances not controlled by "first world" movements. With the composer Leroy McCullough she finds a home away from home; his "blackening up America" with his music gives her dispersed African rhythms with which to celebrate her African-American survival. In "Journal Entry #692" she writes, "That's what it means that black folks cd dance/:

> it
> dont mean just
> what we do all the time/ it's how we remember what
> cannot be said/
> that's why the white folks say it aint got no form/
> what was the form
> of slavery/ what was the form of jim crow/ & how
> wd they
> know. (168)

Shange has said that only a collective voice can revive the emotional language needed to direct rage at oppression and forge new contexts beyond it ("foreward/"). In her writing she uses such a voice: the seven selves clothed each in a different color in *for colored girls*, the family of women speaking from a shared past into a collaborative future-present in Sassafrass, Cypress & Indigo, the use of language not bound by generic category or linguistic convention throughout her work—all this forms a cumulative context of multivocity in which discursive authority is rendered nonhegemonic by being decentered. Even so, one could wish that Shange's efforts to claim female energy did not sometimes lapse into heterosexist assumptions of power: Cypress is almost destroyed by Idrina who is referred to as "the vampire," yet is so completed by the "perfect man" Leroy that his offer of marriage unproblematically diverts her from her political activism; the "safest" relations among women are most often familial—mother to daughter, sister to sister, selves within a self; the sexual energy by which the women

measure their significance is more often stereotypically generative than creatively disjunctive. Considering the promise of texts
that so thoroughly confront oppressive paradigms, these elements
are at the very least curiously disturbing.

Nevertheless, despite these not insignificant problems, the
voices Shange brings to her writing are vital and necessary ones.
They form a collectivity that never rests but is always moving,
making complex wholes out of a multiplicity of parts—like
threads in weaving, ingredients in cooking, letters sent and received,
singers blending each her own voice in song, dancers moving apart
and together in tactile visual patterns, like words of an incantation.
While *Sassafrass, Cypress & Indigo* does not employ what Shange calls
her "verbal gymnastics" to the extent that *for colored girls* does,
adhering most often instead to a prose form with more or less conventional sentence structures, both texts rely on overall narrative
structures that are anything but conventional. The recipes, stories,
spells, letters, journal entries, and poems of the later novel function much the same way as the unconventional uses of punctuation, spelling, and diction in the earlier choreopoem: they produce
language that is at once performance and written text, a dance of
possibilities unavailable in the images and practices of the symbolic order of dominant patriarchal culture. Like Indigo, Shange's
writing is particularly itself.

As with Shange, myth and tradition play an important part
in Broner's work, but differently. Broner's women are surrounded
by and resist patriarchy but do not regard it as the test of their
worth. Broner presents Judaic patriarchy as that which has shaped
as well as silenced her women, rather than as a colonial imposition of one culture on another. The women of Broner's texts fight
their own silences to remake themselves whole within a shifting
process of collectivity based not so much on family likenesses as on
the realization of differences as gathering forces. For both writers,
however, making stories possible outside Western culture's mythic
structure is necessary to their ability to speak as themselves. Their
use of ancient traditions does not replace one myth with another
but dislodges the hegemony of myth as it has been understood in
the history of Western patriarchal thought. In the mouths of
women, who *are* myth in that history, the telling of stories to and
for each other is a way to break the code of law by which narrative
is inscribed. As outlaws they form a community unto themselves.
But it is not merely a community apart; rather, as in the new city

of women at the end of Broner's *A Weave of Women*, it is a place without doors and without boundaries, a place of movement on its own terms.

Beatrix Palmer of *Her Mothers* is a wanderer among wanderers. She is looking for the threads of her own experience; she is looking for herself. The women of *A Weave of Women* have all wandered into a little stone house in the Old City in Jerusalem; there they come together for the hard work of claiming themselves as their homeland. None of these women is on a hero's quest. There is no representative figure in their stories who must conquer all obstacles to win his rightful place among men. There is no bearer or taker of The Word who must come to maturity through (re)possession of Meaning. Broner's women must break through patriarchal scripts, not to become writers of scripts but to free themselves for the immediacy and specificity of ritual without scripture. They have no Talmud to authorize them, no forebears to best. They look far into the ancient past and far inside themselves for what they know; theirs is a process of know-ing. They are engaged in the work at hand. They do their work together, in many voices at once, speaking in and out of turn. Language cannot settle their differences, but is for them a form of action, an unsettled, unsettling community of experience.

In both novels, the movement of the text and of the women's realizations of consciousness takes shape as a never-ending series of questions and answers, the telling and retelling of stories. This movement does not proceed in an orderly fashion; it is not linear, nor even progressive, but a kind of purposeful wandering. It is always its own destination, yet is anything but static. Like Woolf's circuituous investigations on and off the path, or Richardson's self-inscribing stranger, or Shange's interdisciplinary performances, Broner's search for a heritage not lost by not ever being remembered the same twice resists co-optation because it does not recognize as necessary a hegemonic relation between knowledge and experience. Broner's women are in constant motion; motion is life. The questions these women must ask require mobility, for the sources they seek have been dispersed, covered over, and deformed in the name of the Father's right to name. The stories these women must tell require freedom of movement, for the possibilities they can feel in their bones have been pronounced unlawful in the Father's house. They must leave home, for home has always been designated as a matter of going from one father to another. Their truths will sound like lies to those who have been dutiful sons and daughters.

These women make their own stories as they go; their words rely on the unreliability of everything they have heard. Between the lines they find what they need to know; it is their access to their own lives.

"Are your parents alive?" asks Beatrix of Naomi in Tel Aviv (*Her Mothers* 157). Bea has traveled to Israel in search of her daughter, Lena, who is at home nowhere. "Oh yes," replies Naomi. In America Naomi's mother "sleeps without dreaming" and her father dreams "of his return to the Land," the Land to which his daughter has come alone. "Is he proud of you?" asks Bea. "No. He disinherited me," says Naomi, "for leaving him to come here." Bea moves on to Ein Hod where she meets Ilana, a Russian potter whose father is "a man of culture" and whose mother is paralyzed. Ilana identifies herself as "the daughter of collectors" who spent her childhood admiring her father's treasured objects. "Then he is pleased with you, Ilana, that you are a potter?" "No. He has disinherited me. . . . Because I would not stay home and be part of the collection" (170). In Jerusalem Bea questions Rut'y whose father "was a labor organizer" and whose mother "was organized by my father" (170). Rut'y works with immigrants, but her father has disinherited her too. She tells Bea, "Fathers are always disappointed in us. We bear the dreams they have already shed" (171). Bea's search for continuity among daughters of fathers can yield only disjuncture. It is among daughters of mothers that she must find what she needs to know:

> "Mother, I'm pregnant with a baby girl."
> "What does she want to know?"
> "Will her mother be her friend?"
> "No, her enemy."
> "And her father?"
> "He will court her but he will destroy her."
> "She wants to know how."
> "He will dance with her and hold her close in order not to
> see her. He will sing to her in order not to hear her." (25)

It is the daughter's questions of the mother about bearing girl children that set the text in motion and punctuate it throughout, constantly shifting and altering what can be known. Bea is both daughter and mother. She is collecting stories, hoping to find what she has lost. To do this she has learned to ask questions and to understand each answer as the beginning of another question. "Mother, I'm pregnant with a girl. What will she be?" "What she was." "What if she doesn't want to be what she was?" "Then she will change, slightly" (57). Bea is looking for the fissures, the tiny crevices between fact and fiction that will open the way for change. For thousands of years her ancestors have proceeded this way. For thousands of years they have passed on questions and stories to secure the father's house against annihilation. Within those stories the mothers and daughters could not ask the questions but only embody them. In this way they have disappeared. The ancient texts, passed on father to son, teach Bea only about women who "made a contest of the womb" in desperate efforts to be the mothers of sons. "Sister against sister, woman betrays woman. The man is the seed and the woman the gourd, filled with seed and rattling or dried and to be discarded" (164). Her history is not her own. In her attempt to be a good daughter Bea has lost all trace of herself. She must search through "remnants" for the bits and fragments by which to interrogate the terms of her loss.

Remnants becomes the title of the book Bea is working on. She is writing the text while another woman takes photographs of the World War II survivors Bea interviews. She says of them, "They are circus people. The Tattooed People. The Experimented-On People. Still they live" (163). On the page preceding the text of *Her Mothers* is a photograph of faces from a 1944 high school yearbook. Bea grew up in the American Midwest, safe but not so very far from the camps in Europe. She surveys these faces, looking for clues. Those she was meant to emulate display the same standards of fair-skinned, fair-haired beauty worshipped by the camp builders. She could never meet their standards. "Beatrix wrote a report for Ninth Grade Social Studies: 'The Nazis and their Death Camps.' The teacher pointed out Beatrix's misspellings and disbelieved her information. The class was informed that this was an example of historical bias and racial exaggeration" (57). But there are the faces; the faces themselves can never be exaggerated.

As she researches the words of "historical mothers," women writers such as Emily Dickinson, Louisa May Alcott, Charlotte Forten, and Margaret Fuller, Bea studies their faces in old photographs. She has two of Margaret Fuller, one earlier and one later. "What has her face given up from Portrait One?" Bea asks herself. Weariness shows where innocence once was; the mouth is tighter, the eyes more focused, the body more solid. The woman in Portrait Two has traveled. "She will never be able to return from experience," Bea tells herself (91). Nor will Beatrix.

Bea remembers the friends she had at school, the girls who did not fit in. Their faces look out from the yearbook page already marked by the losses they will suffer. These are the daughters who resist annihilation by trying to be themselves. But the cost of a daughter's resistance is high. One has retreated from knowledge of the world into the silence of her father's attic. Another rebels by "marrying Black" and is disowned. A third loves chemistry, has been forbidden to pursue her love, and has married a doctor as a dutiful substitute. When Bea tries to contact them years later, no one answers her inquiries. They have scattered beyond her reach and disappeared. Only their faces remain, leftover images for Bea to study as she tries to locate the moment at which possibility is silenced and loss takes over.

Beatrix herself married a man who has left her. She bore a daughter, Lena, who has mistaken the father for her home and has gone after him. From within the stories handed down mother to daughter, through the fathers, Bea could not stop her. "Mother, I'm pregnant with a baby girl and she has left me." "Then you must spend the rest of your life looking for her" (172). But of course it is only when Bea stops looking that Lena can come to her. And she can stop looking only when she has found enough of herself to stop passing on duty and silence as her legacy. "Primer: Ten Ways to Lose Daughters": "Talk too Much"; "Compare"; "Be Helpful"; "Have Historical Perspective"; "Be Silent"; "Have Goals for Your Daughter"; "Be Organized"; "Teach Politeness"; "Teach Caution"; "Be Energetic" (175-77). As Bea passes on lessons one through nine, Lena's response is to tell her mother to "shut up." By lesson ten, Lena has stopped listening. "'Did you hear me?' asked Beatrix. 'Never again,' said Lena" (178). She is silent, then she disappears. Bea follows, but cannot find her; she is a remnant that does not want to be found.

There is nothing for Bea to do but to keep moving. Her search is for her daughter but also for her own words. Broner's text begins again and again, never settling on any one story as that which will render Bea whole or reunite her with what she seems to be missing. *Her Mothers* takes shape through accumulation. Daughters chant questions over and over to mothers whose answers will not stay still but shift and change with each new circumstance; each story told must be retold with other names and places to ensure that it will not encode silence; photographs are studied again and again only to yield further speculations; the titles of Bea's travels break the narrative continually, circling back on themselves with new material to alter their accountability each time they appear. This is a text of remnants, each both only itself and one part of a complex collaboration. When Beatrix Palmer reaches the last chapter, she begins again with these words: "This is a story"—it is open to telling and retelling, and Bea is the gatherer of its possibilities (223). She has decided to age, move to Florida, look through old photos, and collect shells on the beach. One day Lena appears. Bea lets her go. Lena comes back. Once the ancient prohibitions have been set aside and the photos have cracked, mother and daughter are free to choose one another at will. Each has traveled and neither can return from experience. That, of course, is the point. It is where they can begin, where words between them are no longer forbidden, no longer contests of will, but ongoing interactions between women of experience.

It is difficult not to read *Her Mothers* as a prelude of sorts to *A Weave of Women*. When mother and daughter come together as independent but connected women, they set the stage for larger and more complex gatherings. Beatrix Palmer's dispersed encounters with the past release its hold on her while allowing her to see it anew, much as she and Lena come to see one another. It is this sort of difficult re-visioning that is intensified in *A Weave of Women*. There women of disparate backgrounds come and go at will from a "house of women," a house created out of their presence to one another and complete with the contradictions and clarifications such a house must imply.

In the Old City of Jerusalem women from Israel, Britain, Germany, and the United States pool their experiences of the world to make the world new just where it is at its oldest. They are fifteen in number, off and on; they are writers, scholars, several young "wayward girls" of the streets, a social worker, a scientist, a mystic, a singer, a political administrator, an Orthodox religious wife, a divorcing woman, a Christian, a convert to Judaism, and a mother giving birth to a girl. They live in The Land where coming together makes uneasy alliances, intimate ties of hatred and love alike, and too many laws. Lines are easily crossed; borders are everywhere. What restores the old ways of the fathers leaves little room for these women who, by the very act of gathering their lives together as they do, are Wayward daughters. Says Broner of the text of their lives,

> It is a story of women who are ceremonious and correct with each other, who celebrate sermons and hermans, birth rites, death rites, sacrificial rites, exodus rites and exorcism rites.
> It is the story of sanity and madness in the house of women. (9)

This story and these rites are not the ancient ones handed down through the ages; the women speak this story and its rites into being for themselves, neither discarding nor keeping the old traditions. Like spells, their words take action. Broner's language is compact, direct, like a chant or song. Her sentences gather energy inside themselves; they do not rely for meaning on sequences of events ordered through narrative progression but are active in and of themselves. Her use of language has about it a sound as old as The Land itself, yet comes onto the page as if only just now in the process of becoming. Hepzibah, the religious wife from Haifa who lives in the house of a husband who studies the law of father-right from which all laws in his house come, says of herself and her daughter Rahel, "We are both fiction writers until we can change circumstances" (78). Broner is a fiction writer; her fiction is an act of changing circumstances.

Like Shange, Broner uses collectivity to form her text. The voices, styles, and conditions she writes do not depend on the law, such as the Law of Narrative or the Law of Universal Meaning through Difference, but on experience enacted in words as if they could say anything. Such a feat cannot be accomplished in a single voice but requires all the women's voices together in all their diversity and common intimacy. Broner says of divorcing Mickey, whose words in court are never heard because she insists on speaking as a woman and not as a wife, "Yet she can say anything to these women and they have heard it from another's lips or recognize it as the truth of women" (103). When the women prepare curses in a rite of revenge for the stoning of one of their number, some fear the consequences of speaking outside the law: "Terry reminds the Three Wise Women, Hepzibah, Gerda, and Antoinette, there is nothing they do that is legal. There are no laws yet for these women. Are they, therefore, lawless? No. . . . No one knows better about law and lawlessness than they" (233). They are taking action in words, changing their circumstances.

The first rite the women perform after Simha gives birth to Hava is a "piercing." It takes place in the little stone house they live in across the street from the Home for Jewish Wayward Girls. "I am acting upon the command that is not yet written," says Simha (22). The women gather around the infant while Gerda the scientist carefully pierces Hava's hymen. Says Dahlia the singer, "May she not be delivered intact to her bridegroom or judged by her hymen but by the energies of her life." Says Deedee the American, "May she never suffer again from piercing, of the body or of the

heart" (25). The wayward girls are shocked; the women remind
the girls and themselves of why they have made this ceremony by
telling each of her own "piercing." Deedee concludes the stories
by conferring on Hava what the women did not have: "'Hava, let
your piercing be among friends. Let it be ceremonious and correct.
Let it be supervised. Let it be done openly, not in anger, not in
cars'" (27). In this way the women make ritual without scripture.

Terry the political activist tells old stories in new ways to the
girls from across the street. She begins in the traditional way, but
then departs from tradition and applies her own words to the
story of Esther. "'We are our politics,' says Terry, 'and all decisions
are political. Queen Esther was a political animal'" (118). The girls
dislike this description of Esther, for it does not fit the images
they have always treasured; if Esther is political she can no longer
be the beauty queen, the dutiful daughter who sacrifices herself
for her people. Instead she is a woman who consciously chooses
to think back through her mothers to the Semitic Goddess Ishtar,
creator and destroyer of life. "The girls boo and sound their noise-
makers against Terry who would change fairy tales into history. . . .
The changing of names for accuracy is not allowed in legend"
(120). But once Terry's Esther takes her strength from her ancient
but broken history, she can act as she must, according to her own
knowledge rather than according only to others' needs. So it is to
be with the women. Broner brings them together to make stories
that will not trap them in old fictions.

Interspersed with the story of Esther-made-history is the
ominous progress of a young Bedouin prince and his companion,
to whom he is telling the story of his encounter with Dahlia. Theirs
was a sensuous moment in the desert that has left him obsessed
by her; the prince's obsession has spurred his companion to avenge
what he regards as a seduction by a wanton woman of the enemy
camp. Just as Terry finishes her story, the two men burst into the
house. In an attempt to save his beloved, the prince points to Simha
when the zealot demands to know which woman has wronged him.
The avenger's hammer misses Simha and strikes the baby Hava,
killing her outright. Amid the wailings of the women Broner writes,
"The Megillah, the tale, is told. In the legend there is relief from
the enemy, sorrow is turned into gladness, mourning into holiday.
In life, only some of this is possible" (132). The changing of names
for accuracy is not allowed in legends.

The sound of women's voices or the sight of women's bodies
outside the codes of law is a powerful disruptive force. Broner uses

this force by writing a house of women in which the women speak as they do and as they must. One night, standing near the Wall, Gloria and Simha hear singing from the men's side. Since it is a song they know, they sing too. From the other side of the Wall the rabbi shouts at them, "It is forbidden to distract the men"— for that is what women's voices do. Gloria and Simha sing louder, and the rabbi shakes his finger at them while covering his eyes so as to avoid the Evil Eye—for that is what the sight of women means when uncontrolled. Simha calls to him, "You would know me and yet you pretend not to see me. But I see you. I stare at all of you" (65). The men scream at them as Gloria and Simha shake the mehitzah, the partition; it remains, but they have seen and been seen as themselves. Then Terry and Vered organize against Vered's former lover, a politician who calls for the protection of the sanctity of womanhood by taking a stand against abortion and birth control and promising to imprison Terry's wayward girls for soliciting and to shut down their Home. The women demand to be heard and are denied. They speak anyway, marching and shouting in public demonstrations. At that moment, "a transformation occurs. Not one woman is recognized as the gentle sex, the tender sex" (154). The police attack, the women fight back, and the public is confronted with women "giving battle." They elect Terry to Parliament for this, and Terry learns that she, like Esther before her, can act as she must, as herself.

Broner's women make of their words living forces. They do this in the context of a history of violence and misogyny, refusing to disappear into its deadly silences. Men occupy Broner's text and the women's lives both as sources of partnership or comfort and as sexual terrorists. The women accept freely given moments of sharing, confront directly those men who do them harm, and every day use their experience to stop their own victimization, to heal the wounds inflicted by it, to turn away from the patriarchal order of dominance that surrounds them. They laugh with each other, using laughter as their most radical resistance to annihilation. They retain their sense of belongingness in Jewish culture, but fight hard the patriarchal need to control, punish, consume, and possess them. The danger they face is as often physical as emotional, a matter of literal deaths or maimings in which race and sex have been reproduced as challenges to power cuing time-worn responses of conquest and extermination. Thus is the body of Woman othered and destroyed, consumed by a voracious appetite for (and fear of) the power of life and death it seems to represent.

Such is the fate of Shula, a wayward girl invited off the streets and into the house of women. Like so many before her, Shula dies on a train. Among the women she has taken back her body as her own and found her talent as an artist. She is on her way to study at the Munich Art Academy, the recipient of a stipend for Israeli exchange students offered by Germany in the wake of the massacre of Israel's Olympic team. The train is crowded. Unable to find space in the safety of cabins crammed with young people and students, she travels warily in the company of three men who watch her closely. She is polite, accepting the food they offer her and listening to their talk. Soon they regard her as theirs and begin to force themselves on her. She yells for help but no one hears. When the train arrives in Munich incoming passengers find Shula "sleeping, or parts of her visible around her sleeping bag" (274). Broner says of her, "She was the communal lunch, the licked bones. Of the whole her curled fingers, her foot, and loose hair remain. In the lands of the Minotaur, the lion and the crooked cross there is never enough of sacrifice" (275).

Back in the house of women the mystic Simha counts: "She is the third victim" (276). The infant Hava was the first. Wayward Robin, who disappeared rather than be caught in a contest for her soul among the prophets of the street, was the second. Even in this Land of loss and return the women are set apart. They will not be icons and are punished for their iconoclasm. The blows they receive are severe, but they do not give up what they know. "'There are two possibilities,' begins Terry. All learned discussions in The Land begin thus. 'We are what we choose'" (118). One by one the women recite their choices. "I could stay at home, the good girl . . . or I could travel into danger," says Deedee. "We could stay at home, good girls, or we could go on the road into traffic," say the wayward girls. "I could stay in my marriage, a beaten wife, or I could try to strike back at the beater," says Mickey. "I could have stayed home and married, or I could make new births and new prayers," says Simha (129-30). The choices they make are passages through, not over or around, boundaries. It is the space between them they must find.

Joan the English playwright and Tova the American actress make a drama about this. They move back and forth across borders talking to Jewish women and Arab women, making photographs of their faces. They call this work *The City Between Us* and perform it at the Wall when no theater will allow it inside. The crowd that gathers "weeps, hisses, quarrels, shouts, interrupts, shoves the interrupters, applauds, boos" (180). No response is the right one; no response is forbidden. Because of the public stir, TV talk shows talk about the play, university drama classes assign the play, and a prominent theater finally agrees to show it inside—"but *The City Between Us* is not as successful contained" (180). Neither, of course, are the women.

Of them Broner writes, "these women are all, were all travelers before settling down in each other's friendships" (239). Broner brings them together not to recover what has been lost so much as to gather the disparate threads of what is. They know how to make a home of their presence to themselves and to each other, but a home without walls, without doors, in the open. When they lose their little stone house to plans for a new high-rise of male yeshiva students, they travel to the outskirts of the city. "Slowly, singly and together, the women decide to cross borders. None of this is apparent. They scout The Land, climb towers, study, do stretching exercises, squat. They intend a large deed. Something about The Land makes this possible" (285). In the open desert, where battles have been fought for centuries upon centuries, the women set up a new community. They call it "*Havurat Shula,* the friends of Shula," and raise a flag that says only "Wayward Women." The city sends government officials to convince them to "return to the fold"— but they know that for them "there is no fold. They must enfold their own" (289). It is what they have been doing all along. As she leaves them where they have arrived, Broner asks one last question: "What will happen to them, this caravan of women that encircles the outskirts of the city, that peoples the desert?" (294). She gives no answer. There is none; none is needed. The women, like Broner's text, will do as they must.

In the language of ritual always in the process of dislodging itself, always coming into being, Broner brings fiction and experience together in a house of women. She writes, "Women long ago unlearned the words that preceded weeping, the incantations, anagrams, curses, witchcraft. Now, instead of muttering those words, instead of chanting them, they weep" (40). It is the business of Broner's writing to breathe life back into those "words that preceded weeping," the words that take action. She does not try to stop the weeping as she does this but recognizes it as a part of the history of women's use of-and-as language. Only now the incantations, anagrams, and curses call forth tears of agency rather than tears of passive victimization. Reading Broner's words is like uttering a chant or a curse or a song, not on cue or according to the prescribed text but as a form of action in the world that is ongoing and forever changing. The logic of Reason does not silence her. She breaks into and out of the rules, insisting on her own processes of know-ing. The rituals to which she gives voice do not codify experience into knowledge but release it into possibility.

––––––––

Like Broner, Wittig calls on ancient forms of utterance to make words new. She too uses short, direct sentences, repetition of pace and rhythm, and a ritual-like gathering of diverse fragments into a whole that does not depend on any but its own order, an order continually disrupted and made permeable by its own movement. *Les Guérillères* may almost remind us of an epic—it looks at first glance like a long narrative poem, employs epic tones that might celebrate legendary feats, calls on beauty, love, courage as if they were sources of large deeds. But here there is no hero acting out events that test and prove his or her mettle, no conventions that remain stable enough to reassure us that we are seeing what we have seen before, no mythic figures who take their places in the Story of Man. Instead the text is made up of warrior-women who take apart Story, and Man, whose presence always is about to, is in the process of, taking apart this text too, this text in which they take action as words. Theirs is a collective action, never settling on one or another but made possible by the interaction of all the voices at once. Most of the time Wittig refers to the women as "they" ("elles"), only interrupting their movement with lists of (their) names capitalized in bold-face type, unseparated by space or punctuation, arranged in the middle of pages set at odds with the rest of the text. Disjunctures are everywhere, refusing coopera-tion with the symbolic order. "LACUNAE LACUNAE / AGAINST TEXTS / AGAINST MEANING" (143, virgules mine), chants the page itself.

The women are at war; the words are at war; the symbolic order in which Woman is a form of language is under attack—but this is not an action designed to take over power; rather it is a dis-mantling of power, a scattering of power so that its effects can no longer form hierarchies of meaning. Language is dispersed, pulled apart, cut down, made open and undecidable so that it may no longer make meaning on the body of Difference. Only in this way can the women, can Wittig, meet language head on, dismantle its iconic power, and stop speaking Woman as if she were the shape of their meaning. She, Woman, is after all what Wittig calls an "imagi-nary formation," that myth which sets men's tongues wagging but has no material reality of her own. The material reality of a woman as not-Woman is the forbidden subject whose entrance into the text allows Wittig to say, "Through literature . . . words come back to us whole again" ("The Trojan Horse" 48). But this can happen only when language has been (in Wittig's terms) fractured and estranged, so that Woman is no longer language's cultural symbolic.

The lesbian writer or the lesbian text is in a particularly good position to enact this estrangement, for as Wittig says, "lesbian is the only concept I know of which is beyond the categories of sex (woman and man), because the designated subject (lesbian) is *not* a woman. . . . For what makes a woman is a specific social relation to a man" ("One Is Not Born a Woman" 53). That social relation relies on the categories of sex to produce woman *as* sexuality and women's encounters with sexuality as "a social institution of violence" (53). Women-together, then, exist outside that social relation. That is why the texts that decenter authority by recentering story through the relations between women are so explosive in a phallocentric symbolic order. As Woolf said, when Chloe likes Olivia, everything is changed. As Wittig says, "They say that they are starting from zero. They say that a new world is beginning" (*Les Guérillères* 85).

Like Woolf, Richardson, Shange, and Broner, Wittig writes the sound and shape of women's words in relation to one another. Like Stein, she uses words as things in themselves, as material forms that cannot be dissociated from meaning yet do not overdetermine meaning by re-producing text as "a symbol, a manifesto" in which "one sees and hears *only* meaning" ("The Point of View" 68). In conventional uses of language and story, form disappears as meaning is produced; in nonconventional writing, meaning may be called into question in/as the production of form. For Wittig, the business of the lesbian (not-Woman) writer is to "take every word and despoil it of its everyday meaning in order to be able to work with words, on words" ("The Trojan Horse" 47). This is not unlike Stein's exhortation to "put some strangeness, something unexpected" into one's use of language and "work in the excitingness of pure being," in-and-with words.

Wittig makes of this work also an openly political act of resistance to oppression and exploitation. She aligns language and reality in such a way that women's fictions and the fiction of Woman must collide. Well schooled in the French intellectual traditions that have produced Lacanian theory and a poststructural hunger for The Feminine as the altered space of (former) Man's alienated deification, as well as in feminist analysis, Wittig knows language as the site of both oppression and possibility. Unlike Sappho who may have, as Judy Grahn believes, written in a world free from "lack of safety, fear of reprisal by husband, police or other patriarchal institution" (*The Highest Apple* 10), the modern lesbian writer puts words to use from within the "master" language of a patriarchal ideology that despises and disperses her into nonbeing. Critic Bonnie Zimmerman remarks, "If we have been silenced for centuries and speak an oppressor's tongue, then liberation for the lesbian must begin with language" ("What Has Never Been: An Overview of Lesbian Feminist Criticism" 194). She situates the liberatory capacity of this use of language in "the powerful bonds between women [which are] a crucial factor in women's lives" (178) and credits Wittig with "a 'lesbian writing' that locates the lesbian subject outside the male linguistic universe" (195). Wittig, then, is a writer denied Sapphic freedom yet refusing the restrictions of protective language. She meets language face to face and writes as she must.

In an author's note at the beginning of *The Lesbian Body* (1975, *Le Corps Lesbien* 1973), Wittig writes, "The Amazons are women who live among themselves, by themselves and for themselves at all the generally accepted levels: fictional, symbolic, actual. Because we are illusionary for traditional male culture we make no distinction between the three levels" (9). Both language and the body of woman are cultural symbolics. When the conceptual and the material realities of these symbolics are put into an actual-fictional interaction of dynamic possibility, then "writing the never previously written" is a means to attain "the unattained body" in words (10). Language, form, and meaning come together in an explosively iconoclastic relation. Wittig regards this access to language as proceeding from "the desire to bring the real body violently to life in the words of the book (everything that is written exists), the desire to do violence by writing to the language which I [J/e] can enter only by force" (10). In *The Lesbian Body*, Wittig materializes the "elle" (she) whose "Je" (I) is never assumed as generic subject in the language of Man. Like Woolf's ambiguously fictional "I," Wittig's "Je" must be rewritten from her own experience. "J/e" then becomes "the symbol of the lived, rending experience which is m/y writing, of this cutting in two which throughout literature is the exercise of a language which does not constitute m/e as a subject" (10-11). Her enterprise, in *The Lesbian Body* as well as in *Les Guérillères*, is profoundly daring. Both texts scatter and gather language and the female body so that neither can quite be re-membered in patriarchal terms.

It is impossible to read *The Lesbian Body*, for instance, and retain a culturally familiar image of Woman—it is specified out of existence. The speaker of this text uses words to travel throughout the whole of the body of a beloved, a body like but other than her own. She does not gaze upon that body or recite its characteristics, but uses all her (and our) senses to move through it, inside and out—through every cell, muscle, secretion, excretion, taste, touch, smell. As she moves, the words make melodious, sometimes rapturous, arrangements on the page even as they probe what we have learned to fear and recoil from as well as what we have learned to regard as pleasurable. Consequently, on many levels at once we must give up notions of what is appropriate or not (for language and for the body) and accept instead the impact of the whole. This leaves us with a sense of having seen what has not been (seen). Wittig cues our familiarity with the myths of Western culture but does not allow us to rest there as in an already-known place. As she recites the body, she makes words into experience and the interplay of form and meaning into a specificity that becomes palpable as never before.

> In this dark adored adorned gehenna say your farewells m/y very beautiful one m/y very strong one m/y very indomitable one m/y very learned one m/y very ferocious one m/y very gentle one m/y best beloved to what they, the women, call affection tenderness or gracious abandon. . . . But you know that not one will be able to bear seeing you with eyes turned up lids cut off your yellow smoking intestines spread in the hollow of your hands your tongue spat from your mouth long green strings of your bile flowing over your breasts, not one will be able to bear your low frenetic insistent laughter. (15)

The Lesbian Body does without relation to men or a male symbolic; its "low frenetic insistent laughter" accompanies and is everywhere present in the text. As Hélène Cixous imagines in "The Laugh of the Medusa," all women have to do "for history to change its meaning" (for our sense of possibility to be re-visioned) is to stop listening to the myths about us as if they were true: "You only have to look at the Medusa straight on to see her. And she's not deadly. She's beautiful and she's laughing" (255). Women's relation to old texts has ever been a discomfited one insofar as we find ourselves the enemy, the danger, in them; refusing to die when we look straight on at them is a deceptively simple step with profoundly revolutionary consequences. She who is not defined as in or of the phallocentric symbolic order can withstand the prohibitions of that order; it cannot harm her because she does not partake of its codes. Her laughter is uncontainable.

Despite some resonant similarities such as this one, of course, Wittig's project is generally at odds with that of Cixous; she rejects Cixous's reliance on feminine writing ("écriture féminine") as being a celebration of the female body that accepts the feminization of the unconscious and retains man and woman as oppositional categories, merely valorizing what has been devalued but doing little to radically disrupt political and linguistic oppression. Wittig instead takes on the entire symbolic order in which Woman has been produced. In *Les Guérillères* her warrior-women take that order apart, then reconstitute language as experience of their own unordered realities in which any order or disorder is feasible. *Les Guérillères* makes the writing of *The Lesbian Body* possible, both conceptually and materially. It does battle with that which has rendered the lesbian body impossible and nonexistent. As it does so, *Les Guérillères*'s warrior-women use all the tools at their disposal to bring down the patriarchal edifice, including the radical iconoclasm of laughter. As the women "speak together of the threat they have constituted toward authority," they recount how they have been burned at the stake as witches, have menaced the functioning of armies and governments, have personified the contradictions between life and death, and have, even from within the myths, developed knowledge that "has competed successfully with the official knowledge to which they had no access" (89-90). Throughout it all, they say, despite all efforts to crush them, they remain "as steady as the three-legged cauldron."

> Then they laugh and fall backward from force of laughing. All are infected. A noise rises like the rolling of drums under a vault. The bricks of the ceiling fall one by one, uncovering through the openings the gilded panelling of lofty rooms. The stones of the mosaics fly out, the glass panes clatter down, there are shafts of blue red orange mauve. . . . The laughter does not lessen. The women pick up the bricks and using them as missiles they bombard the statues that remain standing in the midst of the disorder. They set about bringing down the remaining stones. There is a terrible clash of stone against stone. They evacuate those among them who are injured. The systematic destruction of the building is carried through by the women in the midst of a storm of cries shouts, while the laughter continues, spreads, becomes general. It comes to an end only when nothing remains of the building but stones on stones. Then they lie down and fall asleep. (90, 92)

For Wittig, the sound and shape of language uttered by these warrior-women constitute an act of power and will. As she writes, she plays on the patriarchal system's fear of women breaking out of the mythically contained dark and other side of Meaning. In the text's opening incantation of "lacunae" and "golden spaces" where deserts are green and birds immobile, where weapons are piled high and the sound of phoenixes' wings heralds death and happiness alike, "THE WOMEN AFFIRM IN TRIUMPH THAT / ALL ACTION IS OVERTHROW" (5). Then a large circle, a zero, occupies a page of its own. This is how the stage is set. It embodies Wittig's sense of what must be done; she, her words, will enter by force the very systems in which she was never meant to be or to speak, and will so thoroughly eliminate what has been that there will be no chance of getting caught again in its crippling structures of meaning. The logic of reasoning and the symbolic manifestations of it worshipped by Western phallocentrism must be made extinct.

Since conquest is the hallmark of that order, Wittig turns the weapons of conquest against itself, not to conquer but to clear the way. What is most desired and feared by the patriarchal order— Woman—is taken over by the women and used to defeat that order. Woman is not the women, but she is what the enemy knows how to recognize in their stead. When the warrior-women appear at the ramparts of a town, their male besiegers are at first indecisive about what to do. "Then the women, at a signal, uttering a terrible cry, suddenly rip off the upper part of their garments, uncovering their naked gleaming breasts. The men, the enemy, begin to discuss what they unanimously regard as a gesture of submission" (99-100). But the men have misread the women's actions and are attacked instead. "The women, modulating their voices into a stridency that distresses the ear, withstand the siege, one by one" (100). They refuse to function according to the logic of patriarchal order. They refuse to be contained by the symbols that order has designated as innate or essential in them.

"The women are on their cavorting continually rearing horses. They proceed without orders to meet the enemy army. They have painted their faces and legs in bright colors. The cries they utter are so terrifying that many of their adversaries drop their weapons, running straight before them stopping their ears" (102). Wittig plays on the legends of history, here recalling without naming the story of Queen Boudicca (or Boadicea) of the Iceni in early Britain whose battle tactics similarly terrified the Romans. No patriarchal soldier is ready for women's bodies used aggressively rather than as gestures of submission. None is ready for the cries of women used as war cries. All the women have to do is paint themselves into unavoidable visibility and give battle by giving voice to their own presence.

This presence has about it both a historical sense of the material-social conditions in which ideas and actions are produced, and a timelessness in which past or future events take on relevance as intensively present states of being. The garments, buildings, horses, battles, even the incantatory exchanges among the women often seem as old as the most ancient myths. Yet the women also seem to be in a future looking back on remnants of our own time. Past and future become textually undecidable, forming a conceptually material reality based on the interplay of both movement and suspension of time in which the relation between image and experience is both concrete and illusory. The women must take it all into account. It's the only way they can know their presence as the collision and contradiction between representation and reality needed for the opening of the new spaces and new worlds they seek. They know the time has come and that it is marked by no boundaries of linearity or chronological order.

The waging of war structures the text, yet battle scenes do not appear as events in the usual way. One simply comes to know after a while that battle has been engaged. The near-stasis of much of the first half of the text effects a kind of gathering of strength that draws one into a diffused atmosphere of peacefulness charged with motion. The opening and closing poems, the circles that appear at intervals, the lists of women's names interrupting textual cohesion by occupying next pages whether or not previous sentences have been completed, the nonnarrative story that gathers in short paragraphs interspersed by blank space, all actively dislodge the operations of the closed sign system language has been understood to be. Language, text, the symbolic order itself are opened up, made unreliable even as they cue our familiarity with the same conventions this work so pervasively disrupts.

All the while this new world is taking and changing shape, the women play games, tell tales, buy supplies, practice battle techniques, work, sleep, live, and die. They look at old photographs, dig up forgotten artifacts, remember and forget, and continually rework the symbols of the female body. "When they repeat, This order must be destroyed, they say they do not know what order is meant" (30). They ride into battle without orders and are not dispersed. They make no plans and are not lost. They study the past as productions in the present. "The women are seen to have in their hands small books which they say are feminaries. These are either multiple copies of the same original or else there are several kinds" (15). These small books contain myriad descriptions of female genitalia that amuse the little girls. "When it is leafed through the feminary presents numerous blank pages in which they write from time to time" (15). The women are participants in their own texts. The books consist of "pages with words printed in a varying number of capital letters. There may be only one or the pages may be full of them. Usually they are isolated at the centre of the page, well spaced black on a white background or else white on a black background" (15). We are all participants together in this text; it is a text in the process of production as we read.

In the symbolic order of patriarchy, Woman's body is textualized everywhere yet is atextual. It is this contradiction the women expose on their own behalf; it is the fissure that can be widened until the structure no longer holds. When they try to think back to the beginning, they find themselves in an atmosphere of movement without motion, of utterance without sound, of surfaces and reflections that scatter their gestures of lack of control and throw them against one another as they attempt to find firm footing. "They are prisoners of the mirror," Wittig writes (31). And we cannot help but be reminded of Lacan and the Mirror Stage so necessary to the little "hommelette's" recognition of one and another one that will mark his entrance into the Symbolic Order with his utterance of "I" ("Je"). It is this utterance that is denied to Wittig, to any woman, and that must take account of that "lived, rending experience which is m/y writing" by appearing for her as "J/e." The mirror is for women a relentlessly complex denial of presence. In it women see not themselves, but Woman, the image and reflection of Man; through it women do not enter the symbolic order but take up positions as articulations of that order. The women of *Les Guérillères* use this magic tool of phallocentrism to engage their own pleasure and in so doing to turn the force of that excess (for what else can woman's pleasure be?) on the order that has used its reflections to imprison them.

"The women say that they expose their genitals so that the sun may be reflected therein as in a mirror. They say that they retain its brilliance. They say that the pubic hair is like a spider's web that captures the rays. . . . The glare they shed when they stand still and turn to face one makes the eye turn elsewhere unable to stand the sight" (19). This power has always been with them. Now they use it to bring down the system that has been designed to control it. Once the war is fully engaged, Wittig writes of them: "They have modelled their most formidable weapon on the metallic mirror that the goddesses of the sun hold up to the light when they advance on the forecourt of the temples. They have copied its shape and its power of reflecting light. Each of them holds a mirror in her hand" (120). With their mirrors the warrior-women "use the sun's rays to communicate among themselves. When it is used as a weapon the mirror projects death-dealing rays" (120). Turned toward each other, the mirrors create networks of community among women; turned toward the enemy, they kill. Unlike the mirror Virginia Woolf knew so well, these mirrors do not give man to himself at twice his normal size but knock him to the ground writhing and groaning. The women "dance while uttering cries, swaying to and fro" until he and all that is of his world, including Woman, dies.

"The women say that they perceive their bodies in their entirety. They say that they do not favour any of its parts on the grounds that it was formerly a forbidden object. They say that they do not want to become prisoners of their own ideology" (57). Consequently, they must "now stop exalting the vulva"—it is "the last bond that binds them to a dead culture" (72). In preparation for the "great gathering of women" that will bring down the patriarchal order, the women have to believe in their own integrity. When everything has conspired to keep a woman's knowledge of herself fragmentary, divided from herself, there seems to be no access to integrity that is not forbidden. It is not surprising, then, that one would comb through old tales for evidence of how it might be otherwise. So it is that the women tell a story of a woman with thousands of snakes for hair who questions her favorite snake Orpheus as to which fruits of the tree in the garden to eat and, eating, grows beyond all bounds in strength and knowledge. The women respond to this story by "giving voice to a song from which no coherent phrase emerges" (52-53); none is needed, for language without bounds does not depend on old patterns of logic. "Beware of dispersal," they say; "remain united like the characters in a book. Do not abandon the collectivity" (58). But of course this is no easy task in a world that conceptualizes them, in which they have learned to conceptualize themselves, as enigmatic effects of division.

"You say there are no words to describe this time," they are told, "you say it does not exist. But remember. Make an effort to remember. Or, failing that, invent" (89).

The language the women use to begin a new world is "invented" out of what already is but has gone unheard. It is in the gaps and interstices of the language appropriated by men for Man. "The women say, unhappy one, men have expelled you from the world of symbols and yet they have given you names . . . they have exercised their rights as masters" (112). The authority to name is one that "goes back so far that the origin of language itself may be considered an act of authority emanating from those who dominate" (112). It is this seemingly endless mastery the women must invade and destroy. The women remind each other that "the language you speak" poisons them, that it is made up of signs that enslave them. But "precisely in the intervals that your masters have not been able to fill with their words of proprietors and possessors" is to be found "the zero, the O, the perfect circle that you invent" (114). This, then, is the language of overthrow.

The women celebrate it everywhere, in the subverted "symbolism of the Round Table," in "the circle, the circumference, the ring, the O, the zero, the sphere" (45). They collect their words and gather under names of their own making: "the Ophidian women the Odonates the Oogones the Odoacres the Olynthians the Ooliths the Omphales the women of Ormur of Orphise the Oriennes have massed and gone over to the attack" (103). Their actions are in the sound and shape of their words. They are starting from zero. With it, they turn the world upside down. "They foster disorder in all its forms. Confusion troubles violent debates disarray upsets disturbances incoherences irregularities divergences complications disagreements discords clashes polemics discussions contentions brawls disputes conflicts routs debacles cataclysms disturbances quarrels agitation turbulence conflagrations chaos anarchy" (93).

Chaos, that most feared mark of the loss of phallocratic order and mastery, is turned on the logic of dominance, on those who revere slavery and the violence of acquisition. It is a devastating rage that sweeps the land. With it the women reject the roles of dominator and dominated alike, exploding the only possibilities imaginable in the system of binary opposition that has structured the old world. They say, "I refuse to pronounce the names of possession and nonpossession. They say, If I take over the world, let it be to dispossess myself of it immediately, let it be to forge new links between myself and the world" (107). When the battles subside, when the war is over, the women bury the dead, weep, mourn, tear their hair, and begin to build anew.

The links they now forge break with "the tradition of inside and outside" (131) that have divided one from another, men and women, women from themselves. One among them sings, "Like unto ourselves/men who open their mouths to speak/a thousand thanks to those who have understood our language/and not having found it excessive/have joined with us to transform the world" (128, virgules Wittig's). "They say, take your time, consider this new species that seeks a new language" (131). Language is the starting place, as it must be. They examine it word for word, turning it over and upside down. The war they have waged fills them with sadness and grief, but has given them a place to stand for the first time in memory. "The women say, truly is this not magnificent? The vessels are upright, the vessels have acquired legs" (142). Wittig leaves them, and us, "melancholy and yet triumphant" (144). It may be difficult to imagine a new world that rids itself of violence by the use of violence; we may wonder if this isn't really just another trap. But Wittig's way is through, not over or around. Clearly she sees her entrance into language as being possible only by force and only through the gaps and spaces no symbolic system of oppression can quite control. What she works to bring into being is not a reversal in which women instead of men will control language, but rather an *asystematic* relation to language for all.

> ARISE NO/ SYMBOLS MASSED
> EVIDENT/ THE DESIGNATED TEXT
> (BY MYRIAD CONSTELLATIONS)
> FAULTY
> LACUNAE LACUNAE
> AGAINST TEXTS
> AGAINST MEANING
> WHICH IS TO WRITE VIOLENCE
> OUTSIDE THE TEXT
> IN ANOTHER WRITING
> THREATENING MENACING
> MARGINS SPACES INTERVALS
> WITHOUT PAUSE
> ACTION OVERTHROW. (143, virgules Wittig's)

Violence written outside the text, emptying the text, yet through and in the text—the empty space wherein no name, no definition, no sense of mastery can fix or limit possibility. Form and meaning, symbol and materiality make uneasy alliances in Wittig's writing, and purposely so. We are continually confronted by our assumptions and expectations on these pages, finding old categories of good and bad, correct politics and cooptation all of little use. Wittig determines to unspeak the language that is Woman so as to be free to speak as herself. No act of naming will, finally, do; names must be multiple and unstable, forming lists of excess that must exceed their limitations. "The shock of words," Wittig has written, "is produced by their association, their disposition, their arrangement, and also by each one of them as used separately" ("The Trojan Horse" 48). The shock of Wittig's words enacts an "estrangement" so thorough that we are left only with the possibility of using everything.

As Broner says, "She will never be able to return from experience." As Shange says, "She made herself, her world, from all that she came from." And Wittig adds, "Despite all the evils they wished to crush me with/I remain as steady as the three-legged cauldron" (*Les Guérillères* 90, virgule Wittig's). All three of these writers use the collectivity of many voices to enter the contradictions of being women whose differences will not be contained by Difference. Their words are as complex and loaded as spells. They are everywhere at once, speaking in tongues and refusing to choose among selves, refusing to conceal what they know, and in breaking silence, breaking the codes by which their silence would otherwise be enforced. Having read them with attention, we too should never be able to return from experience, but would rather find ourselves free to enter experience as if its categories of meaning were always profoundly ambiguous moments of contact with possibility. The trick is to know our words without leaving out the processes of know-ing.

And so we are back to Stein. Stein, as I have said, is the most uncategorical writer I know. No matter how insistently her radical freedom is read as rejection, opposition, imitation, or lack, no matter how often her writing is named so as to fix it in place, always at the moment of contact it is already elsewhere. In Stein we can see that anything is possible. In Woolf and in Richardson we can see that when it is a woman who asks what a woman is, categories of definition become highly unstable. In Shange and in Broner and in Wittig we can see that women among women take on a diversity of experience rich with all the tensions, conflicts, and coalitions of collaborative possibility that implies. All these writers together blur the boundaries between truth and fiction and destabilize the relations among categories of form and meaning. Their writings resist complicity with dominative processes and realize the dialectic interrelationships of the internal and the external not as a matter of making merely meaningful distinctions, but as enactments of shifting connections that are never the same twice.

For all these writers Woman is a form of language that will silence them if they do not do without her. Stein does just that—without her. Woolf and Richardson enact their contradictory relationships with her so as to disrupt the constructs of the cultural feminine. Shange, Broner, and Wittig step away from her by specifying women multiply, not only to enact female selves but to refuse to limit the selves they know so variously. Each and all of them make writing that makes Woman somebody else's fiction. There may, as Woolf believed, remain phantoms to be slain and rocks to be dashed against when any woman sits down to write a book, but these women have done much to clear the way into post-phantom enablement. What they bring to the page is will, laughter, rage, collectivity, the experience of subjectivity in cacophonous process, the witchery of knowledge that will not be official, and language as we have never seen it before. Such an act has implications far beyond the reading of unconventional texts. Given the central and pervasive role of language in our ability not only to conceptualize human communities but to effect change in the configurations of those communities, the work these women have done to produce language that resists "what we already seem to know" in favor of realizing the continuous activity of know-ing deserves our very closest attention.

I have called these women experimental writers. Insofar as that term signals a break with conventional literary realisms and the illusions they enforce, it is a useful enough term. However, I emphasize again that the term *experimental* tends to imply categories of signification which these women's writings do not settle into. They do not write against a norm so much as they write for and as themselves. All-too-convenient associations of "the feminine" with "experimental" distort the radical strategies these writers consciously employ and serve only to regender women's words when they do not speak Woman as they are expected to do. Only when the sense of something unstructured or not prestructured is activated in the term *experimental* can we more clearly see these writers' words just as they are. Their status as *women* writers, of course, has everything to do with their problematic critical reception as capable practitioners of nonconventional forms, as well as with their abilities to think of themselves and be thought of by others as speakers. Given the cultural script, they can as writers do no less than create their own voices on their own terms.

Gertrude Stein, Virginia Woolf, Dorothy Richardson, Ntozake Shange, E. M. Broner, and Monique Wittig—among others—make Western culture's insistence on the primacy of universal truth untenable. They scatter, gather, recenter, uncenter, look forward and back, and stand where they are. They envision wholeness in no one shape and speak language as if we all were already involved in the process of know-ing for ourselves. They make categorical accesses to language and experience unreliable. It is that which draws me to them, for I am convinced that without their unsettled and unsettling voices our ability to speak as we must, each in her way, is severely and artificially limited. With them, the "lively words" of post-phantom cacophony keep us aware that anything is possible. These writers enter the text from so many different angles that what we are able to see and hear is always more than we have learned to expect. These writers are immeasurably important to our ongoing histories, for they teach us to speak as if we always could.

> The reason that nothing is hidden is that there is no suggestion of silence.
>
> —Gertrude Stein

Bibliography

Barthes, Roland. *Image, Music, Text.* Trans. Stephen Heath. New York: Hill and Wang, 1977.

Belsey, Catherine. *Critical Practice.* London: Methuen, 1980.

Benstock, Shari. *Women of the Left Bank: Paris, 1900-1940.* Austin: University of Texas Press, 1986.

Bernikow, Louise. "The Light and the Dark: White Women Are Never Lonely, Black Women Always Smile." *Among Women.* New York: Harmony, 1980. 225-68.

Blake, Caesar R. *Dorothy Richardson.* Ann Arbor: University of Michigan Press, 1960.

Bloom, Harold. *The Anxiety of Influence.* New York: Oxford University Press, 1973.

Bremond, Claude. *Logique du récit.* Paris: Seuil, 1973.

Broner, E. M. *Her Mothers.* Bloomington: Indiana University Press, 1975.

———. *A Weave of Women.* Toronto: Bantam, 1978.

Christian, Barbara. *Black Feminist Criticism: Perspectives on Black Women Writers.* New York: Pergamon, 1985.

Cixous, Hélène. "The Laugh of the Medusa." Trans. Keith Cohen and Paula Cohen. *New French Feminisms.* Eds. Elaine Marks and Isabelle de Courtivron. New York: Schocken, 1981. 245-64.

Cowie, Elizabeth. "Woman as Sign." *M/F* 1 (1978):49-63.

Daly, Mary. *Gyn/Ecology: The Metaethics of Radical Feminism.* Boston: Beacon, 1978.

de Beauvoir, Simone. *The Second Sex.* Trans. and ed. H. M. Parshley. New York: Knopf, 1952.

DeKoven, Marianne. *A Different Language: Gertrude Stein's Experimental Writing.* Madison: University of Wisconsin Press, 1983.

de Lauretis, Teresa. *Alice Doesn't: Feminism, Semiotics, Cinema.* Bloomington: Indiana University Press, 1984.

————. "Feminist Studies/Critical Studies: Issues, Terms, and Contexts." *Feminist Studies/Critical Studies.* Ed. Teresa de Lauretis. Bloomington: Indiana University Press, 1986. 1-19.

Fadiman, Clifton. Rev. of *The Making of Americans,* by Gertrude Stein. *New Yorker* 9 (10 Feb. 1934):84-87.

Fiedler, Leslie. Foreword. *Dorothy Richardson.* By Caesar R. Blake. Ann Arbor: University of Michigan Press, 1960. vii-xii.

Fox-Genovese, Elizabeth. "To Write My Self: The Autobiographies of Afro-American Women." *Feminist Issues in Literary Scholarship.* Ed. Shari Benstock. Bloomington: Indiana University Press, 1987. 161-80.

Gaur, Albertine. *The Story of Writing.* London: British Library Board, 1984.

Gilbert, Sandra M., and Susan Gubar. *No Man's Land: The Place of the Woman Writer in The Twentieth Century.* (Vol. 1: *The War of the Words.*) New Haven: Yale University Press, 1988.

Grahn, Judy. *The Highest Apple: Sappho and The Lesbian Poetic Tradition.* San Francisco: Spinsters, Ink, 1985.

Haas, Robert Bartlett. *A Primer for the Gradual Understanding of Gertrude Stein.* Los Angeles: Black Sparrow Press, 1971.

Hanscombe, Gillian E. *The Art of Life: Dorothy Richardson and the Development of Feminist Consciousness.* Athens: Ohio University Press, 1982.

Hanscombe, Gillian, and Virginia L. Smyers. *Writing for Their Lives: The Modernist Women 1910-1940.* Boston: Northeastern University Press, 1987.

Hoffman, Michael J. *The Development of Abstractionism in the Writings of Gertrude Stein.* Philadelphia: University of Pennsylvania Press, 1965.

Husserl, Edmund. *Cartesian Meditations: An Introduction to Phenomenology.* Trans. Dorian Cairns. The Hague: Martinus Nijhoff, 1960.

Irigaray, Luce. *This Sex Which Is Not One.* Trans. Catherine Porter. Ithaca, N.Y.: Cornell University Press, 1985.

Jardine, Alice A. *Gynesis: Configurations of Woman and Modernity.* Ithaca, N.Y.: Cornell University Press, 1985.

Kaplan, Sydney Janet. *Feminine Consciousness in the Modern British Novel.* Urbana: University of Illinois Press, 1975.

Kramer, Heinrich, and James Sprenger. *The Malleus Maleficarum.* 1484 or 1486. Ed. and Trans. Montague Summers. New York: Dover, 1971.

Lacan, Jacques. *Écrits: A Selection.* Trans. Alan Sheridan. New York: Norton, 1977. *Écrits.* Paris: Seuil, 1966.

Liston, Maureen R. *Gertrude Stein: An Annotated Critical Bibliography.* Kent, Ohio: Kent State University Press, 1979.

Lorde, Audre. *Sister Outsider.* Trumansburg, N.Y.: Crossing Press, 1984.

Lugones, María C., and Elizabeth V. Spelman. "Have We Got a Theory for You! Feminist Theory, Cultural Imperialism and the Demand for 'The Woman's Voice.'" *Women's Studies International Forum* 6, no. 6 (1983):573-81.

Marks, Elaine, and Isabelle de Courtivron, eds. *New French Feminisms.* New York: Schocken, 1981.

Mellow, James R. *Charmed Circle: Gertrude Stein and Company.* New York: Avon, 1974.

Moi, Toril. *Sexual/Textual Politics: Feminist Literary Theory.* London: Methuen, 1985.

Monteith, Moira, ed. *Women's Writing: A Challenge to Theory.* Brighton: Harvester, 1986.

Moraga, Cherríe, and Gloria Anzaldúa, eds. *This Bridge Called My Back: Writings by Radical Women of Color.* New York: Kitchen Table: Women of Color Press, 1981, 1983.

Morales, Rosario. "We're All in the Same Boat." *This Bridge Called My Back: Writings by Radical Women of Color.* Eds. Cherríe Moraga and Gloria Anzaldúa. New York: Kitchen Table: Women of Color Press, 1981, 1983. 91-93.

Norris, Christopher. *Deconstruction: Theory and Practice.* London: Methuen, 1982.

Rich, Adrienne. *On Lies, Secrets, and Silence: Selected Prose 1966-1978.* New York: Norton, 1979.

Richardson, Dorothy. *Pilgrimage.* 4 vols. London: Virago, 1979.
Volume 1: *Pointed Roofs, Backwater, Honeycomb* (1915-17)
Volume 2: *The Tunnel, Interim* (1919)
Volume 3: *Deadlock, Revolving Lights, The Trap* (1921-25)
Volume 4: *Oberland, Dawn's Left Hand, Clear Horizon, Dimple Hill* (1927-38), *March Moonlight* (1967)

Rubin, Gayle. "The Traffic in Women: Notes on the 'Political Economy' of Sex." *Toward an Anthropology of Women.* Ed. Rayna Reiter. New York: Monthly Review Press, 1978. 157-210.

Sartre, Jean-Paul. *The Transcendence of the Ego.* Trans. Forrest William and Robert Kirkpatrick. New York: Noonday-Farrar, 1957.

Saussure, Ferdinand de. *Course in General Linguistics.* Eds. Charles Bally and Albert Sechehaye, in collaboration with Albert Riedlinger. Trans. Wade Baskin. New York: McGraw Hill, 1959.

Shange, Ntozake. *for colored girls who have considered suicide/when the rainbow is enuf.* Toronto: Bantam, 1975.

———. "foreward/ unrecovered losses/ black theater traditions." *Three Pieces.* New York: Penguin, 1981. ix-xvi.

———. *Sassafrass, Cypress & Indigo.* New York: St. Martin's, 1982.

Sinclair, May. "The Novels of Dorothy Richardson." *The Egoist* (Apr. 1918): 57-59.

Sorell, Walter. *Three Women: Lives of Sex and Genius.* New York: Bobbs-Merrill, 1975.

Spillers, Hortense J. "Interstices: A Small Drama of Words." *Pleasure and Danger: Exploring Female Sexuality.* Ed. Carole S. Vance. Boston: Routledge and Kegan Paul, 1984. 73-100.

Stein, Gertrude. *The Autobiography of Alice B. Toklas. Selected Writings of Gertrude Stein.* Ed. Carl Van Vechten. New York: Random, 1946. 1-237.

———. *Four Saints in Three Acts. Selected Writings of Gertrude Stein.* Ed. Carl Van Vechten. New York: Random, 1946. 577-612.

———. *Geography and Plays.* 1922. New York: Something Else Press, 1968.

———. *Lectures in America.* New York: Random, 1935.

———. *The Making of Americans: Being a History of a Family's Progress* (Complete Version). 1925. New York: Something Else Press, 1966.

———. *Selected Writings of Gertrude Stein.* Ed. Carl Van Vechten. New York: Random, 1946.

———. *Tender Buttons. Selected Writings of Gertrude Stein.* Ed. Carl Van Vechten. New York: Random, 1946. 459-509.

———. *Three Lives.* New York: Random, 1909, 1936.

———. *Wars I Have Seen.* New York: Random, 1945.

———. *What Are Masterpieces.* 1940. New York: Pitman, 1970.

Steiner, Wendy. *Exact Resemblance to Exact Resemblance: The Literary Portraiture of Gertrude Stein.* New Haven: Yale University Press, 1978.

Washington, Mary Helen. *Invented Lives: Narratives of Black Women 1860-1960.* Garden City, N.Y.: Anchor-Doubleday, 1987.

Wilder, Thornton. Introduction. *Four in America.* By Gertrude Stein. New Haven: Yale University Press, 1947. v-xxvii.

Wittig, Monique. *Les Guérillères.* Trans. David Le Vay. New York: Avon, 1971. Paris: Editions de Minuit, 1969.

———. *The Lesbian Body.* Trans. David Le Vay. Boston: Beacon, 1975. *Le Corps Lesbien.* Paris: Editions de Minuit, 1973.

———. "One Is Not Born a Woman." *Feminist Issues* (Winter 1981):47-54.

———. "The Point of View: Universal or Particular?" *Feminist Issues* (Fall 1983):63-69.

———. "The Trojan Horse." *Feminist Issues* (Fall 1984):45-49.

Woolf, Virginia. *A Room of One's Own.* New York: Harcourt, 1929.

———. *Three Guineas.* New York: Harcourt, 1938.

———. *Women and Writing.* Ed. Michele Barrett. New York: Harcourt, 1979.

———. *A Writer's Diary.* Ed. Leonard Woolf. New York: Harcourt, 1954.

Zimmerman, Bonnie. "What Has Never Been: An Overview of Lesbian Feminist Criticism." *Making a Difference: Feminist Literary Criticism.* Eds. Gayle Greene and Coppélia Kahn. London: Methuen, 1985. 177-210.

Index

Agency: masculinized or feminized positions of, 3, 14, 17, 19, 23, 29, 74, 85, 99, 133-34; in structuralist narrative theory, 12. *See also* Subjectivity

Aldrich, Mildred, 76

Althusser, Louis, 21

Angel in the House: as a critical metaphor, 6, 9-10, 15, 82. *See also* Phantom

Anzaldúa, Gloria, 128

The Autobiography of Alice B. Toklas, 41-42, 43, 46, 52, 59, 61, 76

Automatic writing: and Gertrude Stein, 42, 58, 72

Barnes, Djuna, 18

Barthes, Roland, 69-71

Beach, Sylvia, 76

Belsey, Catherine: on ideology of Realism, 15, 21-22; mentioned, 3

Benstock, Shari, 18

Bernikow, Louise, 127, 130

Blake, Caesar R., 118-19

Bloom, Harold, 61

Boundary: blurring of, by women writers, 6, 7, 11, 36, 85, 91, 142, 173; Woman as, 25, 27-28, 87-88, 89, 102-3, 134-35; racial and sexual, 36, 128-29; textual blurring by Woolf, 91, 92-96, 100, 102-3, 106

Braque, Georges, 61

Bremond, Claude, 12, 27

Broner, E. M.: the writing of, 135, 136, 138, 139, 150-61, 162, 172, 173, 174; use of Jewish myth and tradition, 150, 152-53, 157; use of nonconventional narrative, 151, 154-55, 156; on fathers and daughters, 152; on mothers and daughters, 152-55; and differences among women, 155, 160-61; violence against women in, 157, 159; mentioned, 4, 6, 7, 20, 35, 105

Cézanne, Paul, 50, 55

Chaos: and women's words, 2, 5, 43; and female experience, 35, 81, 82; woman as, 134-35, 170

Christian, Barbara, 125, 130, 140

Cixous, Hélène, 165

"Composition as Explanation," 45

Cone, Etta, and Claribel Cone, 76

Consciousness: modern, 17, 119-20; female, in *Pilgrimage*, 6, 83, 106-18 passim; female, 18, 118-19, 125-26, 129-30, 131, 151-52; "stream of consciousness," 119-20

Cowie, Elizabeth, 64

Daly, Mary, 39, 96

de Beauvoir, Simone, 11, 23-24, 82

DeKoven, Marianne, 70-71, 118

de Lauretis, Teresa: on female subjectivity, 12, 26-29, 30-34, 87, 91, 94-95, 124; on narrative as hero's quest, 27-28;

on Oedipal desire in narrative,
28-29; on *A Room of One's Own*,
30-31; on differences (race, class,
sex), 126, 139, 142; mentioned,
3, 45, 64, 85, 93, 121
Derrida, Jacques, 68-69, 70, 89, 90
Desire: in Lacanian theory, 23-24; in
narrative theory, 24-25, 26-29
Diaspora: as a critical metaphor, 7,
136; the Diaspora, 138
Difference: as ideological construct, 1,
13-14, 17, 26-27, 64-66, 75, 84; and differences among women, 6-7, 29, 126-
27, 128-29, 131, 138, 139, 150, 156,
172; as linguistic construct, 13, 68-69;
and women writers, 33, 36, 87-88,
102-5, 111, 117, 121, 140-41, 161

Eliot, T. S., 17, 118
Ellis, Havelock, 75
Experimental writing: as a term, 2-3,
4, 5, 7, 72, 131-32, 173; as presymbolic or preverbal, 4, 71, 118-19;
and women writing, 10-11, 16-21,
33-34, 36, 73-74, 173; as departure
from Realism, 13, 15-16, 21-22.
See also Post-phantom writing

Fadiman, Clifton, 73
Faulkner, William, 119
Female consciousness. *See* Consciousness
Female experience: as a term, 3, 14,
18, 29, 30-32, 81-82, 85, 89, 90; and
women writing, 21, 82-84, 90-91,
91-121 passim; and female subjectivity, 30-34, 96, 126, 128. *See also*
Subjectivity
Feminine, the: as cultural construct,
3, 4, 5, 24, 33, 34; as excess, 18, 70;
as presubjective space, 70-71, 86-91,
118-19, 126, 162, 165. *See also*
Phantom; Woman
Feminist theory: the project of, 1, 3,
18-19, 32, 36, 63, 126
Fiedler, Leslie, 118-19
Fitzgerald, F. Scott, 17
*for colored girls who have considered
suicide/when the rainbow is enuf*,
137, 140-45, 149

"foreward/ unrecovered losses/ black
theater traditions," 137, 149
Four in America, 56-57
Four Saints in Three Acts, 76
Fox-Genovese, Elizabeth, 123, 124-25,
126
Freud, Sigmund, 23, 27, 82, 90

Gaur, Albertine, 67
Geography and Plays: "Miss Furr and
Miss Skeene," 76
Gilbert, Sandra M., and Susan Gubar, 18
Grahn, Judy, 129, 163

Haas, Robert Bartlett, 43
Hanscombe, Gillian, 18, 113-14
Hemingway, Ernest, 17, 60-62
Her Mothers, 138, 151, 152-55
Herself: as a concept, 1, 11, 16-17, 22,
23-24, 34; and women writing, 82,
83, 91, 99, 104, 106-7, 109, 119,
144-45. *See also* Consciousness,
female; Female experience; Woman
Hoffman, Michael J., 54-55
Hurston, Zora Neale, 18, 129
Husserl, Edmund, 23

Ideology: as a term, 21, 31, 35
Irigaray, Luce, 65-66

James, Henry, 108
James, William, 42
Jardine, Alice: on Woman and the
"speaking subject," 86-91, 102-3;
mentioned, 3
Jewish women: in Bernikow, 127,
130; in Broner, 136, 138,
151-61
Joyce, James, 17, 60-62, 108, 118, 119,
120

Kaplan, Sydney Janet, 117-18
Kramer, Heinrich, and James Sprenger,
134-35
Kristeva, Julia, 89

Lacan, Jacques, 24, 33, 61, 87-90
passim, 92, 165, 171
Lack or recipience, feminized positions
of. *See* Agency

Language: gendered accesses to, 3, 4,
19, 20, 30, 37, 62-66, 133-34, 135-36,
139, 163; and experience, 5, 30, 36,
131, 135, 140, 173-74; as "a real
thing," 5-6, 44-60 passim, 69; as
communication, 48, 66-68, 72-73;
presymbolic aspects of, 70-71, 86-91,
118-19; among women, 122-23, 129,
131; as action, 133, 135, 137, 138,
139, 150-51, 156, 160, 161, 165-66
Larsen, Nella, 18, 129
Lawrence, D. H., 17, 118
Lectures in America, 41, 49, 58, 75
Lesbian: and Woman, 29, 125-26, 162-
65; and language, 73, 136, 162-65;
and sexual-inversion theory, 75
The Lesbian Body, 163-64, 165
Les Guérillères, 138-39, 161, 163,
165-72
Lévi-Strauss, Claude, 64-65
Lorde, Audre, 126-27, 128, 129
Lotman, Jurij, 27
Lugones, María C., 136-37
Luhan, Mabel Dodge, 60, 76

The Making of Americans, 47, 76-79
Mansfield, Katherine, 18
Mellow, James R., 42, 51, 76
Modernism: as a literary period,
16-19; and gender, 17-19
Moi, Toril, 87-88, 103
Moraga, Cherríe, 128-29
Morales, Rosario, 131

Narrative theory: and universal grammar, 12; structuralist, 12-13, 26-27,
48, 64; quest patterns in, 17, 23,
27-29; poststructuralist or deconstructionist, 32-33, 68-71, 85, 86-91
Nonrepresentational art and writing,
49-56
Norris, Christopher, 68-69

"One Is Not Born a Woman,"
124-26, 162

Peirce, Charles Sanders: semiotic
theory in de Lauretis, 33
Phantom: as a critical metaphor, 6, 9-10,
88, 90, 173. *See also* Angel in the
House; Feminine, the; Woman

Picasso, Pablo, 53, 55, 61
"Picasso," 80
"Pictures," 49-50
Pilgrimage: discussed, 83-84, 91,
98, 101, 105, 106-21; *Dawn's Left
Hand*, 101, 109, 110; publishing
history of, 107; *Pointed Roofs*, 108,
113-14; *Backwater*, 115; *Honeycomb*,
115; *Revolving Lights*, 120; *The Tunnel*,
120
"Poetry and Grammar," 58
"The Point of View," 162
"Portrait of Mabel Dodge at the Villa
Curonia," 60, 76
Post-phantom writing: as a term, 4, 7,
34, 173-74; and Realism, 15-16.
See also Experimental writing
Pound, Ezra, 17
Proust, Marcel, 108

Race, class, sex: as cultural constructs,
13, 25-26, 29, 35-36, 122-32, 134; and
writing, 18, 25, 62-63, 72, 123, 124,
129-30, 136-37; in Richardson, 104-5,
117; in Woolf, 104-5; and differences
among women, 127, 128, 138. *See also*
Broner, E. M.; Shange, Ntozake;
Wittig, Monique
Realism: in narrative, 11, 14, 21; as
ideological concept, 14-16, 21-22;
in relation to Reality in Western
thought, 21-22, 35, 84-85, 133
Rhys, Jean, 18
Rich, Adrienne, 6, 102, 122, 145
Richardson, Dorothy: and female
consciousness, 6, 18, 83, 106-7, 110,
113-14; the writing of, 81-82, 83-84,
85, 91, 98, 101, 103-4, 105, 106-21;
on race and class, 104-5, 117; narrative form of *Pilgrimage*, 107-8, 111-12,
113-14, 119; on women's writing,
108-10; rejection of gender codes,
114, 115-16; and stream of consciousness fiction, 119-20; mentioned, 4, 20,
35, 135, 139, 151, 162, 172, 173, 174
A Room of One's Own, 30-31, 52, 83,
91-100, 114, 133
Rubin, Gayle, 64-65

"Sacred Emily," 49, 52, 56

Sartre, Jean-Paul, 23
Sassafrass, Cypress & Indigo, 137, 140, 146-50
Saussure, Ferdinand de, 12-13, 64
Self and Other: as model of Difference, 13, 24-25, 61-62; in de Beauvoir, 23; and postmodern alienation, 86, 87, 88-89
Sentences proper to one's own use: as a critical metaphor, 6, 36, 92; in *A Room of One's Own*, 96-99
Shange, Ntozake: the writing of, 6-7, 135-36, 137-38, 139-50; use of African-American heritage, 137, 143, 148-49; use of form and language, 137, 139-40; on breaking silence, 141-42, 145; use of the collective voice, 142-43, 145, 149-50; violence against women in, 143, 148; use of "women's languages," 146-48; mentioned, 4, 20, 35, 105, 150, 151, 162, 172, 173, 174
Silence: and women, 1, 3, 16, 19, 29, 85, 94; the breaking of, 1-2, 122-23, 135, 137, 138, 139, 141, 145, 150, 154, 158, 162-63, 172, 174
Sinclair, May, 119, 120
Society of Outsiders: as a critical metaphor, 6, 92, 106; in *Three Guineas*, 101, 103-4
Solomons, Leon M.: and automatic writing, 42
Sorrell, Walter, 73
Spillers, Hortense J., 128
Stein, Gertrude: the writing of, 5-6, 19-20, 36-37, 38-80, 172, 174; on other media, 42; and automatic writing, 42, 58; and the continuous present, 45, 77-78; her "lively words," 45, 47, 57-58; and "a rose is a rose is a rose is a rose," 49, 52, 56-57; on non-representational art and writing, 49-53; compared to painters, 52-55; and Ernest Hemingway, 60-62; and James Joyce, 60-62; on experimental writing, 71-72; as a woman, 74-76; and "bottom nature," 76-78; mentioned, 4, 18, 35, 91, 118, 120, 121, 123, 135, 139, 162, 173
Steiner, Wendy, 54

Story of Man: as cultural paradigm, 25-26; mentioned, 7, 16, 19, 25, 161
Subjectivity: female, 3, 5, 6, 21, 22, 24, 28, 32, 62-63, 74, 84, 86-87, 90-91; as "site of differences," 4, 6, 91, 126-27, 135; and experience, 30-32; as "the speaking subject," 66, 86-91; in Woolf, 91-106 passim; in Richardson, 106-7 passim, 114-18 passim
"Susie Asado," 58

Tender Buttons, 45, 47, 54, 56, 58, 62
Thomson, Virgil, 42, 51
Three Guineas, 83, 91, 101-6, 115
Three Lives: "Melanctha," 47, 76
"The Trojan Horse," 53, 139, 162, 172

Washington, Mary Helen, 129
A Weave of Women, 138, 150-51, 155-61
Wells, H. G., 101
What Are Masterpieces, 45, 50-51, 57, 79
Wilder, Thornton, 42, 56-57, 72
Wittig, Monique: the writing of, 7, 53-54, 135-36, 138-39, 161-72; on lesbian as not-Woman, 124-26, 162-63, 163-64; use of language and form, 139, 161, 162-63, 166, 167; use of violence by women, 138-39, 161-62, 165-72 passim; and lesbian writing, 162-63; and a new language, 164, 165-66, 167, 169-72; mentioned, 4, 6, 20, 35, 105, 173, 174
Woman: as cultural construct, 1, 3, 10-11, 15-16, 23-24, 33-34, 69-70, 87-88, 121, 125-26, 134, 161-62, 166; and Difference, 1, 13, 27, 74-75, 131; as language, 1-2, 4, 18-19, 24-25, 32, 33, 36, 62-63, 69-70, 73-74, 86-87, 89-90, 131, 136, 139, 160-61, 168, 172, 173; and subjectivity, 3, 19-20, 21-22, 28-29, 84, 121, 129; as repressed material, 28, 69-72, 86-91; and race, class, sex, 29, 124-26, 127, 128, 161-62, 164; in Richardson, 82, 84, 112-13, 115-16; in Woolf, 9-11, 82-83, 84, 91-95, 96-97, 99; *See also* Feminine, the; Phantom
Women and Writing: "Professions for Women," 9-11

Women's language, 4, 98, 108-10, 122-23, 129, 131-32, 135

Woolf, Virginia: critical metaphors from, 6; and the nature of Woman, 9-11, 83, 93-95, 99; the writing of, 9-11, 20, 52, 81-83, 84-85, 91-105, 119-21, 133; in de Lauretis, 30-31; boundary-crossing in, 91, 93-96, 99, 102-3, 105-6; on Society of Outsiders, 92, 101, 103-4, 105; on women's writing, 95-99, 120; on "aggressive masculinity," 100-102, 105; on race and class, 104-5; on Dorothy Richardson, 119, 120-21; mentioned, 4, 5, 16, 18, 22, 35, 36, 107, 109, 135, 139, 146, 151, 162, 169, 172, 173, 174

A Writer's Diary, 99, 101, 106, 120

Zimmerman, Bonnie, 163

Note on the Author

NANCY GRAY earned her Ph.D. in 1988 from the University of Washington and is now on the faculty of the English and Foreign Languages department at California State Polytechnic University, Pomona. She has contributed to *The Women's Studies Encyclopedia* and *Changing Our Power: An Introduction to Women Studies* and has written essays and reviews on feminist theory, women writers, and women's studies.